Protecting Home

Protecting Home

Class, Race, and Masculinity in Boys' Baseball

SHERRI GRASMUCK

PHOTOGRAPHS BY JANET GOLDWATER

RUTGERS UNIVERSITY PRESS

NEW BRUNSWICK, NEW JERSEY, AND LONDON

LIBRARY OF CONGRESS CATALOGING-IN-PUBLICATION DATA

Grasmuck, Sherri.
    Protecting home : class, race, and masculinity in boys' baseball / Sherri
Grasmuck; photographs by Janet Goldwater.
        p.   cm.
    Includes bibliographical references and index.
    ISBN 0-8135-3554-9 (hardcover : alk. paper) — ISBN 0-8135-3555-7 (pbk : alk.
paper)
    I. Baseball for children—Social aspects—Pennsylvania—Philadelphia—
Case studies.   2. Boys—Pennsylvania—Philadelphia—Social conditions—Case
studies.   3. Philadelphia (Pa.)—Social conditions—21st century—Case studies.
4. Masculinity—Case studies.   I. Goldwater, Janet.   II. Title.
    GV880.4.G73 2005
    306.4'83—dc22   2004016355

A British Cataloging-in-Publication record for this book is available from the British
Library

Manufactured in the United States of America

To Soren and John
who gently led me into the mystery of boys' culture
and
Tessa
my best girlfriend along the way

CONTENTS

LIST OF TABLES AND MAPS

Tables

Maps

ACKNOWLEDGMENTS

Many people connected to Fairmount Sports Association went out of their way to facilitate this research. Others tolerated me. I am deeply grateful for both kinds of help. The many parents and coaches who provided hours of conversation in their homes, at picnic tables, or trapped for hours in my car are owed special thanks. I am especially indebted to the parents and coaches of the four teams we followed an entire season for their openness and casual acceptance of our presence. The president of the organization, John Dunn, set an early tone of cooperation I appreciated and often had an amusing spin on what it was I was up to. Among the individuals who deserve special recognition for their patience in answering my stream of questions or for tolerating my lurking presence: Ed Hanlin, Tony Demuro, Susan Tripp, Joe Stankiewicz, Diana Stankiewicz, Ernie Leonardo, Tom Hagerty, Stanley Fleishman, Tom Dunn, Tom Gleason, Betty Montowski, Art Gallagher, and Joe Muldowney. Countless other adults and children connected to FSA, too numerous to mention, offered me important insights into the many meanings attached to "the field" for which I am deeply appreciative. No one mentioned here bears any responsibility for the interpretations offered. I apologize to the boys on the teams we followed who were disappointed to discover that I would not be mentioning them by name or including their home run totals. I also want the boys on the teams I followed who played outfield and didn't get many hits to know how much they taught me and how much space there is in life outside these games. I thank them all for letting me press into their dugout.

This research was conducted with the aid of a study leave from Temple University and several research grants from the Department of Sociology, Temple University. In my three years as Associate Dean of the College of Liberal Arts, I was lucky to have a boss, Morris Vogel, who understood the importance of supporting the research activities of those willing to do institutional service at this level. His commitment to translating the cutting edge of research to our students in clear and appropriate ways was a constant reminder to me of the importance of our audience beyond the academy. The research support of then Associate Dean Anne Shlay and the continued support of Dean Susan Herbst made possible the incorporation of color photographs with the ethnography.

Janet Goldwater had a clear idea from the beginning of how enriching it could be to add a visual dimension to this project, especially since aesthetic comfort was half of what made the collective experience of this baseball league work. It was a congenial collaboration every step of the way as we negotiated the balance between the visual rewards and the sociological content of the selected images.

Chapters or preliminary versions of this manuscript were read and commented on with care and insight by Gül Ozyegin, Susan Hyatt, Rebecca Alpert, Michael Messner, Nancy Theberge, Gideon Sjoberg, Tessa Landreau-Grasmuck, Susan Tripp, Joe Muldowney, and several anonymous reviewers for the *Sociology of Sport Journal*. Critical emotional and intellectual support along the way was also provided by other colleagues and friends, including my adopted sister Laura Barbour, Rosario Espinal, Julia Ericksen, Howie Winant, Ramón Grosfoguel, Joyce Joyce, Kevin Delaney, Magali Larson, and Alice Gordon. Debbie Rogow, who personifies humane efficacy, intellectual acumen, and astute friendship, read every chapter and prodded me forward at many difficult junctures. With Debbie as a friend, anything is possible. I am also grateful to Joshua Freely and Dylan Galaty for their generous research assistance in the fieldwork for this project, and to Nadine Sullivan for her careful assistance in editing, tracking down bibliographic materials, and the pre-production preparation of the manuscript.

I owe a deep and running intellectual debt to Gideon Sjoberg, who in the 1970s chaired my dissertation on Scottish nationalism and who returned to my life after a lapse of almost twenty years. We then picked up right where we had left off, with his arriving at dinner with detailed notes about what was novel, what was undersold, and what was still unresolved in an early draft of my manuscript. Thereafter he read every chapter and worried for hours with me on long-distance telephone calls about tone and fairness. It took me a long time to understand fully how deep had been his early impact on my intellectual development, how much it had meant to be taken so seriously in that early fragile era of feminism.

I have a knack for entering subfields of scholarship just as they are moving away from what sent me to them in the first place. Once, in the early 1990s, I embarked on a course of study in family therapy just as the field seemed to be discovering culture and ethnicity, staples of sociology. These discoveries, from the perspective of my discipline, took an astonishingly naïve form, and I became disillusioned. Something similar happened as my interest in community boys' baseball led me to the sub-area of sociology of sport. As I was wallowing in the wonders of community connection, the complex negotiations among folks of different backgrounds made possible by this sports encounter, critical sports scholars had become increasingly united in a negative assessment of sports as a cultural institution. This took me by surprise—I had assumed that the subfield was dominated by nostalgic former jocks and uncritical physical education trainers. How wrong. Several from this field, especially Michael Messner, Nancy Theberge, and Jay Coakley, were particularly welcoming and supportive as I made my way through this underexplored literature. As I was finishing the last sentences of the manuscript, Michael Kaufman offered valuable insights as well.

I am indebted to Alison Brooks of Wainswright Agency for leading me to Kristi Long, whose early enthusiastic support of the project, beginning at another press and sustained through her move to Rutgers University Press, contributed to the momentum and direction of the book. Her background in cultural anthropology nicely complemented my sensibilities. Working with Adi Hovav, whose timely professional interventions speeded things along, was also a pleasure. Evan Young's respectful and precise copyediting improved the manuscript while remaining faithful to the goals of my project.

For more than ten years I have depended on the mentorship of my son, Soren Landreau, for this project. His wisdom about boyhood and the need to read between the lines in male relationships, his struggle to find a place in the world, and his friendships with loyal neighborhood boys became an important barometer for this research. Along the way, important conversations with Tessa Landreau-Grasmuck helped me to keep perspective about the bracketed meanings of the male sports world. Finally, it is beyond my capacity to express the depth of gratitude I owe to John Landreau for his support through every step of this project or to sort out which layer of his help was most strategic. His academic expertise in masculinity themes in literature along with his passionate appreciation of baseball formed one layer. Beyond this, there was his willingness to tolerate my discomforting scrutiny and second-guessing of his every move as a coach and the reflective, undefensive way he untangled the social knots related to his involvement in the league I studied. Not only did he read every chapter multiple times, but his greater literary confidence and hunger for game details shaped my narrative approach to the games in chapter 5. More to the point, his masculinity is dazzling; there is no one I know who prioritizes caring for his loved ones as much as he. His personal and professional sacrifices for his family have not only enriched us but have saved each one of us.

I am grateful to the City of Philadelphia and the Fairmount Parks Commission for having permitted a community of people to hold onto a valuable piece of city property for the public use of neighborhood baseball. The ragtag baseball that went on in this block of parkland, bordering some of the city's most impressive monuments and valuable real estate, depended on this civic concession and inspired this book.

Protecting Home

1

===

Seeing the World
in Neighborhood Baseball

After watching my son strike out three times during a game early in his first baseball season, then come up to bat for the fourth time and get two strikes, I left the bleachers and walked quickly to the women's bathroom to calm the nausea that was overwhelming me as I sat in the stands. How had someone with as little interest in male sports as I had come to care so deeply for the outcome of a game played by seven-year-old boys? What had become of me? Evidently, the same thing that happened to countless other parents I watched over the ten years of my family's involvement with the neighborhood baseball organization, Fairmount Sports Association (FSA), that is the subject of this book.

My son did end up striking out four times in that game, and even now, years later, I still see clearly in my mind his sobbing face as he threw himself with heaving shoulders into the dugout. The intensity of my reaction at that moment was not because he was an athletic flop. In fact, over the next seven years he proved to be among the more talented players in the league (but don't take any parent's word on such matters). But perhaps because of his talent, and a thousand-year history stressing physicality as a time-honored path to manhood, he cared deeply at age seven about his performance on this field. He already saw sports as his primary identity, and failure had no place in his imagined future. Between games he talked of nothing else. Also on this ball field, he overcame his profound shyness and forced himself to step forward in front of crowds of strangers and to stand with acute longing alone at the plate. That day, watching him, I understood this. My identification with his profound longing to not bomb out (something notoriously hard to avoid in baseball) caused me to sit in the bleachers knotted with an anxiety that seemed better suited to fighting off muggers than to supporting my child's play pursuits.

As a coping mechanism, I began over time to observe other parents and to monitor how they reacted to their boys' plays and errors on the field, what they said about the coaches, and how they placed praise and blame for the outcomes of games and plays. I soon realized that there were interesting differences among parents in their levels of involvement, in their judgments about coaches and coaching styles, and, more basically, in what they wanted for their children from this organization. The coaches, too, varied greatly in how they approached the game and the boys, how they communicated with the boys and taught the games. I saw from those bleachers some of the most tender human gestures by men encouraging vulnerable boys, and some of the most ruthless, almost sadistic, treatments of those same boys that I had seen anywhere. And not all of the children dealt with the coaches, the game, or the victories and losses in the same way. Some seemed propped up, waiting for it to be over; others stared into the field with the seriousness of statesmen, and still others specialized in inventing fun in every space outside the logic of the game.

Over the years as I watched, I noticed other interesting ripples just below the surface of life in the bleachers and on the playing field. Old tensions around class and race in the neighborhood often resonated in encounters between coaches, parents, and children, but in relatively subdued ways, and always in the context of a space defined by the common goal of instructional baseball. I regularly noticed the undercurrent of these tensions, and wondered at their meanings for other parents. In that context, I was also intrigued by the history of FSA, an organization that had transformed itself from a white baseball league into a visibly multicultural one in less than twenty years. And all of this in a neighborhood notorious for its racial exclusion, and in a city renowned for racism in its professional baseball history. How and why did baseball become the site for this integration?

I never intended to do a study of FSA. My academic area of sociology takes me far afield from sports or even children's activities; I have concentrated on Latin American immigration, and gender and kinship. So as I began to realize what a rich sociological context this neighborhood sports organization of ours was, I regularly suggested it to my graduate students as a dissertation topic. Several years went by, and several cohorts of students, but no one took the bait. Meanwhile, time passed, and I watched my daughter come up through the league. Gradually she lost interest in the game and dropped out completely (to my husband's chagrin). At the same time, my son's passion for the game intensified, until the horizons of his existence nearly ceased to extend beyond the happenings on that neighborhood field. His passion for knowing its daily details reminded me of nineteenth-century obsessions. And he wasn't alone. I saw many adult versions of what he was becoming—neighborhood men and women who spent a majority of their waking hours outside of work at "the field." This scared me. Initially, I resisted the encroachment of his sports talk on all aspects of our family life, periodically defining sports themes as off limits for ten-minute intervals during family dinners. Of course, my son was understanding; he would sit in absolute silence waiting for the moratorium to be over and then return immediately to his buoyant and cheerful rehearsal of the same minutiae we had left hanging ten minutes before. But over time, my resistance weakened. If I was to have any kind of relationship with my son in the future, I realized it would have to involve embracing his passions. This meant delivering myself over to the poetics of the game. In the process I also donned my sociologist's cap and slowly delivered myself over to observing, and later recording, the politics, social divisions, human connections, and emotional contours of the league.

Although I continued to suggest the topic to any graduate student who would listen, eventually I realized that part of my interest in the space of FSA came not only from its formal research potential but from my personal involvement, from comparing my intense feelings and reactions with those of other parents, from comparing my husband's and son's reactions and judgments with those of other fathers and sons, and from seeing myself and my family enter as newcomers into what felt like a sacred space. In this way I decided to study this organization myself, and on my own terms, in a way that would draw heavily not just from my perspective as a sociologist, but also from my perspective for over a decade as a "baseball Mom," and, as it later turned out, as a coach's wife, and even very briefly (and to my horror) as a commissioner's wife. Interestingly enough, as I deepened my engagement in the research, there was a parallel increase in my family's involvement with the organization. By the end of my project, my son was playing on three different teams connected to the organization, and my husband had become a coach, then a commissioner, and had even had a briefly conflictive period with the leadership before settling in as a regular manager of one of the ten-to-twelve-year-old teams. Needless to say, studying such an organization under these circumstances was a messy but fascinating adventure.

I knew from the beginning that "getting it right," in a way that would be as fair as possible to those involved, would be vitally important if I was to continue living calmly in my neighborhood (and household). There were certainly doubts along the way. For example, I remember the day my son, at age ten, standing behind me and reading from the computer screen my description of an outrageous intervention by one of his favorite coaches, walked out of the room muttering, "Oh God. Now we're gonna have to move." Then there was the day at the ball field when I heard a lunatic in the dugout screaming at the top of his lungs at a parent and, from the bleachers, suddenly recognized it as my husband's voice. Moments like these made me wonder about the project's viability. But, somehow, I never lost my conviction that, however messy the process, there was a powerful human story connected to this baseball field and to FSA that offered a qualified hope for race relations and community in America and captured many of the tensions and ambiguities of encounters among adults and children of different class and ethnic backgrounds as they tried to play together at the end of the twentieth century.

Let me say a few words at the outset about the way my personal involvement with the league informs, enhances, and interferes with my work. To the extent that it is possible, in the course of this writing I try to make my vantage point visible to the reader. While in some ways my personal perspective enhances the study by providing a more empathetic dimension to the story, in other ways it is a limitation. For one thing, being female means that I am never really able to penetrate the inner sanctum of the male-dominated organization in an informal way, the way my husband, for example, did. His role as a volunteer coach sometimes provided privileged insight into the workings of the organization, but it also often made things harder, since some people found it hard to imagine that his position on an issue or conflict might not be the same as mine.

For another thing, part of the tensions that are explored here relate to the different social backgrounds of the folks who come together in this space. I moved into the neighborhood only nineteen years ago, in 1985, making me a "newcomer" in the locals' eyes; and, as a professor, I further fit the association of "newcomers" with "yuppies" in this gentrifying neighborhood. So, to the extent that I focus on some of the tensions between the newcomers and the old-timers, my social position, and most of my early networks, linked me initially more to the newcomers.

My husband and I both speak Spanish, which gave me access to interesting conversations with Hispanics about some ethnicity and race issues. But being white also positions me in such a way that possible negative experiences of folks of color might not reach me in their pure undiluted form, or as readily as they would a nonwhite researcher.

Finally, experiences in neighborhood baseball are highly conditioned by the skill level of one's child. The parent of a child who regularly succeeds in the field or at the plate, regardless of the approach of any coach, has a baseball experience very different from that of the parent of a child who does not. The fact that my son played on the higher-status traveling teams of the organization throughout his career meant that we saw both in-house and traveling perspectives, but it also meant that the entire space was a source of self-esteem for him, and that may have made many frustrations with the organization tolerable in ways they might not have been to parents whose children experienced less individual success.

As I was writing my field notes, I often put italicized comments in square brackets to signal my personal reactions to moments I was describing. I wrote them to remind myself of my feelings about the moment, in case those feelings would unconsciously influence my description. Eventually, however, I opted to include them, at various junctures, in this text to permit the reader to see the internal static of my observations—in order to become, if not a more reliable narrator, then at least a more exposed observer, or in Ruth Behar's terms a more vulnerable one.[1] This seemed important since I was simultaneously a sociological observer of many events, the mother of a player, the wife of a coach/manager, and a white woman seeing a male space that was racially changing. I was also, often, not sure which of these roles was at work in filtering my observations. In common usage, bias is a word with highly negative connotations. I prefer to think of subjectivity as also capable of enhancing our insights. Indeed, as the hermeneutic and many feminist philosophers would say, awareness of subjectivity is necessary to the process of understanding and interpretation. So from time to time in my descriptions of games, coaches, parents, and boys in the chapters of this book, I include lines that reflect my passing reactions to the moment. This bracketed commentary is between all the lines we read; I'm just trying to bring a tiny bit of it to the surface.

Because this is a story of baseball, it can't be told with words alone. Janet Goldwater's photographs both illustrate some of the themes of the book and capture a different parallel story. The playing fields of the Fairmount Sports Association sit on a green triangle of trees and lush grass, bordered by three busy streets, only ten blocks from City Hall. The sheer aesthetic pleasure of sitting on the bleachers on a June afternoon surrounded by green fields, colorful uniforms below the smiles and grimaces of children's faces, and the glittering skyscrapers of Center City is central to the Fairmount baseball experience. Goldwater, a documentary filmmaker, also lives in the neighborhood and had spent twelve summers watching her daughters play softball in the Fairmount league. About four years into my fieldwork, Goldwater, armed with a very general idea of the themes of my project, began bringing her camera to the field often when I was hunkered down in the stands furiously taking notes. Both having been fixtures on the bleachers for more than a decade, we aroused little curiosity. We usually ignored each other while at work, and later found that the images and words we had gathered had a growing resonance. This resonance, or shared vision, became the backbone of our collaboration.

Doing Fieldwork in One's Own Back Yard

I warmed the bleachers at the Fairmount baseball field continuously for fifteen years, watching the games and practices of my son and daughter between 1987 and 2002. My daughter played for four years, in T-ball and softball, before she dropped out abruptly because she thought her coach was mean. I found the coach gruff but not mean. My daughter never played again. My son then played for nine years, between 1994 and 2002, on in-house teams in the seven-to-nine-, ten-to-twelve-, and thirteen-to-fifteen-year-old-divisions, as well as on various

Fairmount "traveling teams" representing the neighborhood in different city-wide leagues. It wasn't until 1997, ten years after my first contact with the organization, that I began an ethnographic study of the baseball league, its changes over time, and its relationship to the neighborhood. I then became an "observing participant" on the boys' side of the organization.[2] Over the next three years, I completed two phases of data collection. First, I completed ethnographic fieldwork in which, working with two graduate students, I followed selected coaches and their teams from the seven-to-nine and ten-to-twelve divisions over two baseball seasons, and spent many evenings and weekends hanging out at the field over many more summers. And second, I conducted in-depth interviews with a sample of the coaches and parents of FSA. In the following section, I highlight those aspects of the research most important for understanding how my sources of information and methods ground my exploration of this space. Further details of the process, as well as a discussion of broader methodological issues, can be found in the Appendix.

Following Boys' Teams

When I began the ethnographic dimension of the study, in the spring season of 1997, I was interested in observing different coaching styles in the league and the different reactions of parents and boys to these styles. I wanted to track how the old-timer/newcomer divisions in the neighborhood related to the range of coaching styles and reactions to them. I had already seen these differences and listened to countless conversations among parents that referenced the differences. I began, working with a graduate student, by observing coaches from different backgrounds, in order to develop a series of themes and strategic points of observation that I could investigate the next summer with a broader range of coaches and age divisions within Fairmount Sports Association.

Since FSA had undergone dramatic changes over a fifteen-year period, with a new stream of incoming participants from more professional backgrounds as well as many more children of color, I was especially interested in understanding how race, ethnic, and social class differences got negotiated in these interactions, their salience for participants, and their impact on the organizational politics of FSA. I also searched for ways to explore how masculinity styles informed the different strategies of the coaches, and how parents and boys reacted to them, as the boys made their way through this highly diverse cast of characters within the FSA of the late 1990s. For the next summer, I wanted to follow much more closely the rhythm of the entire season from the perspective of the various teams and to compare the boys' experiences in different age divisions, to see how their reactions and others' expectations for their behavior changed as they grew older.

The in-depth observations of games occurred during the 1998 season. Working with Dylan Galaty, a Temple sociology graduate student, I selected four teams at the start of the season: two seven-to-nine teams and two ten-to-twelve teams, equally divided among old-timer Fairmount coaches and newcomer coaches. I was interested not just in the background or style of coaches, but also in that season's mix of boys and parents on each team. During this second season, we observed and recorded field notes for a total of eighty-one games and twelve practices. We systematically monitored only these four teams in these two divisions, but because these four teams played all the other teams several times over the course of the season, we also regularly witnessed games of all the teams and coaches in the two divisions. So, monitoring these four teams meant attending the entire season of games and many practices for each of them, as well as attending the playoffs, the championship games, and the All-Star games in both divisions. I also informally observed most of the games of my son's two teams that year, another ten-to-twelve team, and the eleven-and-under traveling team that competed in the city-wide Devlin league. Beyond these games, for more than seven years I also attended all of the seasonal events of the organization, such as the annual fundraiser called "Booster Day," their opening-day ceremony, and "Trophy Day," as well as numerous team barbeques.

During the fieldwork, I blended in as just another mother, which, in fact, I was. Once, another mother, walking by and seeing me stationed at a game of boys she knew to be younger than my son, commented, "My! You are gung-ho about this, even watching games without a kid on the team!" Dylan looked slightly too young to be a parent of an adolescent boy and was asked about his note-taking more often than I was. But he was a large man who looked athletic, and he culturally seemed to belong more than I did. To me, he often looked like an assistant coach keeping score.

There were interesting advantages to having Dylan working with me in the field. There were clear gender differences in our experiences. I tended to know more about what mothers thought and to hear more of the gossip about the organization, because mothers talked more to me about this than to they did to Dylan. As a mother myself, and as a participant in the space for a decade, it was very easy for me as I stood on the sidelines to "interview by comment,"[3] and thus to learn a great deal. As a guy, and a big one at that, Dylan heard more than I did of the commentary from the coaches he followed about the technical faults of other coaches. In part this was because what coaches do strategically matters more in the older boys' league, where boys pitch to each other rather than relying on a pitching machine as they do in the seven-to-nine division. But perhaps also, they assumed (correctly) that he had greater baseball knowledge than I did, and this was a more common topic among the men. He was certainly popular among the coaches who knew him, and when I was there and he was not, or later when his part of the fieldwork was completed, coaches persistently asked me, "Hey, where's Dylan?" or "Where's the big guy?" I considered wearing a sign saying, "No, he's not here today."

Although the coaches had introduced me to the boys, and although they had a vague understanding of my project (they knew I was writing a book), they only occasionally referred to this. They treated me like just another parent hanging over the fence. Over time, some boys came to treat me as a convenient source of desired objects, such as paper if they wanted to draw something, gum, or candy. As a diabetic, I always carry candy with me for emergency glucose needs. Many of the boys quickly learned that I was a guaranteed source of "life-savers." I happen to prefer the red-hot cinnamon kind. Some of the Marlins, who wore red uniforms, saw this as a sign that I favored their team over the Blue Jays. Sometimes they would monitor when I wrote something down and try to guess why I was writing at that particular moment. A couple of boys convinced themselves that I was there to document the number of home runs they hit in the season and regularly asked me if I had seen that last one. This happened more with my teams than with Dylan's teams. Their occasional but bold interest in me was both a function of their younger age and, I think, of the fact they sometimes saw me as an adult female, available for their random mothering needs. Yet because I never criticized or reprimanded them for their clandestine bench behavior and speech, as did some of the other adults standing around, they also didn't seem to fear that I was interested in getting them in trouble and worthy of much avoidance. In short, despite these periodic expressions of interest, most often the younger and older boys ignored us.

Interviewing Coaches and Parents

In the final phase of the project, over the summer and autumn of 2000, I conducted forty-one semistructured interviews with coaches and parents. I interviewed eighteen current FSA coaches in the boys' divisions, four former FSA coaches or officials, and twenty-one parents whose children had played at Fairmount within the last year. For balance, I selected equal numbers of longtime residents of the neighborhood and newcomer professionals for the coach and parent interviews. Three of the newcomers interviewed were black. In addition to the coaches, I interviewed four former coaches or individuals with a long history of participation in the organizational leadership of the FSA in past decades. Of the twenty-two coaches interviewed, only two were female.

Following the coach interviews, I interviewed twenty-one parents who had boys who had played in either the seven-to-nine or the ten-to-twelve division of FSA within the last year. I tried to balance the selection of parents to get a representative mix of Fairmounters and newcomers, and to include representative racial and ethnic diversity. Three selected parents were black and three were Puerto Rican. I also sought an even mix of skill levels among the children—sometimes aided by the penciled rankings on their registration forms, sometimes as reported to me by coaches, and sometimes determined from my own fieldwork observations.

Approximately half of the parents interviewed were from Fairmount and half were newcomers, with equal numbers of fathers and mothers in each group. The socioeconomic backgrounds and educational levels of the two groups differed significantly. The jobs of Fairmounter parents ranged from plumbing, barbering, mechanical repairs, janitorial work, and babysitting-homemaking to support teaching and sales. With one exception, none of the Fairmounter parents had attended college and none held professional jobs. All of the newcomer parents were college educated and, with one exception, all held advanced professional or graduate degrees. With one exception all newcomers worked in professional occupations as medical doctors, lawyers, university professors, teacher-administrators, and governmental management.[4]

Sociologist, Baseball Mom, and Coach's Wife: My Messy Role

The above description makes my research sound smoother and less knotty than it was. All researchers confront awkward moments where their personal interests or viewpoints interfere in known and unknown ways with the interests or viewpoints of their research subjects. All ethnographers must also select, from an array of moments and events, which ones to present in telling the story of a community. The fact that I was a mother of a ballplayer, personally drawn into the drama of every season; the wife of a newcomer coach; a white professional in a gentrified neighborhood; and always, at every second, a female observing boys and men in a male-controlled organization, marked my experience. There is no question in my mind that I learned more about this social space than I ever could have had I not been so personally involved and lived this world so intensively with my family for so many years. In fact, I was rarely able to completely turn off my brain to my research. It was present at almost every dinner-table conversation during, and even before and after, every baseball season, for more than a decade. But this privileged involvement, and therefore the additional insights that come from such access to the deep impact of the organization on people I love, comes at a cost that the reader will ultimately have to assess. To compensate for my personal involvement, I struggled hard to set up observations and conversations with participants whose experience was different from my own, to regularly express the perspectives I had heard in the bleachers from parents and coaches occupying positions different from my own (such as old-time Fairmounters or newly entering parents of color), and to regularly (at dinner) listen to, and challenge, my son's and my husband's interpretations of many of the FSA moments they recounted.

By way of disclosure, I acknowledge that the moment I finally resolved that I would conduct a study of this baseball space came after watching a deeply disturbing encounter between a raging coach, an eleven-year-old boy, sobbing and cringing with humiliation, and an utterly silent audience of parents. I still remember the acute anxiety I felt sitting in the bleachers, trying to understand the moment, and also trying to figure out what to do. I long fantasized about walking out onto the field, lying down on the pitcher's mound, and refusing to move until either the coach agreed to resign or someone carried me out. I also understood that my son would never speak to me again if I even came close to such a body-on-the-mound strike. What I didn't know was what other parents and coaches felt at such moments, how they reconciled their expectations and hopes with the realities of any game as it unfolded. Something about that moment, and my inability to decide whether I should or should not have intervened on behalf of a boy I didn't even know, pushed me over the line into deciding that this space would be my next research project.

This doesn't mean that my original concern with FSA was negative or was focused on the destructive behavior of some adult coaches. On the contrary, well before this moment my family had already come to love this space and to deliver ourselves to the passion and joy that my son felt as a player there. I had long admired the dedication of the neighborhood men and women who kept the organization alive. Long before that moment, I had observed that much of the social change marking the neighborhood was also sitting on these bleachers in starkly visible ways. The Fairmount old-timers and the newcomers, including the new parents of color, were negotiating, as we sat on those bleachers season after season, the meanings of masculinity and multiculturalism for the next generation of boys. And, I learned, the boys had their own negotiations, quite independently of the adults.

I can think of countless moments in the research when my social role as a mother and coach's wife had possible consequences for what, and how, I learned about FSA and the neighborhood. There was the year my son opted not to play on the higher status traveling team, closely connected with the organizational leadership, and to play instead for his father's lower-status, in-house team. The organization had decided that boys playing on traveling teams would play as an intact team with the traveling coach, against the in-house teams, rather than being assigned to two different teams, one in-house and one traveling, as in previous years. Rather than give up his chance of being on my husband's team for his last year in that division, my son dropped off the traveling team. While the traveling team coach himself never expressed any animosity about his decision, others in the organization grumbled about it, and it may have defined him, for a period at least, as "less serious about the game" than the others. Try as I might to transcend this brief judgment, it annoyed me.

Then there was the long phase in which my husband succeeded in antagonizing the organizational leadership, at precisely the time Dylan and I were wandering around observing games as part of the fieldwork. There are several possible reasons for why, and how, my husband shifted from his early-years status of "good guy trying to help out" to his middle-years status as "yuppie pain-in-the-butt coach" to his 2001 "manager of the year" status, complete with trophy. Regardless of why he fell in and out of favor with the various sectors, and despite the fact that I learned an immense amount by listening to these accounts of who said what and how, I found his salient role mortifying, as did my son. Often, we both cringed at the dinner table listening to his account of new evidence of hostility against him—my son worrying about how it would affect his own game time, and me wondering how it would affect my ability to get people to talk to me. I discuss some of these difficult moments in the context of the chapters. But in some ways, it does not matter why my husband's position shifted over time. His mysterious return to the fold was accomplished in the same way other things happened in the organization. Whatever brought him into periodic disfavor was overcome by the additional years he spent coaching younger boys after my son had moved up. In a volunteer organization, volunteering your labor for years trumps many other cards.

I do not mean to emphasize his role as a primary interference with my own research objectivity. The most dramatic impact made on my research was that made by my own social role because of gender, made by the fact that, as a woman, I could never be part of the male social networks that formally and informally maintained and controlled the organization, could never be part of even the outer periphery of marginal men who supported the organization, who drank beer together and freely entered the concession area and field house. While I might more easily have entered the dense network of FSA women coaches, they were webbed across the world of girls' softball, not the boys' side that was my primary interest.

Then there is the issue of baseball expertise. Let's just say that I am beyond where my Turkish friend, Gül Ozyegin, is. (One afternoon, as she sat on the bleachers with me, she asked loudly, "Do they always run in the same direction?" At that moment, I was very grateful for her salient accent.) I understand things like the infield fly ball rule. I can sometimes spot a pickoff move before it happens. And I understand how sinful it is to "bail out." But I'm still not sure when a batter is pulling his head out or swinging too late. And I'm still not sure of many of the interference rules. I didn't grow up, as other women who have written about baseball did (like Doris Kearns Goodwin and Adrienne Harris), deeply attached to the game through their communities and going with their fathers to see the Brooklyn Dodgers, or attending the Triple A games in Toronto.[5] From my childhood in Texas, I only remember football, and that with no fondness. My deeper connection to the game came as an adult, after I moved to the Fairmount/Spring Garden area. There, there was baseball fever, and I caught it at my own dinner table. My knowledge of the game has increased over the years, and over time I have certainly learned more about baseball than is known by the casual observer. But I have also learned enough about baseball to feel humbled by the many subtleties of the game still beyond my grasp.

Over the years that my son played ball at FSA (from the age of seven until fifteen), he came to prefer the company of boys from the neighborhood, the children of the old-timers, to that of the "yuppie kids" (notwithstanding his being one). He wanted to be on "the neighborhood teams" at FSA, hung out with the Fairmounter kids on street corners on many weekend nights, and in general found them to be, in his words, "more real" than the kids he knew at the nearby private school he attended until he was fourteen (dominated by children of professionals). This identification with, and the tenderness he felt for, the neighborhood boys and coaches helped him to find a welcoming community at a time of considerable difficulty in his life. He was among the small, interracial group of boys stopped by the police and "rescued" by Fairmounters in the incident described at the beginning of chapter 2. One of the policemen that night recognized one of the leaders of the local ball league and approached him asking, "Is one of these boys yours?" Because the Fairmount man answered, "They're all mine," they were released without arrest. This acceptance and recognition of my son as part of the community provided him with a base of local social support. He learned an immense amount of sociology, not just by hanging with the local boys, but also by learning about how some of the teachers at the school he attended at the time perceived him given these associations. Evidently, a teacher from this private school whom he did not really know, a new professional living in Fairmount, did not enjoy the street-corner life of the Fairmount teenagers near his home. My son was enraged to learn that this teacher had discussed his association with these neighborhood boys at school as something problematic, and this and other such events fortified his identity as a "crossover" to the Fairmounter world.

At one point my son decided that he did not like my project happening in "his space" and suggested strongly that I put it aside (after two years of investment in the research) and find something else to study. After discussing this for hours with him one night, I went to bed despondent, because I realized that it might be necessary to give the project up if we couldn't find a solution he could live with, as the space was too important to him. So there was a brief limbo period in which all bets were off about the project's future. But he came back and negotiated, saying that as long as I never took notes at any game he was playing in and my role at his games was just as his mother ("not doing anything weird"), then he didn't really care what I did at the other boys' games. Over time, his attitude evolved from suspicion and irritation to interest, especially as he was reassured by reading segments on my computer that no one he knew was personally identified and found that the issues I wrote about were things that actually impacted what he really cared about—baseball. I am immensely grateful for his patience and insightful observations as my sometime co-researcher.

SOMEWHERE ALONG THE WAY I became as interested in telling a story as in building sociological theory. This goes beyond the idea of the importance of the case study for situating human actions in their natural settings, keeping the flesh and bones intact.[6] I am convinced that part of the marginalization of social science in contemporary public debates relates precisely to our lost capacity for storytelling. It is up to the reader to judge how much further an understanding of this social space is advanced by these narratives and how much might be distorted in their telling. My intention was to prioritize the capturing of multiple meanings as they played themselves out in the flow of events.

The various chapters visit different levels of local space, moving from the neighborhood and its place in the city, to the site of neighborhood baseball and the baseball clubhouse, to the baseball field and dugout, and, finally, to the dugout benches. Chapter 2, titled "The Neighborhood and Race Sponsorship," chronicles the demographic, social, and racial transformations in the two adjacent neighborhoods that set the stage for racial integration and new class encounters at the ball field. Residents' claiming and defending of urban public space for the neighborhood passion of baseball defined the space and the sport as central to neighborhood identity. Despite apprehensions by white working— and lower-middle-class residents, and despite a history of racial tensions with bordering areas, the ongoing viability of baseball depended on opening the space to new children. This chapter explores how racial integration unfolded on the baseball field by means of a changing urban political landscape, by the social sponsorship of new children of color, and by the intrinsic features of baseball itself.

Chapter 3, titled "The Clubhouse and Class Cultures," documents how broader neighborhood tensions that accompanied gentrification in Fairmount and Spring Garden crystallized in tensions between Fairmounters and the new professionals at the ball field. What was often unspoken in the neighborhood surfaced at the ball field around issues of organizational leadership, time dedicated to the voluntary baseball league, and competing values related to individual and collective responsibility, group solidarity, and how best to promote children's interests. Yet as these encounters evolved over time, Fairmounter and newcomer parents also forged fragile, cross-class and cross-race understandings as newcomers' loyalty to the local space deepened.

Chapter 4, titled "The Dugout and the Masculinity Styles of Coaches," explores how the changing space of neighborhood baseball foregrounded competing styles of masculinity, as expressed by coaches in their approaches to boys and by parents in their preferences for different coaches. I explore the extent to which dominant narratives about "neighborhood coaches" versus "yuppie coaches" match my empirical observations of a range of coaches over several years. These comparisons offer insight into the group process of "othering" and the important symbolic role played by "outliers" in contrast to the empirical salience of social hybrids. To give a more textured feel for the different styles of masculinity, as revealed through such different dimensions of coaching as expertise, competition, and emotional styles, I offer a series of portraits of coaches whose behaviors typify contrasting approaches to the game and to the boys they teach.

Chapter 5, titled "The Bench and Boys' Culture," explores what boys make of this changing landscape, steeped with neighborhood tradition and tinged with competing adult expectations about the game and masculine behavior. The writing strategy of this chapter differs from that of other chapters in that it relies on "ethnographic drama" to tell the story of boys' interactions on the bench.[7] By considering the unfolding dynamics among the boys in a constructed time sequence that draws on the logic of game time, we see some of the elements that lend distinctive character to teams as they pool their differences. This chapter highlights the fragile emergence of a range of masculinity styles, which evolve not merely as responses to adult messages but through ongoing interactions among the boys, as they duplicate, modify, and sometimes reject traditional scripts of masculinity.

Between the chapters of this book are three vignettes, or stories of "saturated events." Saturated events for me are stories or anecdotes that illustrate the way a set of relationships in a given social space often plays out. They are not necessarily typical in the sense of occurrences that are frequently repeated. They may in fact be extreme instances of the way typical dynamics unfold. But their time-sensitive drama is what permits us to see some of the boundaries that limit social action and the constraints and consequences of behaviors in a given space. While there are stories within each chapter that complement the analytic points of the chapter, the stories framed between the chapters treat multiple themes that crisscross the chapters, give a feel for moments that go beyond the specific issues of a chapter, or just stand alone without need of sociological framing. The shifting of narrative approach, from the more "realistic narrative" of the early chapters to the more "grounded fiction" of the final chapter, interspersed between chapters with vignettes of poignant moments, defines the overall book as a "mixed genre" of presentation with the goal of drawing on the strengths and limitations of distinct ways of representing the swirl of social life.

The Meaning of My Quotation Marks

Since my research consists of multiple sources of data, the meaning of the quotation marks I use throughout the book needs clarification.[8] First, and most obviously, most of my quotations are direct quotes from the verbatim transcriptions of the taped interviews with parents or coaches. Second, some of the quotations come from the direct observations of games. When something happened, or someone said something that I was fairly sure I would want to use, I would often walk away and repeat the comment into my small hand recorder as precisely as I could. If this was too awkward, or if the scene was evolving too quickly to risk missing anything by walking away, I would take notes on the spot in which I would record as much of the precise phrasing as I could get down by writing rapidly. This kind of quoting obviously involves more slippage than the direct transcriptions of taped interviews, which can be played and replayed for clarification and for understanding of nuance and emphasis. Third, in my narrative vignettes of "saturated events" and in chapter 5, we find the most slippage of all. Here I often relied on notes in which I had recorded fragments of quotes, or strategic phrasings of a set of comments. I also sometimes had to reconstruct the quotations based on my memory of the moment or combine these reconstructed quotations with more precise quotations from the field notes. Thus the more narrative accounts of particular events, such as the case of Donald's father in the vignette titled "How Parents Get on Base," can be considered a kind of documented reconstruction meant to contextualize in a deeper narrative way the sociological meaning of the precise quotations woven throughout. Nothing in these narratives is "invented," as every person speaking said something very close to what I present. It is just that I cannot guarantee that I captured it precisely.

I present the real names of these two neighborhoods, Fairmount and Spring Garden, following norms of journalism and history rather than of sociology, as I believe the actual historical identities of these spaces matter to the storytelling. Since one of my broader goals for this project was to prioritize sociological storytelling as an equally valid way of representing an inevitably partial truth,[9] and since these are communities with particular identities and histories within Philadelphia, I think it is important to the meaning and integrity of the story to preserve their distinctive identity.[10] However, I did not extend this "real naming" to individuals in the community. Although some neighborhood folks did prefer that I use their real names, many did not. For consistency's sake, all of the names of persons presented here are pseudonyms, even in the case of those who played recognized historical roles in establishing FSA as an organization.

Clifford Geertz once said: "Anthropologists have a number of advantages when addressing the general public, one of them being that hardly anyone in their audience has much in the way of independent knowledge of the supposed facts being retailed. This allows one to get away with a good deal."[11] This is certainly not my case. My situation is much more delicate. Most of my "subjects" know where I live. This added more than the usual incentive to strive for a balanced viewpoint in a space of multiple realities. I tried, despite my peculiar social position, to use the criterion of fairness to the diverse social groups participating in neighborhood baseball as my compass for objectivity.[12] It remains to be seen if anyone will come looking for me.

2

===

The Neighborhood and Race Sponsorship

"A Dropped Third Strike"

In the late 1960s, white residents of a neighborhood called Fairmount, north of Center City, regularly ran off blacks who walked through the neighborhood, often with the support of police. A red-faced Irish-Ukrainian Fairmounter, looking back at his teenage years, described the neighborhood this way: "They called our neighborhood ''white island' because we were surrounded. . . . When I was growing up there would have been fighting no matter what. We fought every day. We fought our way to school. We fought our way home from school. We fought every day." Thirty years later, on a summer evening in 2001, three police cars surrounded and detained a group of four boys in Fairmount, two black and two white, under suspicion of attempting a car theft. As the police aggressively questioned the fourteen-year-old boys, a group of Fairmount adults encircled the police cars to defend the interracial group of boys against this "police harassment." Among these adults was the same Fairmounter quoted above who, as a teenager in the 1960s, had fought blacks who dared to walk through the neighborhood. Yet on that summer night in 2001, after this incident, he loudly explained to a group of listeners why the police had really stopped the boys that night. "You want to know what they did wrong? I'll tell you what. They were guilty of 'walking while black.' Or they were white and hanging with blacks. That's what they did wrong."

What had happened in this neighborhood, and to these adults, to produce such surprising changes? One clue comes from the fact that these were not just any boys. They were baseball players, players who had played in the neighborhood baseball league for almost a decade. Another clue is that both of the black boys were middle-class, and one of them now lived in the neighborhood. Many other clues to understanding this moment are uncovered by a look at the changes that swept through Fairmount, and through its adjacent neighborhood, Spring Garden, in the last decades of the twentieth century and at how neighborhood baseball changed over the same period. This chapter explores a process of racial integration in the baseball league and its ballpark adjacent to these two Philadelphia neighborhoods. There are plenty of stories in America of racial conflict and violence accompanying, and following, neighborhood change. Here we explore the opposite—a relatively smooth process of racial integration within a central recreational space in a gentrifying neighborhood.

Neighborhood Changes

By the year 2000, most children who played baseball in either of these two neighborhoods played it on the Von Colln Memorial Field of Fairmount Park, ten blocks from City Hall. Fairmount and Spring Garden physically meet here on their western borders just opposite the impressive Philadelphia Museum of Art. The ball field is just one block down from the museum at the southwestern corner of the Spring Garden neighborhood (see Map 1). However, before this ball field evolved into a site of social unity for the two neighborhoods, residents of the two neighborhoods lived in different social worlds.

In the early 1950s, both Spring Garden and Fairmount were predominantly white, working-class neighborhoods with a strong representation of Irish, English, Ukrainian, Polish, and Italian ethnic groups. Fairmount remained subdivided into a number of small pockets where, often, different blocks were dominated by first- and second-generation white immigrants from different European countries.[1] As a white enclave bordering poorer black neighborhoods to the north, Fairmount had a strong race identity. A sixty-year-old barber who had grown up in Fairmount remembered this period:

> You had the Italians living on Aspen Street and 23rd Street. The Irish were throughout the neighborhood. The Ukrainians were down this way and a lot of Greeks were at 27th and 28th. It was pretty mixed with those groups. . . . Blacks would try to come down here, through here and all. This was a tough neighborhood, so it would be like hand-to-hand combat. There were some black families, around 23rd and Oliver, and I went to school with some blacks and Puerto Ricans, but it was mostly white. This area just seemed to hold on. I called this "Custer's Last Stand." We got the city here [signaling south], got the park over here [signaling west], Girard College on the north and then the prison [signaling east]. So kind of like boundaries. . . . But things have changed now. The old-timers were more racial than we are.

While Fairmount remained an almost exclusively white area through the 1950s, Spring Garden underwent considerable racial change. First, because of its relative proximity to the first Spanish-speaking church in the city, Spring Garden

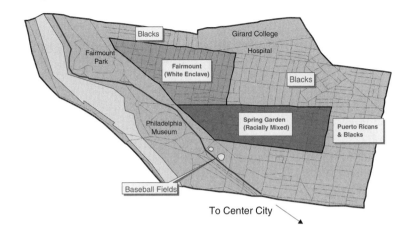

MAP 1. Fairmount/Spring Garden and Surrounding Areas

became the first area of settlement for Puerto Rican migrants arriving from New Jersey agricultural areas in the 1950s.[2] By the end of the decade they constituted 31 percent of the population in Spring Garden (see Table 2.1). Second, during the same period the proportion of African Americans in the area just to the east of Spring Garden doubled, growing from 15 to 34 percent (Whalen 2001, 186).[3] Overall, then, while Fairmount remained almost exclusively white in the 1950s, almost half of Spring Garden's residents identified as either Latino or black by the decade's end.

This racial transition in the Spring Garden area was far from smooth. White residents of Spring Garden, especially the poorer ones, resisted their new neighbors with racial riots and violence. During the summer of 1953, one of the worst riots in the city occurred at Mt. Vernon and 16th Street, with fighting that involved anywhere from 300 to 1,000 people and lasted more than two hours.[4] Fighting continued for the next four nights and spread over a five-block area. Police, prosecutors, and judges viewed white youth as the instigators of the violence.[5] Wally, a white Irish-American man who had grown up in the area, moved away for ten years and returned in 1974 to live in Spring Garden with his ailing parents. He described an ongoing climate of conflict: "Remember, we were on the Spring Garden side. We were, and were not, part of Fairmount. Here, it was mostly black and Puerto Rican. The rest of the blue-collar whites were more trashy whites, bad reputation. Lot of bars, crime. It was common to see killings. On the first night we moved back here in '74, my wife witnessed a guy get killed in front of our house and leave blood all over our car. The very night we moved back in!" Shawn, a white Spring Garden resident, remembered his youth in the neighborhood this way:

TABLE 2.1.

Racial Changes in the Neighborhoods of Fairmount and Spring Garden and in Philadelphia, 1950–2000

| | Fairmount | | | | Spring Garden | | | | Philadelphia[a] | | |
	Population	White %	Black %	Latino[b] %	Population %	White %	Black %	Latino[b] %	White %	Black %	Latino[b] %
1950	10,764	99.3	.5	—	16,737	84.5	15.5	—	81.7	18.2	.01
1960	8,769	97.2	2.5	0.1	9,289	81.8	17.8	30.8	79.0	20.4	0.5
1970	7,620	93.0	6.1	2.1	7,436	82.0	14.9	27.7	68.6	30.1	2.3
1980	6,532	94.1	4.7	1.8	5,694	69.1	10.7	22.4	59.2	35.9	3.7
1990	5,882	91.0	6.7	2.7	5,483	74.2	12.8	14.0	53.5	39.6	5.3
2000	5,962	84.1	8.2	2.9	5,386	73.9	16.0	10.4	45.1	43.1	8.5

Source. Years 1950–1990, compiled from an aggregate file of the U.S. Census created by William Yancey with the assistance of Joshua Freely, Social Science Data Library, Temple University; 2000 data from the U.S. Census 2000 Website, Summary File 3.

[a] Philadelphia is defined here as excluding the two census tracts represented by Fairmount (136) and Spring Garden (134).

[b] Census questions relevant to the categories of race and Latinos changed twice between 1950 and 2000. Throughout the period, census forms have operationalized "race" and "Hispanic origin" as separate variables. In 1960, for the first time, a separate ethnicity question was added to the race question; respondents were asked if they were "Puerto Rican." This was the only possible Hispanic response offered on the form. Beginning in 1980, all respondents were asked if they were "Latino." (Before 1980, the Latino origin question was only asked on a sample basis.) Therefore, one cannot always compare tabulations on Latinos on the census tract level between the 1960/1970 period and the 1980/1990/2000 period. Then, starting in 2000, people were permitted to check off more than one race, making new mixed-race categories possible, and lowering the proportion of respondents answering "white" or "black." These changes explain why in this table the categories "White," "Black," and "Latino" sometimes total more than 100 percent for a given year (e.g., in 1960 and 1970) and sometimes drop below 100 percent (e.g., in 2000, when mixed-race categories were added to the census, but are not reported here).

Twenty years ago this was a bad neighborhood. . . . You wouldn't walk past here. The Puerto Ricans would just jump you. Blacks couldn't walk down through the neighborhood. We had fights at the Art Museum all the time. . . . I had a hard time because I lived above Fairmount [in Spring Garden], and we hung out below Fairmount. But I had to go home at night. Puerto Ricans would actually wait up at night. But we had one Puerto Rican kid who lived on Fairmount Avenue, and he used to walk me home at night. . . . But mostly, we used to get in fights just because they were black, and we were white. . . . It was Fairmount. Blacks weren't supposed to walk through Fairmount.

For many Fairmount residents, this racial transition in the area to their south reinforced their longstanding sense of being a white oasis. The Fairmount area was indeed racially distinct from its surrounding areas (Map 1). As one resident put it,

[Blacks were] up above us, above the college, and on the other side of the prison. . . . That's why we fought so hard, so they wouldn't tear the prison down. Then the other side would be wide open [to the black neighborhood on the other side]. In the '70s, in 1972, when they made the lot down here, our friends' houses were all torn down. They all had to move away. Then, we thought, if the prison gets torn down too, this neighborhood is done. And it would have been done.

Fairmounters' fears of racial integration were not realized. Throughout the period of Spring Garden's racial transformation, Fairmount remained almost 100 percent white. Cybriwski, who studied Fairmount in the 1970s, identified three factors central to the neighborhood's racial stability. First, Fairmounters were much more likely to own their homes, which made the rate of population turnover during this period considerably slower in Fairmount than in Spring Garden.[6] This lower turnover meant fewer opportunities for newcomers in Fairmount than in Spring Garden. Second, when vacancies did occur in Fairmount, they were often managed informally through relatives or by word of mouth. A village-like cohesiveness made it relatively easy to discriminate against blacks or Puerto Ricans, to prevent them from entering the housing market. Jessie, who lived in the heart of Fairmount all her life, described how it worked:

JESSIE: Thirty years ago this was a very prejudiced neighborhood. I mean everybody in it was prejudiced, and that's just . . . the way you were brought up. . . . They kept everything closed-mouthed. . . . They called this neighborhood the "Oreo." That's what they used to say, "We're an Oreo cookie. . . . " And to hold strong, you stuck together like glue. [You didn't] put a sign on your house if you were selling it. It was word of mouth. . . . I've even been guilty of that. Ten years ago, a woman was renting her house on this block, and I said to her, "Watch what you rent to because, while you are out in Bryn Mawr, I'm across the street from the garbage you put in the house."

S.G.: And what you had in mind then was someone black?

JESSIE: Right. And she knew what I was saying, and she said, "I wouldn't do that to you." [Laughter] I think she was afraid I'd come for her. [Laughter]

Third, beyond the closed housing market, Fairmount's youth had a well established reputation for violently defending its space against transgressors.[7] An active street-corner life in the community, especially among teenagers, facilitated very tight control over outsiders and contributed to a neighborhood sense of security. Well after Puerto Ricans and blacks had established a strong presence in surrounding areas, Fairmount corner youths continued their violent confrontations with blacks who passed through the neighborhood.[8] And although lower-class families were harshly criticized by other Fairmount residents as "white trash," they also were often the ones "taking care of business" by enforcing racial boundaries, just as the poorest whites in Spring Garden were associated with street fighting with Puerto Ricans in the 1950s.[9] These internal divisions, however, had always paled in comparison to the boundaries drawn between this white enclave and the surrounding areas. Then, as the neighborhood to the south changed again, this time with the arrival of new, higher-income whites, a new "other" emerged. This both alleviated the racial fears of Fairmounters and posed a threat of a different nature to the old neighborhood.

Gentrification

If the high concentration of rental property in Spring Garden helped facilitate the entrance of Puerto Ricans in the 1950s, it also helped push them out. In the 1970s, Spring Garden began to gentrify. With its close proximity to downtown Philadelphia and its large stock of historic townhouses and rental properties, Spring Garden started to attract many young professional newcomers. Table 2.2 compares the neighborhoods of Fairmount and Spring Garden with the entire city over a thirty-year period and illustrates how dramatic these economic changes in the two neighborhoods were. In the early 1960s, Spring Garden was notably poorer than its Fairmount neighbor, with almost triple the poverty rate and significantly lower than average income levels. Fairmount was a solidly working-class area resembling overall city averages, with comparable poverty rates and slightly lower income levels than the city as a whole, although its average housing values lagged behind city averages. Over the next thirty years, Spring Garden changed dramatically, from being much poorer than Fairmount to being very similar, and in some ways considerably more affluent. Table 2.2 shows that the median income in Spring Garden rose dramatically, from a low of $2,508 in 1960 to $34,691 in 1990, with the biggest jump occurring in the

TABLE 2.2.
Economic and Housing Changes in Fairmount and Spring Garden Neighborhoods Compared to City-Wide Changes, 1960–2000

	FAIRMOUNT				SPRING GARDEN				PHILADELPHIA			
	Owner Occupied %	% Poor	Median income $	Average housing value	Owner Occupied %	% Poor	Median income $	Average housing value	Owner Occupied %	% Poor	Median income $	Average housing value $
1960	51.3	16.3	5,015	6,700	14.5	44.1	2,508	7,400	59.9	17.6	6,039	9,842
1970	48.5	9.7	9,009	7,100	10.4	21.1	9,083	9,200	56.2	12.2	9,834	12,683
1980	50.9	10.7	17,249	37,700	16.6	24.0	15,005	73,900	55.4	17.6	17,336	30,760
1990	48.6	9.8	34,503	94,400	31.3	16.8	34,691	168,200	62.0	20.7	24,603	48,400
2000	58.5	11.0	46,250	100,600	40.0	19.1	41,536	191,300	64.4	22.9	30,746	61,000

Source. Years 1950–1990, compiled from an aggregate file of the U.S. Census created by William Yancey with the assistance of Joshua Freely, Social Science Data Library, Temple University; 2000 data from the U.S. Census 2000 website, Summary File 3.

Note. Poverty was not officially computed in 1960; the 1960 numbers in this table are based on a calculation using the 1970 poverty level, the rate of inflation, and changes in the consumer price index between 1960 and 1970. Philadelphia is defined as excluding the two census tracts represented by Fairmount (136) and Spring Garden (134). "Owner occupied" is based on all housing units. "Median Income" is based on the household. "Average Housing Value" refers only to owner occupied residences.

1980s. Fairmount incomes rose rapidly as well, so that by 1990, median incomes for the two neighborhoods were comparable, and considerably above the city-wide average.

Average housing values in Fairmount and Spring Garden in the 1960s were below city-wide averages ($6,700 and $7,400, compared to $9,842). By 1980, average housing values in Spring Garden were more than double those of the city ($73,900 compared to $30,760), and by 1990, average housing values in Fairmount as well were nearly double those of the city ($94,400 compared to $48,400). These changes in housing values reflect the arrival of a new group of more affluent residents, first into Spring Garden in the 1970s, and then into Fairmount in the 1980s. These more affluent residents were able and willing to either renovate properties or pay the higher prices that developers were asking for renovated homes.

The rapidly rising rents and housing values of the 1970s hit hard in the poorer sector of Spring Garden, the struggling Puerto Rican community. The Spring Garden Civic Association might have helped resist this process, but it was dominated by property owners and developers and failed to include Puerto Rican representation.[10] Organized sectors of the Puerto Rican community protested the negative consequences for them of gentrification and HUD inaction.[11] Despite this resistance, however, the poorer sectors of the Latino population were pushed out and moved toward the growing community of Latinos in northeast Philadelphia. Latinos constituted 30 percent of the Spring Garden area in 1960, but by 1990 they represented only 14 percent, and only 10 percent by 2000 (Table 2.1).

From a working-class area with significant pockets of poverty, numerous basement bars, corner taverns, small industries, and three neighborhood Catholic schools in the 1960s, grew a visibly more affluent one. As the price of real estate in Spring Garden rose, gentrification extended into Fairmount. By the mid–1990s, the Fairmount and Spring Garden areas contained numerous upscale restaurants, gourmet delicatessens, a greatly reduced Catholic school attendance, and a radically diminished Hispanic population. An exclusive restaurant, located right on the border between Spring Garden and Fairmount and featuring Sunday brunches with Gospel music and evening jazz performances, opened in the late 1990s and regularly drew an upscale African-American clientele. By the early 2000s, three other fashionable restaurants lined a three-block strip along Fairmount Avenue, complete with outdoor seating. Regular trolley tours began to showcase Eastern State Penitentiary, the first penitentiary in the United States, a historic landmark separating the two neighborhoods. These tours, along with a special Halloween haunted house inside the ominous and imposing prison walls, brought a growing recognition of the area as an important and up-and-coming Center City residential area. Spring Garden was granted certification as a historic district in the year 2000.

TABLE 2.3.

Changes in Educational Background of Fairmount and Spring Garden Residents Compared to the City of Philadelphia, 1970–2000

Year	Fairmount college graduates (%)	Spring Garden college graduates (%)	Philadelphia[a] college graduates (%)
1970	7.4	16.4	6.8
1980	19.4	27.8	12.8
1990	45.2	56.7	15.2
2000	54.3	57.4	17.9

Source. Years 1950–1990, compiled from an aggregate file of the U.S. Census created by William Yancey with the assistance of Joshua Freely, Social Science Data Library, Temple University; 2000 data from the U.S. Census 2000 website, Summary File 3.

[a]Philadelphia is defined here as excluding the two census tracts represented by Fairmount (136) and Spring Garden (134).

Both neighborhoods were transformed by the arrival of the more affluent professional residents, but in different degrees. New grounds for suspicion were established between the two areas by a disparity in the rate of gentrification, a suspicion based more on class than on race. By the early 1970s, with gentrification proceeding at a more rapid pace in Spring Garden than in Fairmount, the proportion of college-educated residents in Spring Garden was already notably higher (16.4 percent compared to 7.4 percent), and it stayed significantly higher throughout the 1980s (Table 2.3). But as gentrification continued northward into the Fairmount area throughout the 1980s, these same educational disparities become more salient *within* the two neighborhoods. Just as the arrival of new professionals in the more southern neighborhood, Spring Garden, had pushed out many Puerto Ricans in the 1960s and 1970s, the continued movement of professionals northward into Fairmount in the 1980s also squeezed out many Fairmount old-timers. As one longtime Fairmount resident described it, "I bought my home in 1976, and I paid $12,000. No. $12,300 to be exact. It was like the '80s came, and the market took off. It just bloomed. And a lot of the people I knew had to move out, because they couldn't afford the property values. A lot of my friends waited a little too long, and . . . they wound up having to move to Roxborough," a somewhat less affluent, mostly white neighborhood. Others took advantage of the rising real estate values, sold their homes, and moved elsewhere.

Despite early tensions and suspicions between old-timers and newcomers, the arrival of new, white professionals marked a consolidation of Spring Garden as a predominantly white neighborhood again. This gradual transition eased racial fears to the extent that the racial riots of the early 1970s in Fairmount, against the entrance of new black families,[12] subsided over the next decade. But this was a gradual process, and although more middle-class professionals entered Spring Garden and Fairmount in the 1990s without incident, some of the first black professionals who had arrived in the 1970s remembered a more hostile reception. One black professor, Helena, whose family moved into Fairmount in 1973, described how they bypassed the closed real estate market with help from an interracial couple and defended themselves in the early years of their arrival:

> It was rough when we first moved here. We used to live in "Pig Alley," in a house two doors down from here. But we were renting. We entered from the back. The first couple of weeks, the local guys threw something into the window. Earl [her husband] had to go out there and straighten them out . . . the teenagers, the white gang that hung out down at the corner. There was a lot of drugs. . . . He knew who the kid was. Earl went up there and nearly killed him. He ran and got him and really shook him up. . . . And another day, Earl was sitting on the front porch, and his wallet was sitting there next to him, and somebody ran by and took the wallet. He chased him down too. He got his wallet back and scared them. After that, we haven't had any problems.

Recounting these events thirty years later in her home on the Fairmount–Spring Garden divide, she contrasted these experiences and her early feelings with her current, extremely positive feelings about the neighborhood. She noted the importance of baseball to her integration. Beyond the fact that Helena and her husband were highly educated professionals, another critical piece of information is that her son and daughter were excellent athletes who had played in the neighborhood baseball league. So again, we see a connection to baseball, not just in this story of a black professional family's gradual acceptance in the neighborhood, but also in the anecdote at the beginning of this chapter of the white Fairmount man who had fought blacks in the area as a youth and yet as an adult in the 1990s defended their right to walk in the neighborhood. Both cases of transformation, however one might understand them, are deeply embedded in youth baseball, the centerpiece of recreation in Fairmount, based on adult voluntary labor.

Over this thirty-year period of neighborhood change, the local youth baseball organization changed even more dramatically. Although historically the association had been an all-white organization, by the mid–1990s approximately one-third of the boys playing in the younger division were children of color. And peace prevailed. Given this neighborhood's past, how did this happen? The answer to this question must begin with a brief history of neighborhood baseball and its evolution from informal play to structured, competitive games.

Claiming Baseball as the Soul of the Neighborhood

Neighborhood play in Fairmount in the 1950s centered on baseball. For years, kids played informal games at 24th Street and Fairmount Avenue, a prominent block between the two neighborhoods. But one day in 1961 they discovered, in place of their rag-tag field, a large pit, the first step toward laying the foundation for a new large condominium, "The Philadelphian." An old-time Fairmounter who used to bring kids down to this field on his days off described this encounter: "We sent the kids out walking ahead of us one day. I told a kid to go ahead to center field. He came running back and says, "We don't have center field!" You couldn't see it because the field was basically level with Fairmount Avenue. I mean, had he run backwards, he would have fell the hell into the hole. We walked out and said, 'Well, there goes the baseball field.' . . . So after that, we played at the Dairy."

Sometime around this same period, a neighborhood man wanted to organize games among the boys. He began a baseball league, originally called simply "The Braves," out of the Catholic War Veterans Post, and recruited boys from the families connected to the post. Since there was no longer a field in the neighborhood, a small group of neighborhood guys would have them all meet at a specified corner in Fairmount and drive the boys, in an old station wagon they called the "Fairmount Bomber," about three miles north to "The Dairy," a section of Fairmount Park off Kelly Drive. They organized teams according to "corners" where different clusters of boys hung out. One old-timer explained how this worked: "When we were growing up, every corner used to have fifteen-twenty guys here. I mean one gang hung here. You go up to the next block, and there'd be fifteen-twenty guys there. We were all born and raised here, and there would be that many children from each block. So on each corner you would go to, there would be a gang of ten to fifteen guys. You either hung with this gang, or you hung with that gang. You didn't fight one another, but that was your gang." This abundance of kids hanging on corners structured the informal drafting of teams by the old-timer coaches. "A lot of people are [now] content with one kid. But when I was growing up there was families in the neighborhood that had thirteen kids, fourteen kids, seventeen kids. . . . Oh, there was kids everywhere. We didn't have any playgrounds or anything, but we would get games against this corner or that corner. Like, if we had eleven teams, they were all from different corners."

Around the same time, when Tom O'Conners (pseudonym), a talented, young ball player from Fairmount, turned twenty-one, he started his own traveling team sponsored by a different veterans' post in the neighborhood, the Parkway VFW. O'Conners recruited about fifteen of the best players from the original Braves. By the next year, O'Conners had fifty players and had to organize several teams. These traveling teams continued to practice at "The Dairy" and began to play competitive games in South Philadelphia. O'Conners looked to his friends to help him out with the coaching, thereby establishing a pattern that was to continue for decades in the organization: coaches were recruited strictly by word of mouth from neighborhood friendship networks. Some of them were parents, and some of them were not. Both the in-house teams and the traveling teams worked as a loose coalition until 1967, when personality conflicts and internal divisions provoked the men, more associated with the travel teams, to break away and form a separate organization newly named the "Fairmount Sports Association" (FSA). The Fairmount Braves and FSA coexisted for a brief period, until the original Braves folded and FSA emerged as the exclusive neighborhood baseball league, still organizationally based at the Catholic War Veterans Post.

The driving of kids back and forth from the neighborhood to The Dairy in Fairmount Park continued until the late 1960s, when the coaches decided they needed to play closer to the neighborhood and selected a nearby city-owned block, formally part of Fairmount Park, the largest urban park in the United States. When the coaches first started using the space, it was unleveled, and the middle of "center field" was lined with shrubs and a large tree. These new games did not please park officials. Gaining the right to use the space was a gradual process requiring street smarts, persistence, and "quiet confrontation" with local police officers. An old-time Fairmounter who was among a handful of coaches who took on this project described the process of peaceful confrontation they used to claim the territory for baseball:

> We had things like sit-in demonstrations on that field, where the cops
> would come by and say, "Come on, guys. We don't want to have to lock
> you up. You gotta do something because we need this field cleared." . . .
> When I say sit-ins, it was like five coaches. We'd just tell them, "Cops, we
> ain't coming out, so you gotta stop the game." We'd tell the kids, "Sit
> down." And it wasn't a nasty protest. We'd say, "What are you gunna do
> about this now? Because as soon as you leave, we're gunna start again."
> Then one cop said one day, "Come on, Joe, you're puttin' us in a position,
> and we're gettin' orders to lock everybody up."

Fairmount coaches defended themselves by complaining to officials that, unlike many other areas in the city, there was no local recreation center in the neighborhood. One of the obstacles to the use of this contested space was that, while it was city-owned, it was not controlled by the recreation office of the city but was officially part of Fairmount Park. The Fairmount Park Commission saw it as an open green space visible from the Benjamin Franklin Parkway (Philadelphia's "Champs-Élysées"), and they wanted its "park" image to remain. "That was one of the gripes. And when you think about it, it was legitimate. We had a legitimate gripe because there was nothing here and that was the only area to play. But the park—it was right on the Parkway—was pretty to look at driving by. Much prettier than watching a baseball field, I guess. They didn't want to give up a part of Fairmount Park, because once they give up a part, what happens to Manayunk [another neighborhood], or here, or there? But after six years, they got tired of the persistence and said, 'We'll let you.' And we told them we'd maintain it."

Their eventual success in securing permission to use this park land is all the more surprising when one considers that this block is strategically located among many major historic landmarks. The broad, tree-lined Ben Franklin Parkway majestically connects the vast Philadelphia Museum of Art, situated on a granite hill at one end, with the impressive, late-nineteenth-century structure of City Hall at the other, and is home to the Museum of Natural History, the Franklin Institute, and the Rodin Museum. After the 1960s, any visitor to the city who might stand, in the springtime, contemplating the outdoor gateway statute of Rodin's Thinker would have only to glance to the left to see the ball games that came to be a regular feature of that vast, public, open space that became known (in the neighborhood) as "The Field."

This case stands in sharp contrast to Goodman's description of the way dominant economic and cultural groups imposed organized sports on working-class youth, in the Lower East Side of Manhattan, to eliminate immigrant street culture in the early twentieth century.[13] Here, we have working-class residents fighting dominant cultural groups for the right to use public park land to serve their own definitions of its legitimate use—in this case, organized baseball. By the early 1970s, they had succeeded. FSA received formal permission to use the land and spent two years leveling the field. The original terms for the use of the public space built in a substantial commitment to maintain the physical appearance of the land as park land. Neighborhood men took up the challenge. They built two batting backstops on the property and transformed the block into a beautiful, lush, green surface of well-manicured grass and turf. And as a condition for the leasing of the park land, they continued to maintain the fields, for the price of one dollar a year, to be paid to the city for the next thirty years.

If local conflicts around issues of economic growth and the profitable use of space are at the center of the organization of cities, this victory for the public "use value"[14] of neighborhood baseball is a clear victory of neighborhood identity and sentiment over the exchange value of land. The timing of this victory coincides with growing conflicts in Philadelphia in the 1970s between "downtown" (growth machine) politicians and emerging neighborhood activism fighting displacement and gentrification.[15] Built on neighborhood labor, this kind of claiming and transformation inevitably instilled a sense of ownership and territoriality about the space. The claiming of this space for community use left with it collective "memory traces" that established baseball, and this voluntary association, as central to the "character" of this community[16] and defined baseball as a "beauty asset" that Fairmounters would defend for the next three decades.

Letting Outsiders In

In the early years of FSA baseball, all the kids came from the neighborhood, and almost exclusively from the three Catholic schools that existed in Fairmount then. Although there was some limited involvement of local Hispanic families who were part of the same Catholic schools, the children were overwhelmingly white. The organization did not draw upon the large population of black children from adjacent neighborhoods. For one thing, the origins of the organization as an informal operation out of a veterans' post meant that it was next to impossible to know when and where to sign up to play in the spring if you were outside the social networks of these neighborhood men. Up until the mid–1980s, registration for the spring season occurred over two weekends in February at the Catholic War Veterans Post, where all of the baseball equipment was stored for the year and where neighborhood men regularly congregated to drink beer together and socialize. The inaccessibility of the registration reflected a culture of racial exclusion that had dominated the neighborhood. One Fairmounter coach described it:

> Listen. We have our own Halloween. We call it "Whiteween." Parents are notified in their mailboxes when our Halloween is, so they don't have to be attacked on regular Halloween, or be run over by wolf packs [black trick or treaters from neighboring areas]. We have our own Halloween separate for that reason. . . . Twenty years ago that's how it would be here [with baseball]. We would notify who we wanted to about registration. It would be delivery to your house, instead of putting it in the newspaper and publicizing everything. That's how it would have been handled twenty years ago. Registration wouldn't be open. It would be closed.

The tightness of the neighborhood, the reputation for racial exclusion, and the inaccessibility of the sign-ups meant few people needed to be turned away. They simply did not turn up. Jessie, who grew up in Fairmount, described how racial boundaries were maintained in the play spaces of her childhood and reflected bitterly on the social costs she had paid for her parents' fears of blacks.

JESSIE: They [blacks] would have known not to even come. . . . There was no advertising, no. This is why Fairmount has never had a playground, a swing set, nothing! Because our parents and their parents said, "You put a playground up, and they'll take it over."

S.G.: So you deprive yourselves of things to keep other people out?

JESSIE: Exactly. . . . "Nope. You can't have that, because *they'll* come and *they'll* take over." Them playgrounds [new slides and climbers built in the late 1990s adjacent to the field], you see where those are? I'm thinkin' to myself, "Hey! We coulda' been swingin!" [Laughter] All those years we were deprived. We were DEPRIVED OF THINGS!

Fairmount baseball first started to change in the early 1970s when several things happened that would permanently transform its insular nature. First, the rapid gentrification of the area meant a rather dramatic loss of population, especially in the relative numbers of children in the area. This meant a relative scarcity of children eligible for baseball. Between 1950 and 1990, the population of Fairmount dropped by almost half, from 10,764 to 5,882. Spring Garden's population declined even more sharply over the same period; by 1990 it had dropped to approximately one-third of its 1950 size (Table 2.1). As the local population declined and the social backgrounds of Fairmount and Spring Garden residents changed, the traditional base of the Catholic schools in the area declined dramatically. The lack of children in the area meant the viability of strictly "local" baseball was at risk. The original leadership of FSA recognized this in the early 1970s, and made a series of strategic decisions to ensure an ample supply of children for the organization and to preserve its ability to launch a full spectrum of teams for each division. The organization would have to be "opened" up, first to the children of the new professionals in the area, who were already entering, and then to other Center City areas. This opening to outsiders began toward the end of the tenure of what I'll call the "founding generation" of FSA leaders, in 1977. They took steps informally to recruit children from a nearby downtown, largely white, neighborhood. While this shift was resisted by some in the organization, it marked the beginning of an important step in the history of FSA. As one of the original founders of FSA described it:

We decided we gotta open this up because, with this exodus out of the neighborhood, we didn't have enough kids. [Fewer kids] . . . doesn't mean you can't operate, but it can get very boring playing four teams instead of seven or eight. So we saw this. We saw the moving-out, the people we knew, and so we opened it. And that was it. We either closed baseball, or we opened it. So I said, "I'm gunna go down and talk to a friend of mine, Morrie Feinstein, who lives by Taney and Pine. I know they're having trouble getting their field, and tell him to come up. . . . No, we didn't advertise anywhere. We never advertised. Word of mouth. And as soon as a few kids from there [Center City] came, everybody came. . . . But some of these [Fairmounter] guys said, "We don't want them. We don't want this!" They're the people we used to tell, "Just go over in the corner and shut up." I think it was, there were ethnic things. . . . First, there were the Jews, and they were the outsiders. Fairmount was always a very cliquey neighborhood. Most of us were kind of rebels within that. . . . But, yea, there was a lot of, "They're outsiders. They're not Fairmounters."

In the mid–1970s, tensions sprang up between this founding generation of FSA and other, younger neighborhood coaches. Although the founding generation of leaders sought to include larger numbers of children in order to continue the viability of local ball, they also wanted to preserve the "purity" of the organization by keeping it strictly focused on baseball games for children, with few extra frills. They were relatively unsympathetic to growing pressures, from younger Fairmounters inside the organization, to build in more social comforts, such as a concession stand, around the games. The replacement of this founding generation, after 1976, by a second generation of FSA leaders marks a shift in the organization away from a "strictly baseball" approach. While the second generation of FSA leaders had different ideas about the acceptability of adult socializing around the children's baseball space, they nevertheless continued the pattern, started by the first generation of coaches, of opening up the organization to outsiders and extended it to include not just white professional children from outside the area, but also the families of color who began entering FSA in the late 1980s.

Second, beyond the scarcity of local children, the friendship networks of local children were expanding to include children from outside the neighborhood. As the neighborhood gentrified, the presence of a growing group of children who attended non-Catholic private schools (Quaker and secular), and non-parish Catholic schools outside the neighborhood, also grew. Because a growing proportion of these children attended schools outside the neighborhood, the networks of information about the neighborhood and its recreational opportunities expanded. Many of these children had strong networks with middle-class minority children. These children, and their parents, played a part in sponsoring middle-class children of color into FSA. Quite a number of black parents I interviewed mentioned that they learned about FSA's programs through these private school networks. Thus, ironically, although the entry of these largely white professionals into Spring Garden had played a part in pushing Latino residents out of the area, their sponsorship of middle-class children of color into neighborhood baseball also played a part in breaking down the racial isolation of Fairmount. But only a part. In addition, the fact that the one surviving Catholic school in the area, St. Francis Xavier, could no longer rely predominantly on neighborhood children to sustain itself, and instead drew increasingly from neighborhoods of color in the surrounding areas, also played a role. As this school increasingly integrated over time, some white Fairmount children also sponsored the entrance of their school friends of color into the ranks of FSA. Both of these sources provided a kind of "race sponsorship" into the predominantly white local space.

Third, several factors combined to give FSA greater visibility and political accountability in the city in the mid–1980s. Prior to this time, there were no physical markers of the organization at the ball field. Children desperate for restroom facilities were often shepherded to a tolerant neighbor's house a few blocks away. Several years after my family had moved to Spring Garden in 1984, I remember driving by the field and seeing kids playing baseball in uniforms. I tried to find out how to sign my daughter up to play T-ball. No one I asked seemed to know, until it occurred to me to ask the mother of two girls on the block who went to the neighborhood Catholic school. She explained that I should go to a back room, "kind of a bar," up at one of the Veterans' Posts in Fairmount, on one of two Saturday nights in the winter before the season starts. They would collect the registration fee and then a coach would call about a month later to tell me what team my daughter was on and where to go for practice. "How would I find all this out if I didn't know you?" I asked. "You wouldn't," she replied.

The ball field remained essentially a large, leveled, lot until 1985, when the president of FSA and the local ward leader persuaded John Street, then local City Council representative, to secure then Mayor Wilson Goode's approval for the construction of a clubhouse with bathroom facilities, a concession area, and a meeting room for the organization. Five years later, in the middle of the 1990 season, the new building with its concession stand and restrooms opened with an agreement from the City that FSA, in exchange for the maintenance of the field, the grounds, and the building by its volunteers, would rent the space and facilities for one dollar a year, ratified in five-year contracts.

From that point on, anyone driving by and seeing large groups of children playing organized games could inquire at the concession stand on one side of the new building and receive information about sign-up procedures. It is of no small significance that both the City Council representative and the mayor who ultimately supported this neighborhood initiative were African American politicians who represented large minority constituencies beyond the neighborhood. The completion of this building, and the involvement of city officials, was a turning point for the organization, a visible index of which was the transition of organizational headquarters from an insulated informal club within a Catholic veterans' organization located in Fairmount, controlled by a small group of neighborhood men, to a highly visible building, constructed with city funds, with a new accountability to public officials.

Finally, after white gentrification in Spring Garden had contributed to pushing out many residents of color, most of them Puerto Rican, in the 1970s and 1980s, the 1990s saw growing numbers of black professional residents beginning to move into the area. The entrance of the children of these black newcomers into FSA, combined with the other, largely middle-class minority children from outside the area who had already entered FSA, meant that, by the mid–1990s, approximately one-third of the youngest children playing organized baseball in FSA were children of color. Anyone in the 1960s, aware of how blacks were excluded and sometimes violently expelled from this area, would have found such an outcome surprising indeed. One Fairmount mother who had grown up playing baseball in the neighborhood said that the rapid racial change in FSA took her by surprise:

> Well I know my reaction to Opening Day, and the day after it, was like, "Did they send flyers out all over the city?" I was just like, where did they all come from? I mean, where did they all find out about us? And it's like, word of mouth. And I mean, there's nothing you can really do. When you have a league and it's opened up for enrollment, that's it.

This racial transformation of neighborhood baseball occurred not only relatively rapidly, compared to the two surrounding neighborhoods, but relatively harmoniously. How was that? Beyond the demographic changes and the new accountability to black politicians, the answer lies in two factors: "race sponsorship" and the nature of baseball itself.

Race Sponsorship

The importance of what I call "race sponsorship" in the smooth integration of FSA cannot be underestimated. Race sponsorship, as I define it, occurs when an individual or family enters a formerly exclusive space through alignment with, or sponsorship by, an individual with legitimate membership status. This is similar to the moment in the early Jackie Robinson days, in 1947, when Pee Wee Reese left his shortstop position to walk to first base and stand with his arm around his lone black teammate on the Dodgers as they confronted racist taunts from the Cincinnati fans.[17] In FSA, mixed-race alliances helped create pockets of safe space for new minority members in this early stage of integration, and later for whites whose race motivations might be misunderstood by new minorities entering. Sometimes this was a "remote sponsorship," where a leader of the organization extended a welcome to a minority stranger in the face of members who were prepared to offer a more hostile reception. The motives for this kind of sponsorship are almost irrelevant, and might have been little more than a strategic move on the part of the sponsor to fill the ranks of the organization. But the importance lay in its function, as the means by which such a leader or sponsor resisted the "race bulldogs," the more overt racists in the organization who had dedicated themselves to "boundary work" (to the exclusion of blacks under almost any circumstance). The race bulldogs were kept in check by fellow insiders. I saw this kind of sponsorship on numerous occasions, done by strategic leaders of FSA, in the 1990s. Several examples illustrate this. Every year, on two weekends in February, the organizational leaders of FSA (some insider coaches, and some their friends from the neighborhood) congregate in the small, windowless meeting room of the clubhouse to await the arrival of parents signing up their children for the next season of baseball. A good deal of socializing occurs over the course of these two weekends. It is also a good strategic place to be if you're a coach who is looking to pick up new, talented kids who might not be known to the other coaches. Once this registration is over, the league selects its coaches and holds a draft. The league has no formal obligations to accept any latecomers; accepting those who come late and charging them a late fee is a discretionary decision. This makes the post-registration period an opportune time for excluding anyone who might be considered undesirable.

During one of these weekends in the mid–1990s, when the number of black children was just beginning to show noticeable increases, I went to this "office" to pay the eighty-dollar inscription fee and to register my son. For those registering, there were two chairs in front of the sign-up desk. I was seated at one filling out forms, while a heavy-set black mother sat next to me, filling out a registration form for her son. After she left, a Fairmounter named Carl, who regularly hangs out at the clubhouse and qualifies as what I have called a "race bulldog," softly mumbled to a small group of men standing around something like, "Watch out, that chair is still warm." I glanced up to see the expression of Brian, one of the leaders of the organization, who was seated opposite me. As he looked up, he frowned disapprovingly in Carl's direction. The reprimand was subtle and involved no overt loss of face for Carl, but it served to silence him, and also the snickers of another listener.

Commentary from two other FSA coaches also confirms the importance of sponsorship by strategic FSA leaders and coaches. William, a black school principal I interviewed, whose two sons had played in the league for five years, also stressed the role of certain strategic FSA leaders in welcoming-in new people of color "without a lot of ruffled feathers":

> I've heard other people who have complained, but when I ask questions about it, I think sometimes they may be overly reacting. You know, overly sensitive to what has been, what someone has said or done to them. . . .
> If there is a problem, I think that there are ways to deal with that problem.

> I think Brian [FSA leader] is very approachable. I think the Commis-
> sioners are approachable. But Brian specifically is very approachable
> about problems, and I think he's very open to looking for solutions.

It would be rather surprising if a social space like Fairmount, with the kind
of history of racial exclusion and racism that had plagued the neighborhood in
the past, would have produced a group of adult men among whom racist feelings or subtle racist behaviors were entirely absent. The integration of the baseball space certainly did not mean this sort of racism-free atmosphere had been
attained. But the extent to which the strategic individuals within the leadership
of FSA reached out on a regular basis to a stream of new black families and
sponsored their entry with a welcoming stance was remarkable. Their willingness to do this, while holding their "race bulldogs" mostly in check, set the stage
for the race integration that followed.

Coupled with the sponsorship of early black children into FSA by strategic
leaders and middle-class kids, their parents' relatively low level of interest in
getting very involved in the organization of FSA meant they posed little threat
to insiders. The first black parents who entered the organization lived largely
outside of the neighborhood, in Center City or in the surrounding areas, and
were primarily interested in a safe space for their children that would not
require a large time commitment. As one black lawyer put it, "I don't feel like
they necessarily need me to do anything, and that's fine. I'm just happy that we
have the league. If they can handle it, fine. But nobody really asked me to participate in any leadership way anyway. . . . But I don't have the time. There's a
lot about FSA that I would like to see changed, but I don't have the time to really
make it happen, so there's no point to complain about something you can't do
a thing about."

Beyond the organizational leadership, the consolidation of black politicians into strategic positions of power at the city level, including as neighborhood representative to City Council, added an additional incentive to facilitate
the smooth reception of new black families into FSA. One white Fairmount
mother contrasted the current openness of the organization with the past she
remembered: "I think it can happen now because of the way the laws are set up.
It kind of ties your hands. Where twenty years ago, I think them laws were like
stuck in a box somewhere. And everybody just closed their eyes to it. Ignorance,
whatever you want to call it." In addition, white leadership dominated the city
of twenty years ago, and baseball was strictly a neighborhood affair. A black
father, William, who gave several FSA leaders the bulk of the credit for welcoming in families of color, nonetheless noted the importance of this background
political climate and the two strategically placed African American politicians:

> Well, I think the leadership set the tone. I think the other thing, from a
> practical standpoint, the leadership, Fairmount's Sport Association, has

received a lot of support from John Street, and he was the councilman then, and now from, what's his name, Darrell Clark. . . . You know, they get state money. They get city money. And I think they understand that part of that, in order to do that, you have to show that there is some, you know some positive, affirmative kind of plan for the, for what they do, and it's worked out fine.

Remote race sponsorship by a few strategic leaders, however, could not bring about the kind of race integration seen at FSA if it were not also occurring in multiple ways at a more grassroots level as well. In addition to sponsorship by association leaders and greater accountability to black civic leaders, more intimate forms of race sponsorship were also significant to the integration process. Numerous black professional parents I interviewed mentioned that they originally found out about FSA through their child's white friends at the private school they attended outside the neighborhood. Thus, some of these early black children did not enter alone, or as groups of black children, but as part of mixed-race friendships, often visible to organizational gatekeepers. One affluent black father remembered how his daughter entered FSA:

> Well, it was when my daughter, Barbara, was at [a private downtown Quaker school]. We found out through Karla [a white girl at the same school], because she was playing ball, and her mother and my wife had a conversation about Karla. And my wife said, "Wow, you know, I'm sure we want Barbara to do something like that." She was about six or seven when we took her down there. . . . And in the case of black people, all of us are connected back to a neighborhood somewhere. We may be middle-class, or upper-class, whatever, but we're all connected. And if we see an opportunity for young kids, we're gonna, you know, bring others in. That's just the way it is. And *dare* somebody to tell us we can't do it.

While this father is stressing his responsibility to offer good opportunities to other black families, he is also linking his daughter's entrance to a mixed-race, private school network. These friendships structured the context of entry, so that an exclusion of one child could easily translate into conflicts with another, whose exclusion could not be justified along racial lines or whose parents might have had more social resources to resist.

Helena, the black professor, and her family—described above as one of the early black families in Fairmount—who had been tormented by hostile white teenagers, provides another example of race sponsorship, in this case through an alliance with a mixed-race couple. In our interview, she stressed how her family's very entrance into the neighborhood had been sponsored originally by a black real estate agent who rented them their first apartment in Fairmount.

HELENA: Michelle [a black real estate agent] used to live above us and owned the building. They were an interracial marriage, and they would catch it upstairs, and we would catch it downstairs. They [the neighbors] would really just throw things at them. So when Earl, my husband, went out there and took care of them, it slowed up a lot, because they just thought he was crazy.

S.G.: So, when you guys lived up there, were those two apartments the only black people in the neighborhood? On that block?

HELENA: Almost in the neighborhood. There were very few African Americans in the neighborhood. Michelle was probably the pioneer. And then she rented to us. Later she sold us this house.

But it was her sponsorship into baseball and her family's active participation there that smoothed the way for their eventual social acceptance in the neighborhood. One year, a very competitive coach who lived on their block "discovered them" before the draft and recruited them into FSA. They entered under his direct personal sponsorship, although they had already formed an opinion about the organization from another professional black mother whose daughter had played the year before with no problems.

> But if it weren't for that [baseball], we would probably never have really gotten involved with the neighborhood. It forced us to become "Fairmounters." That's basically what happened. Real Fairmounters! Accepted by Fairmounters! You know, it's hard to be a Fairmounter. You almost have to be in the sports. One thing that puts you in their league is the sports team. . . . I just think that Fairmount is a unique little area. It really is, when you think about it. There's a two-three mile radius, and it never ceases to amaze me. Even this little block, my neighbors. They are interesting people. There's the different cultures, the different economic brackets. One person lives over here and makes $500,000 and another person doesn't work.

Interracial couples, or mixed-race families, constitute obvious instances of "intimate race sponsorship." For example, those prone to exclude a black child may come to see that child in a different light when his behaviors are regularly interpreted by his white father, who has little social distance from the racially suspicious. One black mother, married to a white man named Fritz who was active in the league for years, explained her son's positive experience in FSA, "Want to know why Sonny had such a good experience down there [the field]? One and only one reason: Fritz. They could all relate to Fritz. So I tried to keep a distance and just watch from far off." Similarly, when two middle-class children of different races demonstrate a casual comfort, as well as an implied history, despite the fact that they may have different cultural styles, their friendship proves a model for those with no such experience. The modeling might be for other racially exclusive children or it might be for their own wary parents. Shawn, a Fairmount league parent who had described his own adolescence as one constant battle with black kids, expressed amazement at how his son, Jimmy, had black friends from the ball field who ran in and out of his house "like nothing."

As a different kind of example, a black parent who suspects a white coach is treating his child unfairly might be less likely to read in racial motives if the coach regularly selects a black parent as his assistant, and if this black parent can testify by example to the nonexclusionary style of the suspected coach. In this case, the black parent is sponsoring the acceptance. Intimate race sponsorship is vital, because the reception and interpretation of the behaviors of those defined as "the other" always happen in a context, and the more the context links the potentially excluded to internal bases of support, via distant or intimate race sponsorship, the more likely the entry will be smooth and judgments about behaviors tolerant, or at least not overtly hostile.

Segmented Integration

The fact that the integration process at FSA occurred relatively harmoniously doesn't mean that it also happened evenly. I noticed over the years, and numerous parents I interviewed also brought up, that the children of color were often not randomly distributed among the white coaches. Certain white coaches were more likely than others to have more black kids on their teams. This pattern of "selective recruitment" resulted from a variety of factors. Some coaches worked hard to recruit known neighborhood kids, most of whom were white. In other cases, either coaches had no such preferences, or once they had a black child on their team they tried to draft him again because he was known to them. Black parents who had had positive experiences with a coach sometimes volunteered to assist with the coaching so as to secure for their child a place on that coach's team. In any case, these more welcoming coaches carved out a safe social space for these new children and their parents, which served as an important filter for the newcomers' overall interpretations of the organization. Sal was one such coach. A Puerto Rican father had included him in his list of a handful of white coaches he viewed as most likely to have more mixed teams. Sal described how he perceived his role in this process:

> The direction of the interview was interesting to me, because it's stuff I think about all the time—when you asked me about race. I watch these interactions all the time. I'm supposed to . . . and I'm not one of these crusaders. I'm not gonna come out and say [pause]. I mean, I have to coexist here. But I don't agree all the time with what's going on. . . . Last

year I had a lot of black kids on my team again. Years ago, I used to work as an exterminator, and I worked in some black homes where the kids would come up to me and touch my arms, like they had never seen a white person in their lives. I always remembered that. My experience here has been such that, having these kids on my team, I don't try to be anything special. I'm jus', I'm just a white guy who's not half-bad. That's what I'm trying to be. White kids get a lot of preconceptions from their parents and so do black children—what to expect. There's a guy, Phil, a black janitor where I work who lives way up North Philly, and he told me he wanted his kids to play baseball and experience other types of children. So he came down, and I got him on my team. The kid got the sportsmanship award, for being there all the time. . . . They said he had a great time and is coming back. . . .

Why is [integration in the league] so smooth? Because of the diversity of the white people. You have people with better educational backgrounds. It's not all the [pause]. I don't know how to explain this. I think about this a lot, but I can't verbalize it. I think there were more non-Fairmount whites who could lessen the impact of the change. Does that make sense?

Jessie, a white Fairmounter whose small neighborhood business brings her into frequent contact with newcomers, also mentioned the impact of more liberal professional attitudes on neighborhood change, "No, I think it [race integration] has been relatively smooth, considering this neighborhood and its background. . . . I guess you gotta give credit where credit's due. If the yuppies didn't move in, I don't think there would be any change. I think they moved in with different attitudes, and you kind of got a little eye opening here and there, and you start to think, 'Well, you know, they're right.' . . . And I think time itself."

Recognizing the segmented nature of the racial integration that did occur in FSA is crucial to understanding the uneven process by which the transformation occurred. Its unevenness also meant that not all families of color who played baseball at FSA came away with good feelings. Some were isolated on teams whose coaches were less sympathetic, or were concentrated on teams whose coaches were in disfavor with the leadership or umpires, and came away with judgments that race issues were still alive and well at FSA. In fact, after my fieldwork was completed, I learned that in 2003 a small group of parents that included some local Puerto Rican parents tried to organize an alternative baseball league at a nearby playground, the Roberto Clemente Park. Though this league never attracted enough support to get off the ground, at least several of these parents were motivated to make the attempt because they felt some of their negative experiences at FSA had a racial basis. But many more families of color stayed and found enough welcoming space at FSA to transform the organization into a multicultural one.

Something about Baseball

Scholars who have studied race and sport have often debated whether sports activities promote social integration or merely reflect broader social inequalities in their games, on their benches, and in their locker rooms.[18] Depending on the context, sport can facilitate racial harmony or contribute to racial division. On the negative side, sport events can become venues for racial hostilities when teams representing different racial groups compete and give fans and players opportunities to vent game frustrations through racial channels. Other sports practices, such as "stacking" (the segregating of blacks into certain team positions) or the underrepresentation of minorities in professional sports leadership or "thinking" positions, inflame racial resentments.[19] On the positive side, sport enthusiasts point to the way sports can bring people of different backgrounds together. For example, three-fourths of high school athletes told Louis Harris pollsters in 1993 that they had made friends across racial lines through sport.[20] Thus sports becomes a means of integration, not just for the participants, but for those who identify with the competing teams.[21] Eitzen has identified some contexts in which sports can help build racial understandings, such as (a) when teams permit players of different races to contribute equally to team success, and (b) when the team with mixed races is successful.[22]

Much of what we do know from the field of the sociology of sport regarding the ameliorative or destructive impact of sport comes from research on the top levels of sports, the college and professional levels.[23] With this elite focus comes a heavy emphasis on how organized sports, controlled by a dominant class,[24] or corporate sports controlled by a power elite, directs spectator attention away from social injustices.[25] This emphasis on "sports as opiate"[26] leaves little maneuverability to human agents, who might find pleasure and community amidst the constraints of sport's rules and ideologies, or who might even resist the status quo within sport arenas.

Critical sports sociologists who have weighed extensive evidence on both sides of this debate point to a more paradoxical verdict: under certain conditions, the consequences of sport can be destructive, by reinforcing dominant power relations and racial and gender inequalities; conversely, under some conditions they can be constructive, by undermining or challenging them.[27] The answer may well depend on the type of sport and level of sport, whether it is informal, organized, or corporate. The challenge is to understand the particular circumstances that obtain when sports experiences are positive and healthy, and those that obtain when they are negative and destructive, and to account for the differences.[28]

This chapter has explored the factors behind a delicate process of racial integration in the neighborhood baseball league of these two Philadelphia neighborhoods. Turning to the role of sports itself, we could extend the question and ask, "Were all the features mentioned above sufficient to bring about the transformation of this exclusive, white baseball league into a relatively harmoniously integrated recreational space? Were all these factors—the passion of the neighborhood men for preserving the integrity of the game, a scarcity of local children, mixed-race alliances and the race sponsorship of new children, the visible lure of the new clubhouse, and the new accountability to black politicians—enough?" We could further ask, "Did it matter that it was baseball? Would the same thing have happened if it had been football, or soccer, or a neighborhood basketball league? Could the social change that happened in Spring Garden and Fairmount have been embodied in any other sport?" My answer would be no. Something about baseball itself did matter to this transformation.

The quasi-religious status of baseball in America is an idea well established among scholars of the sport.[29] For one thing, baseball is a highly structured encounter, inherent in which is a great deal of waiting. And it is precisely because of all that waiting, that requirement of patience while tracking the contingencies and possibilities of a play, that baseball offers such social opportunities. Think of the spectators' experience of the game, not just that of the players. Parents sit together on bleachers, often separated from the parents of the other teams who are sitting on different bleachers, each team's parents sitting with their child's teammates' parents. Parents of different backgrounds sit together, but in a very highly structured context. They do not have to figure out how to relate to one another. The differences that might cause problems among them are not right on the surface, or are at least deflected by the bigger concern: the game. You're part of this team, and you're part of that team. You just sit, and wait, and you don't have to do anything. But at the same time, there is a bonding that goes on, because, at least for this season, you share a common fate. And this common fate produces conversation: what the other team did wrong, what the other coach should have done, what our coach should have done, how Rickie didn't fall asleep until midnight worrying about the playoffs, what if the sun goes down before we score? Over a fairly short period of time, a deep sense of "we" develops. Parents don't like it, for example, when parents from another team forgetfully sit on their bleachers (even when they know one another). They want to be able to feel happy with "their group" when the poor little seven-year-old on the other team strikes out. They want to feel okay about it, to mumble, "Thank God." So there is that structure to baseball. There is enough time between the moments of intensity to permit human connections. Precisely what looks like a boring moment to baseball's detractors is often a deeply felt moment of shared wonder to the informed spectator.

Baseball is also a game of hope, and a game that spotlights individual failures. Pitchers break down. Batters fail. Fielders drop the ball. There are a lot of collectively shared feelings about the errors and mishaps of individual players, most of whom—almost all of whom—will not be your own son or daughter. A kind of identification evolves, not just with the group, but with particular kids over what happened to them that day, that game. We now care intensely about what happened today to the kid we didn't even know three weeks ago. Mothers will commiserate with each other with a "You're gonna have a rough night tonight!" when one of the boys has three strikeouts in a game.

So the slow pace of baseball, punctuated as it is by moments of such intensity and drama—that long plateau with its occasional upsurges—matters. It allows parents of different backgrounds to come together on the bleachers and feel comfortable, without the need to do much, and yet to share the passion, the disappointments, and the triumphs. And just before all this "we" feeling gets out of control (at least usually before), the season comes to an end. And then comes the reshuffling. So that the next season the parents are on the same bleachers, but with a different group of people. And after four seasons, they have come to know a lot of people in the community, and learned a lot, very specifically, about different individuals and their children. While they may at first have thought of a given child as a "jerk," after months on the bleachers with that child's parents they often learn more about why the child behaves poorly, and may feel less removed from that child's "problem."

On the bleachers, parents share that baseball "suspension of time." In contrast, parents who sit together watching basketball do not get the same opportunities. In basketball, too much happens against the pressure of the clock. The same is true for soccer. So, it mattered that it was baseball. Because it was baseball, we waited, and hoped together, and experienced moments of communion, pain, and redemption in the process.

Last but not least, Fairmount baseball is played on that lush, green rectangle of grass and red earth, before the backdrop of the open skyline of Center City Philadelphia and its most majestic museums. This space offers all its participants a constant grounding in beauty on a scale grander than the baseball diamond. The deep longing begins around the end of February. "When will practices start?" "Has your coach called yet?" Opening Day becomes an aesthetic reentrance into a community of friends, neighbors, and former strangers where, just as you feel the first warmth of the spring, you begin tracking the inevitable growth and changes in this year's crop of children. "Oh, my gosh, look at how much Jonathan grew." "I can't believe George is no longer afraid of the ball." "Look at that green! I say to my wife, you want a yard? A yard? This is all the grass I need."

To say that the racial integration of FSA occurred relatively smoothly and without major conflicts is not to say that there were not tensions, grumblings, or conflicts—including stacking, selective recruitment, and questionable calls against outsiders—in which racism played a real or perceived role. These certainly did happen. But given the history of racial conflict in this neighborhood, it is a striking fact that the central cleavages to emerge in this organization were not along racial lines, but rather along lines of class, or along the divide between the old-timers and the new professionals.

ONE OF THE SWEETEST intricacies of baseball is the rule about a dropped third strike. This rule permits a player who strikes out the chance to run to first base, if the catcher drops the ball on the third strike. It builds a strong element of hope into baseball. While individual failures are spotlighted in baseball, small possibilities of redemption like this are laced throughout the game. In reviewing the history of baseball in this neighborhood, we have seen that the Fairmounters cared enough about baseball to turn their backs on their own exclusionary past and to make room for outsiders—first their "class competitors," and then children of color. Did the newcomers get to be deep insiders? For the most part, no. But their children were allowed in, and they gathered rich experiences in a beautifully orchestrated game. And all of this happened in a city that had distinguished itself by its exclusion. In the mid–1950s, Philadelphia had the *last* national league baseball team to integrate.[30] Fairmount, a neighborhood that had represented the ugly racial segregation that marked many American cities, that had defended itself against racial "outsiders" with interpersonal violence, got a chance to redeem itself in the later decades of the twentieth century—and took it. Responding to population loss, and in the post–civil rights era context of the new scrutiny of elected black officials, locals watched as children and parents of color were sponsored in. The neighborhood reformed itself, slowly and unevenly, to move beyond its failures, at least on the turf of baseball. It got a second chance and took it—just like running out a dropped third strike.

====================================

Kate's Quiet Championship

There were teams that Fairmount insiders favored—the clubhouse teams—and teams that needed to be beaten—the "yuppie teams." During certain defining games, like the playoffs or a game that would clinch a team's position in the standings, the size of the crowds gathered behind the two teams was lopsided. Behind the team with a Fairmount head coach, a large crowd would congregate, many of whom were not parents of players but simply neighborhood folks who had come out to root either for this coach or for neighborhood boys they knew on the team. In contrast, for the opposing team, headed by a newcomer coach, the crowd was usually much smaller, even for championship games. The clubhouse teams also tended to have lots of Fairmount players, whereas the newcomer teams were stacked with newcomer kids.

Kate was one of the most unusual women in all of FSA. Her father had been a semipro umpire, so she had a profound experiential and factual knowledge of the nuances of the game. As a single parent, she had moved to the neighborhood precisely because she wanted her son to play baseball there. Kate was college-educated at a local, prestigious university, but had a low-key, self-effacing manner. She was of average height, and somewhat heavy set, and she combined a confident, easygoing style with an easy laugh. Rarely did she parade the extent of her baseball knowledge, nor had she ever aspired to become a coach-manager. Indeed, it had taken years before many in FSA appreciated her expertise. Eventually, she was discovered and regularly called upon to advise informally about technical rule conflicts during games. Her nine years of assistant coaching on multiple teams, keeping score for the older traveling team, and working long hours at the concession stand finally earned her an invitation to join the FSA board. Not only was she one of the first newcomers to be included on the board, she was certainly the only female professional to serve there. She described herself as exactly in the middle between the "yuppies" and the Fairmounters.

Kate had started assisting Dan, the Fairmounter coach of the Marlins, a 7–9 team, when her son first joined his team. Dan was secure enough with his own masculinity that, one year, he came to rely on the considerable baseball expertise of Kate as far as to make her his main assistant coach. He then convinced her to stay on with him as assistant coach for years after her son left that age division. While it was not unusual in the league to have men without sons coach teams, it was highly unusual to have women without sons serve as assistant coaches of boys' teams. This meant that he preferred her assistance over that of any of the fathers on the team. Strong statement. Indeed, Dan stood out, in this regard, for his early public endorsement of Kate's baseball acumen, when she was not defined as someone's wife or mother, but as merely an expert.

In 1998, Kate was again the assistant coach for Dan's 7–9 team, the Marlins, but also for a 10–12 team, the Rangers—with my husband, John, as the head coach. John had also asked Kate to assist him, knowing that when he had to leave the country to teach before the playoffs, she could continue in his place. So Kate found herself serving as head coach for the Rangers, as they prepared to play for the 10–12 championship against a "clubhouse team" with many Fairmount players, coached by a relative of one of the FSA leaders. Kate explains:

> Well, you know, the guys up at the clubhouse always have a team that they are cheering for, and it's usually because one of their kids is on it. Um....And usually, when one of their kids is on it, the team tends to be, not always, but it tends to be a good team because there are just ways that that just happens. Um....And they cheer for them and, rightly so. They're cheering for their kids, but they sort of bring the organization with them when they cheer for their kids. Like this year, when the Marlins played the Senators in the championship, and the Senators were the in-house team. Dutch, the coach, had, sort of, "the guys" on his team. Then the Rangers [her other team] played the Expos, who were the 10–12 house team, so I was beginning to feel *really* not liked. [Laughter] So I was on both of the disfavored teams.

The pressure of that championship was even greater for Mike, the coach of the opposing clubhouse team. After all, he was facing the only female head coach ever to lead a 10–12 team, and certainly ever to take that team to the championship. It was a three-game series. Most assumed Kate would be lucky to win one game. But after she won the first game, Mike, the opposing coach, wasn't so sure. So as they exchanged their lineups by trading clipboards, he placed a little yellow "sticky slip" on his clipboard with a hand-scribbled note with a smiley face on it that said, "Let me win this one." A secret message between the two of them. I wondered aloud as she told me this if he were serious. Kate responded: "It WAS serious. I really didn't know how to take it. I mean he couldn't really expect me to betray my own team like that. What was I supposed to do—switch around the players or what? I suppose he felt it was just too much to deal with, his relatives, and all of them." Compounding her awkward feeling about that note was the fact that so few of the parents from her underdog team came to the game and stood behind her dugout to cheer, compared with the dramatic turnout of Fairmount supporters for the opposing, clubhouse team. Kate continues:

> Some of the guys from the field house were up the hill, but everybody that came to the field stood behind the other dugout. If we had been standing on a scale instead of on a baseball field, it would have tipped over and everybody would have slid into the other dugout. Because there were chairs behind it, people were standing behind it and there were more chairs. Everybody who came down was cheering for the other team, and the few people who were cheering for us, the Rangers, had the intelligence not to do it openly, or to do it from up the top of the hill where nobody could tell what team they were cheering for. Only a few of our parents came. A few of them couldn't come, even the few who usually do come. I was, of course, in the dugout. Pete's dad [a Fairmounter who stuck by her] was in the dugout with me, and Victor's dad was in the dugout with me. A few others. But basically we had three or four people behind the dugout, and there were just scores of people over there.

Then there was the one newcomer parent, Paul, who stood openly behind Kate's dugout during the first game, even though he did not have a son on either team. His loyalty to Kate was understandable, because his son had played on this team with Kate assisting for three years before moving up. However, his son also played on the traveling team that particular year, and Mike, the opposing coach Kate now faced, was also the coach of that team. Evidently Mike had complained to Kate about Paul standing behind her dugout, "What kind of gratitude is that? After I dedicated all this time to his kid"—ignoring that Kate had too, for three years. His pique must have reached Paul, because before the second game Paul came up to Kate and whispered, "I have to stand over there, but my heart is with you." Kate was amazed by both men's behavior; that Mike would even note where Paul stood during the game, and that Paul would subsequently conform to Mike's idea of loyalty. However, once she won that second game, and the pressure had lifted from the young Mike's shoulders, he was able to do what most of the older Fairmount men could not. He came over, stood awkwardly for a minute, and then hugged Kate and said, "I was never someone really who said things like, 'playing like a girl!' But if I was before, I would never again say anything like that again." She continued:

> But apart from Mike, no one else from the clubhouse ever said congratulations about that game. Not a word. It was like it never happened. What I felt bad about was that you couldn't really celebrate. I mean you could have, but it would have been seen as...anything you did would have been seen as overdoing it. And when you come up, and all your kids are happy, you want some people to be happy, and be happy for them in particular. Like Jay and Talib, in particular, both played great to get the Rangers through, and I wanted people to come up to them and tell them that. And I didn't really feel that people did that, and I think in large part, I think if we had been on another team or we hadn't played that house team, I think people would have done that. I really wanted people to go up to them and say, "Jeez, that was a great game! You guys played great." But that didn't happen. I think it's sort of stuck there and won't go anywhere.

But it did go somewhere. And though it might not have been graciously acknowledged in the short run, its formal recognition came four years later when the leadership recruited Kate to coach a prestigious traveling team for FSA. In her first year of coaching in the city-wide recreation league, her traveling team won the championship and played at Philadelphia's Veterans Stadium. Fairmount Sports Association had a "yuppie female" representing them in a city-wide showcase game.

3

==

The Clubhouse and Class Cultures

"Bringing the Infield In"

In 1995, a middle-aged newcomer named Howard took it upon himself to run for an office in the normally uncontested election of the FSA board of directors. A businessman who lived outside the neighborhood, Howard had coached his son's seven-to-nine team at FSA for three years prior to the election. His son, who attended a secular private school in Center City, as did many of the newcomers' children, was a relatively strong player among the younger boys. Howard, with long, hippy-like grey hair, typically dressed in baggy khaki shorts and a polo shirt. Although he had an easygoing, personable coaching style, old-timers often complained that he was unfocused and spacey in his approach to tasks. Beyond coaching, Howard contributed in unusual ways to the organization by devoting himself to maintaining the large fields of grass in the early hours of the weekends. His heavy time contribution was welcomed. But because something about his social style irritated many Fairmount old-timers, he was never accepted as an insider.

Howard loved the league but had numerous complaints about the way newcomers were treated. He decided to lobby other newcomer parents and coaches to come out and support his candidacy as an officer against a Fairmount old-timer who, although formerly active, Howard felt no longer did much beyond sit in the clubhouse. But some insiders felt that the years of service this Fairmounter had put in entitled him to a regular presence in the clubhouse, and making him a board member guaranteed that. Howard's newcomer challenge was resisted by a rapid counter-defense and display of neighborhood solidarity. Sandy, one of the most experienced Fairmount coaches, and someone who had grown up in the neighborhood and played ball as a boy in FSA, recounted the tale, often gossiped about on the bleachers, of this aborted challenge.

There was a campaign a couple of years ago to try to take over, to push Howard Gold as vice president. We were ready for this for years, but it never happened. Three years ago, it happened. . . . [On election night] I noticed early on that lots of people were coming in to vote. They come in to push to take over the leadership . . . "the yuppies," we call them. . . . They hadn't been around long. All of a sudden they wanted to get active coming in the door. Howard showed up late to vote. But he definitely was involved. He's very sneaky, Howard is. And I knew it. The election was from seven to ten. At 7:15, I said we're going to have to make a move here. He [our guy] is going to lose. The normal thirty votes wouldn't cut it this time. . . . [Laughing] I got on the phone. I drove a van around picking people up on the corners to get them to vote. . . . I was driving around the neighborhood, "How old are you? Are you eighteen? Get in the van." "How old are you? Get in the van." Out the door people were voting, all of a sudden. Usually the total votes is thirty or forty. . . . Over 100 voted, because of this movement to get Howard Gold in. . . . Howard got an unbelievable amount of votes. But I got everybody out. I made sure a guy who worked here for years, I made sure he was the winner. . . . I think we proved the point that we can get as many votes as we need to make sure our guy gets vice president or president.

This move to resist a newcomer challenge to FSA leadership was swift and effective. No such newcomer challenge occurred again, at least for the next nine years. The defense reflected a deep sense of entitlement to decision-making on the part the Fairmounters. The conversation makes clear the extent to which the categories of "neighborhood guys" and "yuppies" were part of insider FSA consciousness and the very effective way neighborhood solidarity could be tapped to thwart an overt attempt by newcomers to gain organizational control.

If it is remarkable that the racial integration that characterized the ball association over several decades occurred relatively smoothly given the history of racial conflict in this neighborhood, it is equally remarkable that class came to trump race by the 1980s as the principal social boundary—a transition that carried over onto the baseball field. This is because the white professionals started appearing at the ball field in the late 1980s with agendas that did not match neatly those of the old-timers. So, by the mid–1990s, tensions at the baseball field centered on divisions between old-timer Fairmounters and the newcomer professionals who periodically tested the boundaries of power at the clubhouse and found them firm. If newcomers were not given the benefit of the doubt concerning leadership in the association, it was because many Fairmounters already had a stockpile of resentments toward the new professionals, based on earlier neighborhood encounters. Besides, FSA leaders held onto their influence by holding the boundaries firm.

Class Resentments in the Neighborhood

Fairmounters' feelings of resentment toward newcomers to their neighborhood often lurked just below the surface. Tensions were related not just to the conspicuously more affluent lifestyles of some of the new professionals, with their capacity to purchase homes at skyrocketing prices, but to a social style that Fairmounters perceived as condescending and pushy. Newcomers were overly eager to change things they didn't understand; worse yet, they were perceived as contributing to a fading sense of community.

The village-like feel of the neighborhood had diminished with the arrival of the newcomers. Fairmounters blamed this on the tendency of the newcomers to have fewer children, and to send those children mostly to private, non-neighborhood schools, which minimized local mixing. An elderly Fairmounter, who hung out regularly in the local Vietnam memorial park, the oldest such park in the nation, told me, "[Before the professionals moved in] there was a lot of kids around. But people only have dogs and cats now. They don't have no children anymore. They don't raise kids. We got a lady up here has two, no, three dogs and cats and won't come down here [outside in the park] at all." Frannie, a seventy-plus-year-old Fairmounter whose family members had attended the same Catholic grade school since the late 1880s, voiced a similar critique of newcomers' lack of integration with locals:

> Yeah, and these people who are moving around here now, these couples they don't have children. They might have one, but when they have it, when the child is four years old, the first thing you know, he doesn't go to our school. He either takes a bus and goes to private school, or they move. We've had a lot of people . . . and we can always call the shots. . . . "Oh, they'll be moving soon." If they do stay, they have the private bus pick up the child and the kids usually don't mix with the rest of the kids. . . . They don't let them come out and mix. You know what I mean? They're almost like house-tutored.

He then related the lack of neighborhood solidarity and local responsibility on the part of the newcomers to their focus on their work lives.

> Well, the only time they join a group is if they have a child they want to get on a baseball team or something like that. Because we have these town watches and we can't get anybody. We have the same handful of people who do it all the time. We can't get nobody else. And I don't think it's that they are antisocial. It's that they are so busy paying their bills really. . . . We had a house up here sold for over $300,000. You believe that? Years ago, you could have bought the whole block for that! A young couple bought it. I don't think either one of them is thirty. Now you know, they got to really work to pay that. You're not going to see too

much of them. It's not that they are bad people. They're good people. They are lawyers and doctors, all money people.

Fairmounters who had gained economically from the neighborhood transformation tended to see gentrification more favorably. One Fairmounter who owned a small neighborhood shop stressed this: "The changes have been good. Good for me, the business here. . . . People moved out. A lot of them thought they were bettering themselves too. It's not like they were pushed out. They made more money. My oldest sister bought a house for $58,000 sold it for $110,000, made $62,000 in two years, and moved out. Another example of people raking it up." Another Fairmounter woman, Patty, who also felt positively about the newcomers, nonetheless also stressed their lack of commitment to the neighborhood, local schools, or social networks.

It's nicer but less neighborhoody than it was here before. I hear stories [from her husband who grew up in Fairmount] about having twenty-thirty kids on a block. You didn't have to go anywhere to play, just Pennock, Swain Streets. Now, there are fewer kids and such a variety of kids! They all go to different schools. Private kids, public kids, now Waldron, Masterman, St. Frannies school. Wow! But we like that. All the children get to know all variety of children; whether Catholic, Jewish, Greek, black, white. Pretty good mix of kids. But it drives me nuts how some come and everything is wonderful. Oh they love it, love it. And then, they're gone when the kid is five for schools in the suburbs.

Wally, a longtime Spring Garden resident, offered a harsher critique of the new professionals based on their instrumental approach to relationships with people. Their greater affluence had brought more economic stability to the neighborhood but had weakened the connections within the community, because of the tendency of newcomers to form friendships based on business or economic interests outside local space. "I tend to find that, with the gentrification, there is a different group of people who live in the neighborhood now. I guess what you could call Fairmount or Spring Garden is now made up predominantly of professional people or people with higher incomes. And friendships, although they'll have friendships with people close to them, maybe a block over or two blocks over, most of their friendships form around either business contacts or professional contacts. And that's where the main thrust of their friends and their social activity, through business contacts, is."

Some residents saw the divisions between Fairmounters and newcomers as nothing more than the latest version of the class divisions that had existed in the old neighborhood. One Fairmounter remembered the tensions during his youth between the more securely employed Fairmounters and their poorer neighbors. The Fairmounters currently feeling rejected (including himself) were the ones whose families had formerly done the rejecting,

I used to kid my mother before she died. She'd say, "It's not the same. People [newcomers] are not as friendly." I said to her, "Mom, all you used to do is sit on the step and talk about other Fairmounters. Like, 'There's Joe Schmoe. He's drunk again,' or 'His kid's a little pain in the ass.'" . . . I mean, they [Fairmounters] will tell you, "Well, our people moved out," or "I don't know these new people." Well, I say, "Have you tried to know them? Have you just resented them moving in or have you went across the street?" My wife and I try. But still, there's just some new people here who, apparently, I don't say they don't *like* us, but we're not their style.

Indeed, some Fairmounters felt less negatively about the exodus of some of their neighbors precisely because it was selective and "solved" some of the internal class divisions that had historically existed. Jessie, a longtime resident of Fairmount, explained it this way: "My parents' home cost $6,000. Twenty years later, we sold it for $76,000. The property values, it brings new people in. [Pause] I think it's been good for the neighborhood, myself. I mean, it's gotten rid of a lot of garbage. Because they see dollar signs, and they're out the door, and we say, 'Oh good! We got rid of that family.' And it kind of gives you . . . it's like looking out and seeing some new taste." Jessie's home business brought her into regular contact with many new professionals and their children, and her attitude toward the newcomers had softened over time. In particular, she pointed to their parenting styles as preferable to some she saw among Fairmount families:

In the beginning the neighborhood people were angry. The new people didn't really do anything. It's just that you are in our neighborhood basically. But I think it's kind of like acceptable now. I mean, now I look at it like, oh good, they'll fix up, they'll do that. It's good for the neighborhood. They are family oriented, which is a good thing. A lot of these people, years ago, I mean the father's at the bar and da da da. And these new people are more family oriented with their children. And that's a good thing for the kids. You know, a lot of the kids who might just be hangin' corners would play with the kids who have a family atmosphere. They can see the other side of the coin, so to speak. I think it is good for some children. I mean, it wouldn't affect me whether they lived here or not. But for some of the children who don't have that type of family background, I think it is good for them, they can see other kids, play with them.

But the more gracious view of newcomer professionals apparent in Jessie's comment was frequently undermined, both in this interview and in subsequent conversations with her, by other resentments she held toward the newcomers. For example, several years later when she and I were down at the ball field discussing my recent decision to take my son out of his private Quaker school and the fact that he had never identified with the culture of that school, she blurted out, "I'm with him. I hate every one of those yuppie parents from that school. I work for 'em, but you gotta make a buck somehow!" Despite the obvious irony, she intended this as a statement of solidarity with me. It was a complex moment. As I drank in her words of comfort, I also realized she was probably talking about some of my friends. Still, we found space to bond over our shared resentments.

Fairmounter irritations did not always lie dormant beneath the surface. They were not accustomed to being pushed around by outsiders, at least not in their own neighborhood. Another comment from Jessie illustrates the direct manner in which she confronted pushiness and indiscretion on the part of newcomers: "When a newcomer comes in, I feel like I have seniority. Don't come and tell me you want to make big changes. They [two new neighbors] moved in and said, 'We'd like to get permit parking.' And I said, 'You know what, Neil, you and your wife better go back in the house. There is no permit parking around here, Hon. I'm not paying the city another dime for parking. Not one more penny. You see this block. You're just one vote. So don't even bring it up.' [We both laughed.] It is like, 'Newcomers, you have no seniority!'"

How did the newcomers take all of this? Understanding their responses depends in part on also understanding their social backgrounds and attitudes. Gentrification doesn't happen uniformly. There are phases to the process, phases often identified with different social actors who arrive in new neighborhoods with different sets of motivations, and there are different consequences for traditional residents.[1] Merely knowing that gentrification means that new affluent residents move into modest or marginal neighborhoods is not sufficient to understand the impact of the process on those neighborhoods. It is worth briefly considering what kind of middle-class people choose to live in urban areas like Fairmount and Spring Garden and how they might differ from their middle-class counterparts who prefer the suburbs. After all, most affluent movers facing restructuring American cities continue to choose the suburbs over the central cities.[2] Compared to this suburban backdrop, the gentrifiers are only a "modest urban demographic blip."[3]

Gentrification and the New Cultural Class

The rise of a new middle class of professional and managerial workers in postindustrial societies has drawn considerable attention from scholars over the past several decades.[4] Central to this discussion has been the question of how this "new class" is divided and the implications of these divisions for politics, social inequality, economic development, and urban life.[5] Some theorists have linked this broader debate about the new middle class to gentrification and patterns of urban change similar to the transformation that occurred in the Fairmount and Spring Garden area after the 1970s. For example, Ley ascribes a distinct geographic identity to a specific cadre among the new middle class, a group he calls "the cultural new class," consisting of social and cultural professionals. This sector is concentrated in central areas of large metropolitan areas and is identified with left-liberal politics. For example, in gentrifying neighborhoods within Toronto, Montreal, and Vancouver, the cultural new class challenged conservative urban growth coalitions and supported oppositional reform regimes in city government.[6]

The most liberal sector within the new middle class consists of those in social and cultural fields, such as academics, social scientists, architects, lawyers, and professionals who work outside the private and corporate sector.[7] These metropolitan professionals are also more committed to racial integration, more in favor of government spending on social programs, and more likely to consist of dual-career families compared to their other middle-class counterparts.[8] For our purposes, the relevance of this broader scholarly discussion is that, beyond the economic issues of gentrification, there is often something cultural and political behind the forces of gentrification that may contribute autonomously, or paradoxically, to local economic transformations.[9]

The new professionals who moved into the Spring Garden and Fairmount areas, and eventually entered the neighborhood baseball space, fit quite closely the above description of the new cultural class associated with gentrification in other places. The newcomer coaches and parents I interviewed came almost exclusively from this sector of the middle class. Almost all of the twenty newcomer coach and parent interviewees held professional jobs in governmental, educational, or legal services unconnected to the corporate sector. Almost half of them were educators—teachers, principals, and professors. When describing their motivations for moving to this area of the city, newcomers often spoke of their preference for the cultural lifestyle of the city, and specifically cited the diversity of the city as a plus. Their attitudes are similar to the "diversity seekers" described by Goode and Schneider in Olney, another changing Philadelphia neighborhood.[10] Many had working-class parents who helped them achieve upward mobility through educational advancement, and they remained positive toward, and emotionally comfortable with, the social style of many of the Fairmounters. While Fairmounters might see them as sometimes condescending and distant, the new professionals who chose to live in an inner-city neighborhood like Fairmount often did so as a vote against a suburban lifestyle precisely because of its homogenous, predominantly white culture. They often held liberal social views and welcomed, within limits, the economic and ethnic diversity around them. As one professor who had two sons in the league expressed it, "I guess because I'm a teacher and come from a working-class family, I am very sympathetic to what working-class people are like—even though I don't want to go back. I mean, I worked like hell to escape it, and I'm glad I did. But I'm very sympathetic to Fairmounters. It is easier in some respects for me, dealing with professionals. They're better educated. I understand the neighborhoods they're coming from and their priorities and stuff. But one of the reasons I really like Fairmont is because it is this little sociological melting pot." Another newcomer mother, who had originally moved to Spring Garden as a single woman and spent twenty years slowly renovating her home, described how relieved she was to be raising children in the city rather than the suburbs. "I feel like my kids already live a pretty sheltered existence. They go to a [private] school where things are pretty easy for them, and they don't confront the things there that they might in another setting. And so, there's more reality here, and on the baseball field." Indeed, this group's identity was as likely to be posited in opposition to their professional counterparts in the suburbs than in opposition to their more working-class Fairmount neighbors. In short, many newcomers liked the Fairmounters more than the Fairmounters liked them.

Some, from the first wave of professionals who entered Spring Garden, were worried by the 1990s that the very diversity that had attracted them in the first place was slipping away. One professional couple, a public interest lawyer and a pediatrician, moved to the Spring Garden area in 1967, had worked hard in the early 1970s to defeat local real estate developers who were urging city officials to end scattered-site public housing in the area,[11] and had also fought in the early 1980s for the establishment of a shelter run for and by homeless people in a church at Spring Garden and 20th Street. Yet, by the middle of the 1990s, they bemoaned the rapid "upscaling" of the neighborhood as it began to attract not just comfortable professionals like themselves, but residents of considerable wealth and political influence.

While Fairmounters saw newcomers as uninterested in local friendships and community affairs, newcomers sometimes felt that their participation was not welcome. They saw themselves as the ones being excluded from neighborhood social life. One medical doctor described his treatment by the locals in the ten years since moving to a block in Fairmount filled with residents who had grown up together: "You have to be related to Fairmounters before they talk to you." Marsha, a forty-year-old lawyer who had moved into Spring Garden thirteen years before, described the distance as a social wall between Fairmounters and newcomers that was inevitable and mutually imposed. But rather than begrudge Fairmounters their tendency to exclude people like her, she linked it to a rational way of sharing resources and eyed their sense of community longingly, from a distance:

> I think something that I envy about the Fairmount people, that I don't
> know that we have at our socioeconomic level quite as much, because
> people at our level tend to be more self-sufficient. . . . More affluent

people have more resources available to them because of their financial situation or because of their intellectual ability. They can draw from other places. Whereas, I think when you get down to that level, people don't have many resources, and they actually draw from each other constantly. So there is this real tight-knit community that I am clearly not a part of, and I envy that. And I couldn't get in. I don't belong in. It would never work. I realize that, 'cause even the times that I've tried, we can only go so far and just, the door shuts. But I absolutely think it's two-way. So I envy that, that close-knit thing. And I kind of enjoy that in the summer [at the ball field], 'cause I get a piece of it. But we definitely don't have it otherwise.

Marsha's mostly positive attitude about the neighborhood is fairly typical of newcomers and reflects the partiality of participants' understandings; she gets only a piece of it. Choosing to live in the city did not mean that they wanted an intensive neighborhood social life. Fairmounters' suspicions were on target here. The newcomers were somewhat aware that old-timers were not enthusiastic about their arrival, but they wore the cool reception lightly on their shoulders, for their deeper interests and investments were often in spaces beyond the neighborhood.

The apprehensions between Fairmounters and new professionals operated in the neighborhood mostly as undercurrents. But they surfaced in more overt ways at the ballpark, the symbolic center of neighborhood identity and culture. The two groups essentially wanted different things, not only from neighborhood life but also from baseball.

Baseball and Belonging

Stylistic differences between newcomers and Fairmounters surfaced on the bleachers, in the dugouts, and on the ball field. But the differences were most visible in the social distance between the clubhouse, controlled by old-timer Fairmounters, and the rest of the field. Although who sat on the bleachers, and who coached, changed a great deal at FSA as the neighborhood changed (between the 1980s and 2000), not that much changed in the clubhouse. It was as if a kind of membrane surrounded the clubhouse that protected insider Fairmounters from too much outside interference. The clubhouse became like a family living room, with lots of kinfolk who came and went. The newcomers were unexpected dinner guests. They were invited in and tolerated, but not embraced as kin. From time to time, someone at dinner would do something rude by family norms, and when this happened it was usually a newcomer who did it. As guests, the newcomers never felt completely welcome or comfortable, and they were never sure why. This was because the only way to feel comfortable was to become part of the family, to move in. Some "crossovers" did this and were eventually adopted as distant kin. But most newcomers didn't want strong ties or time-intensive visits. They had too many other dinners to attend, too many other sports to play, and they couldn't really even stay for dessert. And mostly this suited everybody just fine. But there were occasional sparks.

In order to understand how some of the neighborhood tensions played out at the ballpark, it is important to first understand the formal structure of Fairmount Sports Association (FSA) and the critical role voluntary labor always played in its survival. FSA had, since its beginnings, depended on the labor of men who were very rooted, physically and socially, in their community. It evolved from an informal club with loosely organized teams in the 1960s to a formal organization recognized by the City of Philadelphia in the 1990s, with bylaws, elected officers, and support from community development grants. Its transition from informal recreation to a formal sports league paralleled trends in youth recreation across America,[12] a shift from pickup games involving few adults to scheduled encounters mediated and controlled by adults. But despite the shift toward a more formal organization, FSA had always survived because of the time and labor contributed by neighborhood adults.

Those three decades of neighborhood support created for Fairmounters a deep sense of entitlement to organizational leadership and decision-making about the baseball league and the way baseball was to be played. Local tradition held that long-term labor and participation constituted the only legitimate road to influence within the league. From the mid–1980s on, most new professionals entering FSA approached the space with only a vague sense of how its residents had sustained baseball for three decades. They also often came from work experiences where they were in charge and made autonomous decisions. In general, they were accustomed to wielding social influence. Their suggestions for how the organization might be improved upon, which came almost immediately, went over like a lead balloon.

It would be a surprise to most of the newcomers entering the organization in the 1990s to learn that FSA leadership at this time was actually the third generation of FSA leaders. As discussed in chapter 2, the first group, whom I call "the purists," founded the club, secured the right to play in the current field across from the Philadelphia Museum of Art with their sit-ins, and managed the league from 1961 to 1976. They were strictly baseball. They walked to the field just before games, played, and then went home. They prohibited drinking on the field, and they resisted any suggestions for making the space more agreeable to adult spectators. The second generation, in control from 1976 to 1985, oversaw the league during the neighborhood's gentrification, opened the league to the first wave of newcomers to the neighborhood, introduced girls' softball, and received the first middle-class blacks into the league. This new generation of leaders was younger at the time of their takeover than the founders had been when they started the association. They were *not* strictly baseball. Adult socializing and beer-drinking became a regular feature of the space. This was also the group that secured city approval for the construction of the clubhouse, concession stand, and staff room. This building became the organizational headquarters, the site for player registration, league planning, and socializing after games. The third generation of FSA leaders emerged in the mid–1980s and remained in charge through the early 2000s. Many in this third generation had played ball as boys with the coaches of the first generation of FSA leaders and spoke of them with reverence. They had then come up through the ranks; many of them had been coaching since their late adolescent years. They oversaw the construction of the clubhouse, ushered in a large wave of parents and children of color, and confronted real and imagined organizational challenges to their leadership from the newcomers, whose relative numbers had grown. The ball field had been a core part of the childhood of this third generation. Their parents and their parents' friends had kept it going. It was their birthright. They were in charge here. Their social identities seemed more tied to this baseball space than to their world of work, where they more typically received orders rather than gave them. In my interviews with some of the Fairmount men, I was often surprised at the depth of emotions that surfaced as they discussed the overall meaning of their involvement in the league. During one week of interviews, three different Fairmount men I interviewed separately cried over a baseball memory. I began to wonder if something about me made men cry. One FSA leader, Shawn, a sales representative at a machine supply company, whose father had been one of the first-generation coaches, teared up three different times during our interview as he described his feelings about the league:

> Yeah, I mean I love the game. I grew up with it. Well, since I was ten. . . . It's always something. I always tell Jill [his wife], it's the only thing that I'm good at. Only thing, I said, you know, I've got my job, I've got this, I've got that, but . . . there's just something about baseball that . . . it's hard to say. . . . [He pauses as his eyes water.] I can talk to people about it, and I can listen to other coaches, but it's something that I know what I'm talking about, and I know that I'm right. You know? I'll always take in other knowledge, so I feel that I can carry a conversation with anyone. I mean, like politics. . . . A conversation with politics is like, "OK, yeah . . . Clinton's an okay President." But I can't hold that conversation. But if I have a baseball conversation with virtually anyone, I feel like I can stay in that conversation and hold my weight. With baseball I know what I'm doing.

Participation in baseball was a centerpiece of the Fairmount identity of these men. Two different Fairmounters I interviewed used the phrase "Baseball is all we had." It contributed to feelings of social worth and to a sense of place.

Yes, they needed newcomer children to fill the dugouts and help fill out the league to a viable size. But as the relative numbers of newcomers increased, Fairmounters became uneasy. Such large numbers put their control of this birthright at risk. It became increasingly important over time to take steps to ensure control. Someone from the second generation of FSA leaders described the third generation as the group that "circled the wagon against the yuppies."

The Baseball Club and Unequal Participation

How did the organization that needed defending operate? The formal organization of FSA consists of a president and nine officers (vice president, secretary, treasurer, field maintenance manager, kitchen manager, equipment manager, purchasing agent, and umpire commissioner). These members constitute the deep insiders of the organization. There is a formal election every September for these positions; the elections are normally uncontested. Typically, very few parents turn out to vote. In addition to the officers, there is an advisory board that formally consists of the seven or so commissioners of the boys' and girls' divisions, from T-ball to the thirteen-to-fifteen-year-olds, although the president or other officers sometimes nominate supplementary floating members. This means that the size of the board has varied—sometimes more expansive, sometimes strictly the cluster of commissioners and officers. Below each commissioner are the clusters of coaches for each age group, six or seven for the boys' divisions and three to five for the girls. These constituted the positions of power within the organization.

What comes with this power? For one thing, an immense amount of work. As a tax-exempt voluntary organization, FSA depends on donated time to keep the operation afloat. A myriad of tasks are required to launch and sustain a season. Along with maintaining two well-manicured fields and keeping the concession stand stocked and staffed, in early spring FSA volunteers send out registration materials to the families of potential players, order and repair equipment, set up the batting cage, negotiate with the city to deliver dirt, plow the infield, set up the fences, and dig up and reset pitching mounds and base paths when needed. Then the regular seasonal tasks begin, including: staffing the office during sign-ups, recruiting the forty or so coach-managers for the teams (that is, convincing working adults to devote several hundreds of hours during a season to the job), organizing the drafting of teams, ordering the uniforms for every team, recruiting commercial sponsors from the neighborhood to support teams financially, managing the finances of the organization, maintaining the park grounds throughout the entire season, stocking the kitchen and concession area with all the supplies needed to provide hot dogs, hamburgers, and other tasty, non-nutritious food for the four active months of the season, monitoring the kitchen support of inexperienced parent volunteers, filling in when parents fail to show up for their allotted hours of kitchen or field duty in order to keep the immaculately clean concession stand open and functional five evenings a week and all day on Saturdays and Sundays throughout the entire four months of the season, recruiting the volunteer umpires, filling in when umpires don't show, recruiting paid umpires for the playoffs, developing scheduling grids that fit forty teams, each playing approximately fifteen games, onto two fields, redoing the scheduling grids after periods of rain, fending off streams of questions from confused parents regarding changes in the schedules, and listening to complaints from parents about coaches, rules, schedules, and umpires.

Who did all this work? Volunteers did, but in very unequal degrees. Based on my interviews with strategic FSA leaders and coach-managers,[13] I estimated the different degrees of involvement of the 100 or so most active volunteers keeping the organization running over the 2000 season. Table 3.1 illustrates five levels of volunteer participation. At the highest level, there was an inner core of three volunteers, all Fairmounters, who spend most of their waking hours outside of work at the clubhouse, maintaining an almost constant presence. These three men spent an average of fifty-three hours a week for five months of the year, and many unaccounted hours during the winter months, ordering equipment, maintaining the clubhouse and fields, and hanging out at the clubhouse. All three have been associated with the organization for more than two decades. A second level of support is provided by about six core supporters, also Fairmounters, who spend an average of twenty-six hours a week managing a team (sometimes multiple teams), umpiring other games, and supporting the general activities of the clubhouse. A third level of support comes from approximately twelve "super head coaches," who, beyond spending twenty hours a week coaching a team, provide additional support before and after the season in getting the fields ready, and often fill in as umpires during the season. Among this group are also a few Fairmount women who either coach softball or support FSA administratively. Although Fairmounters also predominate in this third group, there are several newcomers accepted here as well. These three levels constitute the "deep insiders."

Next, there are thirty other head coaches, the "fourth level," who support FSA by coaching one team. They spend approximately twenty hours a week during the four-month season on the practices and games of their teams. These head coaches typically restrict their contributions to the managing of their teams, although they may help out from time to time on odd jobs around the clubhouse. While historically, head coaches at FSA were exclusively longtime residents of Fairmount, the proportion of newcomers in coaching positions began to grow in the early 1990s and by the end of the decade the ratio was equal.[14] However, few, if any, newcomers had entered the ranks of head coaches of the older divisions or of the higher-status traveling teams. Finally, at the fifth

TABLE 3.1.

Estimates of the Market Value of the Seasonal Contribution of Unpaid Volunteers at Fairmount Sports Association by Level of Support

Levels of Support/ Positions	Hours per Week	Months per Year	Hours per Season/ Person[a]	Hours per Season/ Group	Cost of Seasonal Labor[b] ($6/hour)	Cost of Seasonal Labor[b] ($10/hour)
3 Core Insiders	53	5	1166	3498	22,667	$37,778
6 Core Supporters	26	5	572	3432	22,239	$37,065
12 Super Coaches	20	5	440	5280	34,214	$57,024
30 Head-Coaches	20	4	352	10,560	68,428	$114,048
60 Assistant Coaches	10	4	176	10,560	68,428	$114,048
Total 111				33,330	$215,976	$359,963

Source: Project Data, Grasmuck

[a]Hours per season is calculated by multiplying hours per week by 4.4 weeks per month by months per season.

[b]Dividing the total hours of seasonal support for all groups (33,330) by the 111 individuals who make up these five levels of support, we arrive at the per capita hours of labor for this entire group: 300 hours per season. The minimum seasonal labor cost is estimated on the basis of paying a $6.00 minimum wage plus 8 percent for FICA and Social Security contribution. This is an extremely conservative way of calculating this, as none of these adult volunteers are earning minimum wage on the labor market. The second estimate uses a $10.00 hourly wage plus the 8 percent FICA and Social Security contribution.

level, the head coaches rely on the contributions of assistant coaches, minimally two per team, who help manage the practices, keep score, or coach first or third base. The devotion of assistant coaches varies greatly, but a fairly reliable one spends approximately ten hours a week during the four-month season. In summary, about 111 adults devote approximately 33,330 hours of labor a season.

After those hundred-plus adults (the organizational leaders down to the assistant coaches), there is a huge drop-off in the amount of time that others, principally parents, devote to the organization. FSA expects the parents of the approximately 500 households, in addition to paying the eighty-dollar inscription fee, to provide four hours of kitchen, field, or bathroom duty during the season. Parents may pay an additional fifty dollars to be exempt from those four hours of work. It is almost always newcomers who take this "I'll-pay-rather-than-work" option.[15] Although most parents are aware that there are many volunteers who contribute more time than they do, few are aware of the amount of time the core volunteers devote.

Think of the organization, then, as a set of concentric circles moving out from a small inner core of Fairmounters who played baseball in the neighborhood and have spent thousands of hours of their adult leisure time at the clubhouse and the field over the past several decades, to a larger, middle group of Fairmount core supporters who have also been affiliated with the organization in most cases since their childhoods and continue to devote hundreds of hours of time each season to FSA. Next we have larger groups of manager-coaches and their assistant coaches who, by the year 2000, consisted of about half old-time Fairmounters and half newcomers who joined FSA more recently, as parents, after they moved into the neighborhood, or who came from nearby areas. Beyond these layers of deep insiders, middle-level supporters, and head coaches, we have the outer group of parent supporters who sign up their children, bring them to practices, attend games, and devote one afternoon or morning in the season to helping out, with varying degrees of devotion and regularity. This outer group has been divided about equally since the year 1998 between parents coming from Fairmount/Spring Garden and those from outside the neighborhood.[16]

The gap in the amount of time dedicated to maintaining FSA by the inner core of volunteers, whose participation ranges from ten to fifty-three hours every week of the season (or an average of 300 hours each season per "activist"), and the outer circle of regular parents, who contribute only four hours once during a season, is a source of significant resentment on the part of insiders in the organization. The cost of these community services, if they were to be contracted on the labor market rather than provided by volunteers, would be staggering. If the community had paid its one-hundred-plus volunteers just minimum wage for their services in 1998, it would have cost over $200,000 for that one season. If paid something closer to a more realistic wage, say ten dollars an hour, the labor costs would have risen to $359,963 for the year. It is not hard to imagine the feelings of those who put in these kinds of hours when confronted with complaints and suggestions for change from affluent strangers who devote only four hours a season, and sometimes fail to do even that.

Wanting Different Things from Baseball

The different degrees of involvement in FSA became a central focus of tensions between old-timers and newcomers in FSA—tensions, as we have seen, already established in the neighborhood. But time devoted to the organization was just one symbolic issue that divided them. Just as Fairmounters complained that newcomers had weak ties to the neighborhood and engaged in little local mixing, held instrumental views of friendship, and offered minimal community support, they saw newcomers approach the baseball organization in a similar manner—for the instrumental needs of their individual children and not as a neighborhood treasure that needed nurturing. Many newcomers were oblivious to this resentment. Others countered with their own complaints about Fairmounters' coolness to outsiders, about unfair access to insider information about teams and opportunities, and about the adult-centered, competitive way Fairmounters ran an organization for children.

Neighborhood Coaches versus Father Coaches

The Fairmount tradition established in the 1960s of neighborhood men volunteering to coach baseball, whether or not they had a son in the league, continued in a modified way for decades. In the 1990s, many teams in FSA were still associated with a Fairmounter coach who "kept his team" year after year. That is, a particular man would coach the Rangers, or the Angels, in the seven-to-nine age division year after year. Teams came to be identified as "The Padres—John's team," or "The Grays—Bob's team." For example, one Fairmounter coach named Jerry coached the Angels for seven years. He had had his son on his team at one time, but he continued to coach the seven-to-nine team after his son moved on. For many old-timers, then, while kids changed each year, the coach stayed the same and to a large extent the reference group stayed the same—namely, other coaches and the old neighborhood. As a result, the coach would build a reputation (for better or worse) with his team, and each new crop of boys represented the potential to help or hurt this reputation. Most newcomer coaches, on the other hand, were father-coaches and often, unlike Fairmounters, coached their sons in other sports, such as soccer. Their reference group was more their own son, and other players and parents on the team, rather than spectators outside this small group. Thus, newcomer coaches spent more time addressing targeted parents and players than on socializing beyond their specific games. They were less likely to stay with the same team or the same age division over time and more likely to move up in age division as their sons did. They almost never coached or maintained contact with the organization beyond the playing careers of their children. Therefore they established less identification with a particular team and less investment with the organization beyond their team.

Why were Fairmounters more willing to agree to coach a team without a son on it, or long after their son had moved up?[17] This pattern of "neighborhood coaches" versus "father coaches" represents a crucial difference in viewpoint concerning the organization between Fairmounters and newcomers; indeed, it reflects different motivations for coaching and joining the organization. We may think of this as different kinds of investments. One is more of an investment in the community or the neighborhood, and the other is more an investment in a life-stage of parenting. This pattern was true at all levels of the organization throughout the 1990s, from T-ballers to the sixteen-year-old traveling team.

These patterns were evident in two teams we followed in the first year of the ethnography, the Angels and the Senators. The Angels were coached by a Fairmounter named Jerry, a manual laborer who also worked side jobs painting houses. This was Jerry's seventh year coaching the Angels but he had coached in years prior to that for other teams when his older children had played. Jerry had nothing to do with the nearby soccer organization. The second team, the Senators, was coached by a lawyer, Kyle, who had coached his son's baseball team at Fairmont for three years and also coached in the parallel soccer organization. Kyle did not live in Fairmount, but in a nearby neighborhood.

Jerry often greeted friends at the field, talking or joking about the performance of his team. He also spent time in the clubhouse and drank beer with other Fairmounters on the weekends between and after games. After he agreed to have Josh, my research assistant (who had grown up nearby in another baseball neighborhood), shadow his team and help with practices, he expected that this meant sharing social time as well, and he generously extended to Josh several invitations to join in Friday-night hanging out at the clubhouse. In contrast, Kyle did little of this. In general Kyle talked less than Jerry to anyone outside of the team, and when he did talk, it was directed to the players and/or parents. Jerry's wife was also very involved with the league, winning an award at the end of the season for her all-around contributions to FSA. Kyle was divorced, and his ex-wife's involvement with the organization was restricted to game attendance. She seemed to know relatively few people in the organization and she was largely unknown to the old-timers.

This practice of equating a team with a coach puts the focus more on the coach and how *he* is doing, rather than on the kids' performance, at least in the eyes of the reference group of friends. Thus, it is quite common at the field to hear someone ask, "How is Dan's team doing this year?" or "How are the Angels this year?" Associating a team with a coach also provides structural pressures that increase competition, by creating a strong identification of a particular coach with the team and the team's win-loss record and division standings. It can also heighten the attachment of the coach's ego to the team's performance. Even Fairmounter coaches who ignored these pressures and minded the boys and their needs as a top priority received regular commentary about their "career record" in the league. For example, one coach, a Fairmounter, is legendary in the league for having won the championship five times, once every other year for nine years, with his seven-to-nine team, the Rangers.

Many times over the years, I observed the tendency of Fairmounter coaches to meet and greet friends during their coached games. Fairmounter coaches were more likely, for example, to stand either along the third base line or near the dugout talking with friends or other buddies who were coaching other teams. It became clear that many Fairmounter coaches felt they were being observed and perhaps judged by peers and neighborhood friends. Thus, the pressure for these coaches to have a winning team comes from the commentary of their buddies in the neighborhood about how well their team is doing. This predisposes these coaches to think about their teams as much, or more, through friends' eyes as through their players' eyes or through the eyes of the parents of their immediate teams. All the insider interest in the outcome of games at Fairmount made some Fairmounter coaches see as their reference group other coaches in the league, and friends and longtime families of the neighborhood. Most of these Fairmount coaches had numerous relatives in the organization—brothers, sons, sisters, wives, and in-laws—who served as coaches and organizational officers in FSA. These Fairmount insiders hung out socially in the FSA office on weekends, relaxed after hours and on weekend nights under the large sycamore tree adjacent to the ball field, and regularly attended social events sponsored by FSA, such as "casino night," when a rented bus would take insiders and Fairmounter friends and relatives to Atlantic City.

One year after one of the traveling teams won the final game of the city-wide championship, the first such victory in the thirty years of the organization, I was selling hot dogs in the concession stand along with the sister of the winning coach, Billy, a six-foot, three inch old-timer, as he entered the kitchen upon arriving from across town. She asked him in a whisper, "Have you called Mommy yet to tell her?" Surprisingly, he reported that he had already done so, apparently within minutes of having completed the game. This was an indication both of how tuned in his mother was to his performance, and of the importance he placed on her knowing immediately. It seemed inconceivable that the newcomer coaches, with mothers far removed from the neighborhood, indeed, perhaps from the city, would make such a call. Moreover, historically it was common for the wives of some male coaches to also have girls' softball teams. Thus there was a complicated network of local contacts, with cousins, in-laws, husbands, and wives from a relatively small number of families holding a considerable proportion of the strategic positions in the organization.

The different ways coaches related to the organization and the divisions between neighborhood coaches and father coaches had a parallel in the form of teams that Fairmount insiders favored and teams that needed to be beaten—the "clubhouse teams" versus the "yuppie teams." After a few years in the league, I noticed how, during certain defining games (like the playoffs or a game that would clinch a team's position in the standings) the size of the crowds gathered behind the two teams would be very lopsided. Behind the team with a

Fairmount head coach, a large crowd would congregate, many of whom were not parents of players but simply neighborhood folks who had come out to root either for this coach or for boys they knew on the team. In contrast, if the opposing team was headed by a newcomer coach, the crowd, even for championship games, was typically smaller. I also began to realize that the teams with Fairmount coaches typically also had a large proportion of Fairmount kids on them. Similarly, the newcomer coaches had a large number of newcomer kids on their teams.

The frequent turnout of Fairmounters for teams on which they had no children was a collective endorsement by Fairmounters of their community. Rarely, if ever, did I see large collections of newcomer parents gather at games in which they did not have a child playing. They seemed to have no such group identity or loyalties. I preferred for my son to be on the Fairmount teams, and so did he. They were more exciting. The crowds were bigger. I learned more about the nuances of the game in these contexts. The conversations with team parents behind the dugout, or in the bleachers, were more frequently about the nuances of the game and less about schools, colleges, or work—common topics among the professional parents. Sometimes, a newcomer parent would come alone to see the team their child had been on before leaving for summer camp, in order to report to the child at camp. But typically, their interest in the outcome of games not involving their child did not extend this far. What this meant was that, if a newcomer coach entered the championship series against a Fairmounter coach, the newcomer team could expect only a small cluster of parents from that team (and even at championships this did not mean all parents), whereas behind the Fairmount team, referred to by some as the "clubhouse team," almost the entire neighborhood might be seated.

My Community versus My Boy

Part of the intensity Fairmounters felt about the outcomes of games and championships stemmed from their definition of baseball as the only sport, perhaps even the only social activity that mattered. As one regular umpire for FSA told me, "Fairmount is 'strictly baseball.' The people who run the building, who control Fairmount sports, are from the neighborhood, and their main interest is baseball or has been baseball up until the last two years when they introduced basketball." Once, as I was working kitchen duty, a Fairmont leader chatting with me shared his frustration that the local soccer league, run almost exclusively by newcomers, had scheduled their "opening day" on the same day as FSA's "closing day." He mumbled something about their lack of respect or willingness to coordinate things, but laughed as he finished off the conversation with, "Besides, is soccer really a sport?" Another Fairmounter coach complained that newcomers' over-involvement in multiple leisure activities and other sports translated into making each a "jack of all trades and master of none." Citing their "general lack of baseball talent," he said,

> The quality of the ballplayers is much weaker now, because of the yuppies moving in. It used to be hard-working, neighborhood people. Every kid was a good player. Now we have people from all over the city, and the talent is worn so thin. Old-fashioned, neighborhood people are better ball players. . . . They played more often. You played with your friends, and they played baseball. . . . They weren't involved with soccer, and Hebrew school on Saturdays, and all those other things. A bunch of people are involved now. The quality of play is down now too.

In interviews with FSA insiders, some complained that newcomers used the league as a day care service, dropping their kids off at practice or games and coming back later to pick them up. They viewed this as particularly a problem with newcomer parents. In part, this is because when it happened with a Fairmounter child, they often knew where the child lived and what other adults were friends with the child and felt less worried if something happened to the child. With the newcomer kids, they didn't have this same sense of security, as expressed in this comment from one of the organization's officers: "We had a kid badly hurt here last season. There was no relative of his in a 20-mile radius."

One set of tensions that arose over the issue of scheduling practices and games relates to the different nature of the ties the boys and their parents have to the neighborhood. Fairmounter coaches seemed to take a more organic approach to the neighborhood, assuming, for example, that people would be around and available for games and practices. To them, it was less important to give much advance notice for games and practices. Fairmount boys were also more organically tied to networks in the neighborhood, like the local Catholic school. The former practice in Fairmount of scheduling sign-ups on several Saturday evenings in February, for a season that began several months later, presented no problem for a community that communicated relatively effectively through word-of-mouth or through the schools. Once the season began Fairmount boys were likely to be around for practices and games, and were unlikely to leave town for expensive sleep-over camps. If their parents were not at the field, chances were that someone else there knew them and could tend to them or walk them home. Everyone they knew was deeply tuned into the cycle of the season and understood the need for the juggling of games after rainouts, or for rescheduling games when there were conflicts with traveling team schedules or with the scheduled games of the local Catholic school, where many Fairmounter boys also played. No such accommodations were made, however, for the activities of non-Catholic schools. This became a major source of irritation to newcomers who were not in the loop of information. Fairmounters sometimes referred disparagingly to newcomer parents as "the summer-camp crowd," a reference to their tendency to disappear during the playoffs in July. This became such a problem that FSA added a question to the signup sheets about plans for summer camp, so coaches could take this into account as they drafted players. One Fairmount mother advocated putting all "summer campers" on the same team, so that their team would self-destruct at playoff time and not "mess up the playoffs for the rest of us." The summer camp issue was a hot-button issue, in part, because it dramatically symbolized the inequalities among the children. While it was never discussed in terms of "who can afford to send them and who can't," the judgment about whether leaving for camp before finishing out the season was fair or unfair was colored by how natural going to overnight camp for a month at the age of ten or eleven seemed to the one doing the judging. One Fairmount mother told me she considered this practice a form of child abuse. After years of having the playoffs disrupted by the exodus of middle-class kids, FSA leaders required that parents specify on their registration if the child was camp-bound. This information in the top right corner of the registration form, almost a certified stamp of "yuppie kid," then weighed into considerations during the draft, somewhat alleviating the problem. But the perception that Fairmounters could be counted on to commit for the season and that newcomers were as likely to turn to other competing interests rattled many old-timers. An old-timer who had held numerous positions in the league over a twenty-year period put it this way:

> Sometimes newcomer parents are uncooperative with what you are trying to do, or insensitive or just ignorant with what you are trying to do. And they place their activities and their kids' activities over the commitment to the team. . . . You had a critical game situation, and if they had to go down the shore, they just went down the shore. . . . If the commitment that you make in the beginning doesn't pay off, and you have the opportunity to leave legitimately, then leave. Or don't sign up again next year, if it didn't work out. If you signed up for nine weeks of baseball, or fifteen weeks of baseball, see it through to the end. No matter if you're the best player on the team who feels unsatisfied because everybody else stinks, or you're the worst player on the team. This is something that happens in life. You don't always have these chances to move around. . . . But I see parents who see things not work out, and they just say, "Okay, hell with it." I think they're sending the wrong message. 'Cause what they're telling the kid is, "You can just shop around, and if this works for you, great, take advantage of it. But if this doesn't work out, then hell with it and hell with them." Fairmounter parents have a different mentality, more stick to it once you make a commitment.

Newcomers sometimes countered that insider favoritism determined how rules were applied, that FSA leaders, for example, cancelled and rescheduled games according to the needs of the high-status traveling teams on which many of the sons of the Fairmount leadership played. It was easy to stick to your FSA commitments when schedules were juggled with *your* competing activities taken into account. There was truth to this claim. In fact, to avoid conflicts for Catholic school players, the entire season's schedule of FSA games was not finalized until the schedule for the Catholic league, in which many Fairmounter boys also played, was established. Thus what looked like "strong commitment" from Fairmounter boys could as easily be interpreted as "participation made easy."

Newcomer kids were also less tied to neighborhood networks, more tied to networks that extended beyond the neighborhood, less familiar and less legitimate to Fairmounter coaches. This put them at a disadvantage sometimes, when information about practices circulated informally among Fairmount boys at the local Catholic school. Moreover, the general social trend in America toward increasingly complex social schedules for children, with few available hours of unplanned leisure, is especially marked among more affluent families.[18] Baseball was typically only one of a number of sports played by newcomer boys and was less likely to be ranked by them as their favorite than it was for Fairmounter boys. Just as Fairmounter parents chafed at the professional classes' inability to make the games and questioned their commitment to the league, professional parents often grumbled over short notice for practices or schedule changes and the difficulty of juggling complex schedules. Last-minute changes to schedules in lives this tightly scheduled set off fits. As one newcomer father complained:

> I tell you, there's a group of people, three or four people, that seem to make the decision about when games are played and how games are played and when the playoffs are played. And then, their decisions aren't always logical. It's based on what's always been, or what's easiest for them, and not based on what's good for all the kids. Like when the playoffs games start, whether people might have vacations, might have other things to do in the summer. No concern for things like that. You really can't talk to them either. You really can't change it. . . . They just don't— they're not open to change, and they don't want to hear from you.

There were also frequent accusations of conflicts of interest against the Fairmounters. There was the fact that Fairmount commissioners, for example, were sometimes also head coaches of a team in the same division. So if a conflict erupted in a game with this coach/commissioner there was no independent party to which an appeal could be made. As another example, each year, tradition has it that the head coach of the championship team orders a personalized Fairmount jacket for Trophy Day for every member of his team who is willing to pay for it. One year, when a team of one of the commissioners was defeated in the championship, he and his team nonetheless ordered and received team jackets with "division champions" sewed on them. Never before had a first-place team which had gone on to lose the championship ordered such an honor for itself. During another season, a middle-class newcomer who lived outside Fairmount, but whose son had played at FSA for five years, exploded one weekend when he heard that the commissioner had cancelled his son's playoff game on a Friday, the day before the game. This father had rearranged weekend plans for the beach in order to be there, only to find out that the commissioner had cancelled it. It seemed that the opposing team (on which the commissioner's son played) did not have enough players, because they were all down at the shore! "I'm sick of this stuff. It happens all the time. I'm sick of those traveling teams too. And don't tell me it is just a few people, 'cause it is Fairmount. The league lets this happen." Newcomers also complained when a coach of one team served as an umpire for a game between two other teams in his own division in which the outcome would significantly impact the umpire's team's standing. Others grumbled about the umpires favoring "clubhouse teams" in which the boys of FSA officers played. Yet, finding newcomer volunteer umpires was difficult, either because many didn't feel competent to umpire or because they were unwilling to volunteer. FSA was therefore forced to draw, from deep within its own internal ranks, individuals who, conflict of interest or not, were more willing to come forward, stand in the often smothering heat, wear heavy equipment, and weather parental insults and grumblings about judgment calls.

An African American newcomer described the central divisions in FSA as being not about race, but about insiders versus strangers. Nonetheless, he explained how the insider culture sometimes fueled race suspicions:

> I think it is not so much race. It's about a group of people who may have grown up together, socialized together. They played in the league as youngsters, and they socialize as adults in the same circles, and they've kind of kept that circle closed. If you're not initially a part of that group, then either you will not feel comfortable in joining that group or there will be discussions or decisions made, or whatever, within that small circle at different times. And pretty much that's what the organization is about. . . . And I'll give you a great example. Last year my son had a really successful year, lots of home runs, plus he was pretty good all around. They started a travel team, basically a ten-year-old travel team. But they had a number of kids who were younger than ten on it, some were just turning nine or whatever, but we were never invited to try out for the team. When we inquired as to what the procedure was, we were told that the kids had to try out. What tryouts? Those folks who were in that inner circle would be privy to that; so their kids would typically have the opportunity to try out and ultimately make the team. . . . And I could

have easily concluded that maybe they didn't want African American boys on the team, maybe they were afraid we would push their kids out from the elite status on the team. One could conclude that there was some racial motivation there, as some other parents did.

A white newcomer mother implied that there was a higher bar for newcomers, black or white, on the traveling teams: "If you are not a Fairmounter, your kid has to be three times as good to get selected for their travel teams." One Fairmounter leader agreed that talent was not the only criterion for selecting which children would "go travel" because with that honor sometimes came a trip to Cooperstown. "We're gonna select kids whose parents have been helping out all this time and deserve some recognition for that. Not just someone who rolls up new this year with a little talent." Men who were putting in hundreds of hours of labor to umpire, coach, administer, or work as commissioner had become accustomed to the prevailing sense that, without them, the league couldn't exist. They merited certain kinds of payoffs, perquisites. Judgment calls were part of their rights, a compensation for the drudgery they put in daily during the season. Misunderstandings came because most newcomers took the requirement of four hours of labor at face value. Even though there was a lot of passive resistance about completing that duty, once it was paid, they expected equal treatment and information in exchange. They were usually unaware that additional labor contributions could translate into more consideration for their children.

Social activities sponsored by FSA that were unrelated to baseball marked another boundary between the clubhouse and the outsiders. Newcomers rarely participated in these outings and were often entirely unaware that they existed. Sometimes these activities involved a group of Fairmounters going to see a minor league baseball game together in Reading or Camden or renting a bus to go as a group to Atlantic City for the evening. One newcomer mother, whose son played ball at FSA for six years, put it this way: "I've never been invited to those events and don't know how you get invited. I've just seen the bus driving away." A professional father, when asked about his participation in these FSA-sponsored events, reflected on his peculiar position of being rather engaged with the organization but outside it at the same time. "Well, I have never been specifically invited [to social events]. I feel that I am not, well—There's the typical Fairmount members, and I'm a newcomer. I'm a newcomer, a professional. And a large part of those people, I feel that we don't have a lot in common. And I feel that they don't want to get to know me, and I'm not sure that I want to get to know them. So I feel there's some sort of social gap or something between us." Once my husband asked Brian, one of the FSA leaders, about an upcoming trip to the casinos he had heard about, thinking that a few of the parents on his team might be interested.

JOHN: Are there any flyers or anything I could hand out to my team?

BRIAN: No.

JOHN: 'Cause some of the parents on my team might want to go.

BRIAN: Aren't they all yuppies?

JOHN: No, you're thinking of me. My team isn't.

They both laughed, but no flyers were forthcoming.

The boundary between those who attended such events and those who didn't was not merely between Fairmounters and newcomers. It only appeared that way to newcomers. In reality most Fairmounter parents did not participate either. These were social activities for the Fairmounters most deeply involved in the day-to-day work of holding together the organization: the inner circle of FSA staff, their family members, and their friends. But the tightness of this group, and the visibility of some of their socializing, underscored newcomers' feelings of being on the outside. It also explained why even many Fairmounter parents did not consider themselves insiders.

To get a feel for this sensibility, I asked all the parents I interviewed if they considered themselves to be insiders, outsiders, or something else. Not surprisingly, none of the newcomer parents I interviewed described themselves as insiders. They were about equally divided between those who described themselves as outsiders and those who answered "something else." Here are some typical self descriptions of newcomers:

— I consider myself an outsider who knows what's going on and is aware of a lot of stuff. I follow all the gossip and hang out there a lot. So I'm not directly involved with them, but I'm not an outsider either.

—I'm an outsider, but a friendly outsider.

—Absolutely 100% outsider.

—A far outsider.

—I'm something else, in the middle. To be an outsider means you don't feel comfortable there. And I feel perfectly comfortably down there but certainly not an insider.

While none of the Fairmounter parents described themselves as pure outsiders, the majority also did not consider themselves to be insiders. This was because they too perceived a divide between the clubhouse and the rest of the organization. More typically, Fairmounters thought of themselves as "something else," as expressed in this sample of their answers:

—Something else. First I was an insider, and then I was an outsider. And now I'm something else. That's how I want it. Plenty of people have been pushed out down there. That's usually how they end up getting out. Why? The clique just decides.

—I feel like I'm in between. Why? There are lots of politics involved in FSA. I don't like politics. I like to see everything positive. If I see any negativity, I stay away. I umped for about seven years, umping and that's it. I went down, umped the game, and said "hi" and "goodbye." I lived in the neighborhood and umped but still wasn't an insider. There's a kind of exclusion.

—We're kind of caught in the middle, 'cause we're not real Fairmounters. But we're not outsiders either. My husband grew up here, but he's an attorney now, that kind of thing. You know, he can talk to them, but he's not them.

—On the outside, right up against the window, but I don't want on the inside. [Laughter] I like it on the outside. I really do. There are some I like down there, but some are obnoxious. I want no part. I could be if I wanted. If I said, "Oh, I'll come down and work the kitchen every night," they'd say, "Oh sure Jessie." But no thanks.

This last comment is especially telling in that she indicates, in contrast to the opinion of many newcomers, that there was one surefire way for a woman to become accepted as a newcomer: to donate long hours at the concession stand. There is some truth to this claim, especially when we consider the case of the only African American newcomer parent I ever saw accepted as an apparent insider. Sometime around 2002, this young mother could be seen sitting in the circle of chairs under the sycamore trees where FSA leadership watched games, regularly selling hot dogs at the concession stand, and joining insider barbecues after games. As one newcomer board member described it, "She is amazing to me. She just walked in, started helping with whatever she saw going on, ignored all raised eyebrows, and years later, she was in."

The Catholic Imagination and Local Accountability

There was something of the "Catholic imagination" that informed the tight cultural feel of the baseball club. Andrew Greeley, a sociologist of religion, argues that the Catholic religious imagination shapes the social lives of practicing and lapsed Catholics in subtle ways that often distinguish them from non-Catholics.[19] An ordered community, close ties among neighbors, and an emphasis on layers of hierarchy or authority flow from this religious sensibility. We have already seen how Fairmounters lamented the weak social ties of newcomers to the neighborhood. Similarly, Fairmounters at FSA, who were overwhelmingly Catholic,[20] often complained about the individualistic, self-serving way that newcomers approached the organization. One Fairmounter who had grown up in the neighborhood, attended college, and achieved success as a professional saw himself as seated right in the middle between the two groups. But he emphasized that central to "the problem" at FSA was the individualism of the professionals and their instrumental approach to the league.

> I think they're more selfish to a degree. I don't say completely, because I have met some really outstanding people. . . . It just seems to be a trait that you notice with a lot more professional people. Maybe they're more goal-oriented, so a lot of secondary issues don't mean anything to them. . . . They also don't have any real connection to the neighborhood, or don't consider themselves Fairmount. . . . It's not a problem for them to use the organization to their benefit like they would use any other organization. . . . "Look, I paid my money. You got me down here doing kitchen duty and field maintenance. I'll do what I want." This isn't a big thing for them. I would say, it would seem to be a trend you would see in more professional people. . . . Maybe they had more opportunities to do other things. They have more choices than those who live up in Fairmount. . . . Fairmounters, on the other hand, aren't that way. . . . They make a commitment. . . . They follow through. . . . The culture in Fairmount, you don't quit teams. . . . You follow through. . . . If you don't like it after it's [the season] done, then you don't come back. . . . I think that trait is more apparent with people who grow up in Fairmount or have a Fairmount mentality.

This judgment, that the new professionals were in it for themselves, was highlighted one year when FSA leaders discovered that two newcomer head coaches had used private connections with city officials to secure permits to use one of the practice fields in Fairmount Park for their own teams and had not offered to share the opportunity democratically with the entire organization. Finding a good place to practice would put any coach at an advantage since, often times, the practice fields were hard to come by. One of the coaches had secured the permit as an individual, but the other had used FSA's name, heightening the general condemnation. The permit was angrily reclaimed by FSA in the name of equal access. Yet, ironically, and consistent with the newcomer complaint of insider advantage, after it was taken away from these newcomer coaches, only selected coaches, mostly Fairmounters, were informed of the availability of the new practice field.

Ironically, while newcomers often felt powerless and shut out from real influence in decision making, or even from understanding the logic of many decisions, some Fairmounters felt that newcomers often got more of what they wanted in the organization because they were less constrained by the opinions of their neighbors in pushing for their kids' interests. The Fairmounters' deeper connections to the neighborhood sometimes operated to make *them* feel more constrained in FSA and less able to "get their way" than newcomers, for fear of alienating old friends and neighbors they saw regularly in church and at school. In short, Fairmounters viewed newcomers as shameless lobbyists for their children's individual interests. This accusation is reminiscent of the way middle-class parents often use their educational credentials to intervene with teachers and principals to secure institutional advantages for their children at the expense of working-class children, whose parents are more reluctant to interfere with teachers' judgments.[21] A Fairmounter named Jessie grew agitated as she described this pattern:

> Most of them who are down on this ball field are my age, a couple years older than me. We've grown up together. We formed that league more or less together. So you watch what you say to each other. New people don't have that same relationship, and they really don't care what they say. And they say what they want. And you know what? They're probably better off, because their kids play where they want to play. . . . They always get what they want. That's the best part. Because I could kick myself in the ass all the time. I'm thinking, look where their kids are playing, you know? My kid's screwed [laughter] all the time . . . because I'm afraid this one won't talk to me, or that one won't talk to me, if I complain because you've grown up all your life together. You just have a different bond. The new people in the neighborhood don't have a problem with saying anything. I'm not a big one for someone from the outside coming in and telling me how to do something after all these years of sweating blood and all this stuff you put into this organization, and that is something that happens. You get the yuppies coming in, and they are being very vocal because they don't know you from Adam. If you are an outsider, you can run your mouth and get more action, whereas I won't run my mouth. But that tends to make like bad blood 'cause you're like, "Wait a minute, I've been here for twenty years sweepin' floors, picking up dirt. [laughs] Who the hell are you?"

In her view the "bonded social capital"[22] of the neighborhood could inhibit insiders as much as it might provide an advantage. The degree to which long-time residence worked as a form of social control that disadvantaged old-timers was echoed by another Fairmounter parent: "If you do something to offend somebody, they are going to remember it. . . . And it might take five, ten, fifteen years before they forget. . . . Like I was saying, the argument I had with that other coach. . . . It's still in existence. . . . And it's been ten years! And when I see him to this day, a cold stare. . . . And we grew up together! And it will be that way till we're dead I guess."

There was also the problem of some newcomers who acted too independently once they were given some responsibility. They seemed to have less sense of the hierarchy of the organization than did the Catholic Fairmounters, less awareness of its subtle requirements for deference to leaders. If a newcomer was permitted to manage a team, or to serve as commissioner for one of the divisions, this didn't mean that he shouldn't run most of his decisions by the leadership on a regular basis. To do otherwise would be considered disrespectful. But as Sennett puts it, "respect is an expressive performance" that requires an artful use of words and gestures that convince others that you mean it.[23] Not all newcomers, even with the best of intentions, found the right words and gestures of respect. One old-timer described the dilemma many newcomers faced (and I had the distinct impression his example referred to my husband's brief stint as commissioner) in searching for the proper deference:

> Sometimes the newcomers feel, they're made to feel, as intruders. They're not that warmly received. If you don't say or do the right thing, or behave right at the beginning, in the right manner, you can isolate yourself. It's very easy to say the wrong thing. You're not even aware that you're saying the wrong thing. . . . [As an example] maybe being too independent, by not letting the front office know what you were about. It's funny, even though you might be the commissioner of the league, it's prudent to run it past the office. Say to them, "You know, this situation happened. Here, this is what I'm going to do." And then listen and see what their reaction is. Their reaction in most cases is, "Yeah, do that then," or "Let's do it that way. That's right. It's the right thing to do." . . . You really get advice. You can sense if it's not a good idea with the front office. You think it's a good idea, but you can sense that they're not happy with it. Then you can try it another way. Or you should just drop it. I found, not to act too independently, and let them find out later. Although 90 percent of the time they would have agreed, but without advice, it sort of strains the relationship. . . . [People who don't do it] they find out when it's too late, after they get yelled at, or after they don't get what they want, or they were overruled. . . . But you're never told this. You're expected to do it. And it's what, if you're from Fairmont, it's what you're expected to do. And you wouldn't think of doing it otherwise. If you're from Fairmont, why would you even think of it? Know what I'm saying? So the contradiction is, if you're not from Fairmont you don't know what you should be doing.

Hierarchical Communalism versus Child-Centered Individualism

If Fairmounters saw newcomers as individualistic and not community minded enough, newcomers would counter that at least theirs was a child-centered individualism. The sharpest newcomer critique related to newcomers' view that

FSA prioritized adult socializing over children's interests. While Fairmounters might devote lots of time to the organization, they argued, a good amount of that time was devoted to hanging out in the clubhouse and drinking beer, which set a bad example for the kids. The clubhouse has a keg refrigerator so that cold beer is always on tap. Insiders have only to grab a plastic cup, pull down a lever, and fill up. One black middle-class father elaborated this critique this way: "If I had a pet peeve [with the ball club], it would be the consumption of alcohol on the premises. I'm not sure if there's a legal issue there, but I think it was poor, it was in real bad taste when you have adults drinking alcohol when there's lots of kids. . . . But I understand it kind of has some history to it. These are people in the neighborhood that kind of grew up together and socialize. I just think because the product is children that we have to adjust our behavior when we're in their presence. So that's what I probably liked the least, the alcohol, and how the parents come down hard on their kids." Another newcomer father, whose son had played in the league for more than eight years, went further: "At FSA, there's drinkers and non-drinkers. I see alcohol as the major problem in the Fairmount Sports Association. The amount consumed by the coaches, amounts consumed in the clubhouse. . . . And sometimes I think that it's an organization, not for the kids but, for the parents, so that the parents, whoever the people in the organization are, will have a place to hang out, drink beer, and be with their buddies. . . . Yeah. A social club for the coaches and parents and not so much for the kids."

Once, when a pediatrician whose son had played in FSA for years found out that my husband had agreed to serve as commissioner one year, he asked me, "Hey, now that he is commissioner, is he gonna start hangin' at the clubhouse drinking until 3:00 in the morning?" The aloof treatment of newcomers fueled the suspicions of some, that little more than drinking was going on in there, that it was a subsidized, inner-city country club for insiders. One Fairmounter coach revealed his awareness of this external critique when he said, "'The clique' they call us. We're the clique. And it's the clique versus the newcomers. It's like the Hatfields and the McCoys. It's been going on forever. . . . But it took a lot of work to be involved in that clique. Sign up to do something, and then you'll know what is going on."

The complaint that FSA was adult-centered went beyond discomfort with beer-drinking in the clubhouse. Actually, many newcomers thought that drinking beer in the staff office and using the clubhouse year round as a hang-out place was perfectly acceptable, even appropriate compensation for the hours they spent holding the organization together. When newcomers said that the organization wasn't enough about children they usually had in mind an emphasis on winning games, winning championships, and winning in the city-wide league. Among the parents I interviewed, it was disproportionately newcomers who felt FSA leaned excessively in the competitive direction and who longed for more emphasis on individual instruction of players. In contrast, Fairmounter parents tended to see the organization as more balanced, with an appropriate balance of emphasis between teaching skills and winning games.[24] Typical among newcomer parents were these comments from one father: "At FSA they are very much playing games to win, very competitive. This is one of the things I don't like. See, certain kids are not going to get a base hit because the coach just teaches them to bunt, so he can win the game. They learn to bunt but should be learning to hit and [then they would] have a slightly better chance to get on base than by [just] bunting. I prefer to teach kids how to play baseball and not how to win. But when games are not competitive it's not as much fun to watch, maybe not so much fun for kids. Still, I would have less emphasis on playoffs, so there's not so much emphasis on winning." Another newcomer father described FSA as "less instructional and more about winning" and related it to the need of coaches to have bragging rights in the neighborhood. This argument relates back to the issue of "clubhouse teams" versus the newcomer teams. Baseball as a central element of the Fairmount neighborhood's identity meant that losing a game, especially for a "clubhouse team," took on added significance. The association of particular teams with insiders focused energy on the importance of winning to prove something to some other group of *adults*. Many newcomers thought that that other group of adults was them. One black professional father who lived in Center City and had spent years in FSA with his children believed that, with the arrival of significant numbers of players of color, the need to win at FSA had intensified.

> I think Fairmount stresses competition more than instruction. . . . Here's the whole thing. Let me see if I can express it. You have this new dynamic of all of these black kids in the league now. It happened. But the league is still controlled by a small group of white people who have been there for a long time. I think the parents have been feeling that, and this is something that black people feel anyway; which is, when we come in, we can come in, but we'll never be able to control it. And, um, I think many parents felt that when it came down to winning, these white coaches who are involved in the league will win at all costs, thus to show that they're still in control of their knowledge, that they know more. . . . The winning carries over to more than just *we win*, but I'm still, *we're* still, *in control* of this thing. We *have* to be here because we know the most about this game. We're not gonna have coaches coming from outside of the league who know more than we do because, although that may be the case, people may know as much, but if you look at the result, the result was that we won, and we obviously won because we know more.

Beyond how parents judged the competitive nature of the organization as a whole, I wanted to know how they differed as individuals in their approaches to competitive games. To understand this, I presented all the parents I interviewed with the following scenario involving a boys' game in the ten-to-twelve division:

> I'd like to ask you to consider the following game scenario and tell me what you think the coach should do: It is the bottom of the last inning of the game. Your son's team is ahead by one run. They are in the field and already have two outs. The other team has runners on second and third, and their clean-up hitter is up to bat. What should the coach of your son's team do?

If the parent was confused about the implied dilemma of the scenario (an expression of lack of baseball knowledge), they were probed as to whether the coach should intentionally walk the batter, since the tying and winning runs were on base, and let the pitcher confront a weaker hitter. There was a pronounced clustering around the different answers to this question. Fairmounter parents almost universally (nine of ten) endorsed the more competitive, "intentional walk" position. Newcomers were more divided, but more (seven of eleven) favored the pitch-to-the-batter solution. Moreover, the justifications for their distinct answers were often emphatic. To see these contrasting sensibilities, consider this selection of typical justifications offered by Fairmounter parents for the intentional walk:

—Fairmounter father: Sure you walk him automatically. . . . If your pitcher's not better than their hitter, you walk him, and you go to next guy and put pressure on him. . . . In ten-to-twelve, you still walk him because the fifth hitter will be more intimidated than the fourth hitter would. It's baseball, that's the way you would do it. [When probed about alternative response] If you moved to high school, what would your high school coach tell you to do? Walk him. That's baseball. The knowledge of the game is, in order to win you put the pressure on the weak link. The weak link becomes the fifth batter. . . . It's not a matter of man against man; it's a matter of position against position.

—Fairmounter father: Automatic walk. It's a beautiful game between both teams, but it's close, and you don't want to lose that game, not like that. I'll take a chance and go after the next guy. We'll get the fifth batter at the plate.

—Fairmounter father who also coached: Walk 'em. Definitely. As long as I know my pitcher can throw strikes, no ifs, ands, or buts. [laughs when probed about the alternative] It's just simple good baseball. . . . I wouldn't be a good coach, if I didn't do whatever I could to make the team, to put 'em in a position to win.

—Fairmount mother: I would walk him. Load up the bases then go with your fifth batter. [When probed about alternative answer] Do you want to win? Everybody always does this thing, "Well, it's for fun." Jump rope's fun. [Laughter] Yeah, jump rope. I hate it when they say that: "It's for fun." Because if it was just for fun, there would be no score. There is a score. There's an object here. Somebody's got to win. Somebody's got to lose. I think they would be better off teaching the children, you know: "Win some, lose some, blah, blah, blah." I can't stand when they do that—the confidence thing, "He has to build his confidence." But it's an important game! You have to win it. It's strictly the game.

—Fairmount mother: Walk. Yeah. I learned that from the real baseball. . . . Yeah, I'm out to win. We're just trying to do the best that we can to win. Of course, I would get mad if it was the opposite. [Laughter]

In contrast, here is a sample of newcomer parents' rationales for letting pitchers confront the clean-up batter:

—Newcomer father: Pitch to him instead of walking. Why? It's an instructional league—even though you're playing the game to win. I just don't think it's fair to the batter at that level and the team. I mean, it's a legitimate move. I just feel, at that level it should be about the kids not the coaches.

—Newcomer father: If it was in the regular season, I would pitch to him. See if my pitcher can face the situation. Let him get their best hitter, to build their confidence. But if it was a championship, I might intentionally walk.

—Newcomer father: I don't get it. [After an explanation of the dilemma] Oh, pitch to him. I'd have confidence in my pitcher and let him have the out.

—Newcomer father: I would encourage the pitcher to do his best to throw strikes. No, an intentional walk would not be my first choice. If the game is on the line, we're gonna either win it or lose it. You're gonna play to win, so take chances—it's an opportunity for a guy to come up after, chances are as good as with the fourth batter.

—Newcomer mother: I probably would not do an intentional walk, but it is an acceptable strategy. I wouldn't find anything wrong with a coach who would walk, but I probably wouldn't. I'm a shoot-from-the-hip kind of person.

—Newcomer mother: I've learned that, in baseball strategy you should walk the clean-up hitter, especially at the higher level. But in little league, let him swing. 'Cause it's little kids, not the major leagues. They should be able to have the experience of batting in a pressure situation. He's in a clean-up spot. When my son was on a bad team last year, they walked him all the time. He was so frustrated and built up a lot of anger because he couldn't swing the bat. He was putting up with all these errors of others and come his turn, if they didn't walk him, the umpire was calling a ball or strike that wasn't.

One black newcomer parent, in contrast to these other newcomer positions, did vote for the walk position. But in discussing her logic, she went on to oppose organized youth sports in general, precisely because of the need to follow the strategic logic of the game rules. "I think he should walk him. If you're playing the game, you're playing to win. You should walk him. But that's why I'm not sold on youth sports, per se. If you're playing the game, you're playing the game. If you want to just hit and have fun, then let kids hit and have fun. But if you're playing organized sports, then it's like playing checkers. What is the objective of checkers? To win, and you have rules. The same thing with baseball and any other sport. As soon as you organize, that's what happens. . . . Unfortunately, in our society, we over-organize. When I was growing up, we formalized our own teams, made up our own rules. We didn't have the parents there. We didn't have all this hoopla. There wasn't the pressure then. But the minute you make it baseball, you make it the real game. You make it organized. You have teams, parents, everything, and then it becomes the real game, the real pressure, and you have to deal with it. I think we have organized baseball too soon. Most of them are not ready for that kind of pressure."

One Fairmounter father challenged the assumption behind my question, that this was a matter of individual choice and not a matter of group culture. He had coached for many years in FSA's past and stressed how important the overall culture of the league was for signaling what coaches should do. "It doesn't matter what I want to do. It matters what the other coaches are doing. More than half the coaches and parents out there will say, "Walk 'em." They want competitive ball. So if that is the case, I'm a sucker if I give my pitcher a chance against their number four, but my number four gets walked every other inning." His point is important and underscores the way frustrations arise when individuals try to introduce less competitive approaches into a setting where more competitive approaches dominate.

The differences in the way Fairmounters and newcomers related both to the neighborhood, as described above, and to the league reflected a competing set of cultural values related to individual responsibility, group solidarity, and how best to promote children's interests.[25] The different orientations toward the community could be described as hierarchical communalism versus child-centered individualism. While there was a range of opinion about most of these concerns within the two groups, when differences did appear they often took this form. Fairmounters, on the one hand, regularly brought up resentments about the way newcomers used the organization narrowly for the benefit of their own children, without appropriate levels of support, or deference, to the needs of the broader group and its leadership—much like their approach to the neighborhood. Brett Williams describes the metropolitan vision of professional newcomers in a gentrifying neighborhood of Washington, D.C., as one riddled with contradictions: "they want a diverse community but they want the best for their children as well." Their quest for variety and for maximum advantage for their children distanced them from local life and from the less affluent residents whose "passions for texture" created human connections in local space and kept street life and the community nourished, despite the stigma of doing so. Although the Fairmount old-timers are different from the poorer "renters" of William's neighborhood, their criticism of newcomers' lack of care for the space beyond the fleeting experience of their children's games is similar. In response, newcomers to FSA complained that their interests were ignored, that Fairmounters too often listened only to other Fairmounters and ran the organization to benefit themselves and their adult friends, with concern for children running a distant second. But newcomers' critique of Fairmounters was less intense than the Fairmounter critique of them; in part this is because the space meant less to them.

Segmented Understandings

Despite the emphasis in this discussion on the divisions and tensions between and among Fairmounters and newcomers, there were also many understandings and feelings of connection forged across these groups. Indeed, the cross-class sympathies may even have been stronger than some of the tensions between the deep insiders and newcomers. After all, you had to be somewhat "in the know" with the organization to even notice some of the divisions. Most importantly, many newcomers cherished being a part of FSA, despite its warts and their somewhat marginal position. But the emerging empathies wove themselves across the space in a segmented manner, similar to the uneven and segmented way racial understandings happened at FSA. In the words of one newcomer, "We represent some of the outsiders. But I think the mixture of kids here is terrific. I'm not aware of any tensions. I think it's one of the few places where kids of different colors, different ethnicities, and different socioeconomic incomes come together for a common purpose in this city. It's wonderful."

The loyalty of newcomers to FSA was tested at one point by the emergence of another baseball organization run predominantly by upper-middle-class professionals. A small group of dissatisfied newcomers whose children played at FSA but who lived mostly outside the neighborhood, in Center City, rebelled against FSA by leaving and starting an alternative baseball organization in a nearby area referred to as Taney. The goal, presumably, was to create a club that they would control and run in a manner more consistent with their needs. This would be a club run in a less competitive fashion than FSA, with more baseball instruction for the kids, and with clinics offering coaches more professional training. There would be no separate softball divisions; girls would play hardball with the boys. Because of the smaller numbers of children at Taney, they only fielded teams through the age of twelve. Once their children reached thirteen, some parents returned to FSA to finish out the thirteen-to-fifteen division. Others who had started at Taney also moved over at this point.

There was an enormous amount of discussion at FSA over the years about what the Taney "breakaway" meant, what it promised to deliver, and the reality of what it did deliver. Occasionally, when a Fairmount–newcomer conflict would erupt, the escape value of Taney would be pointed to, such as the time a Fairmount staff member shouted to my husband, who had complained about the practice schedule, "And if you don't like it, you can always go to Taney." But others acknowledged that there might be a difference between the professionals who opted to be at Taney and those who preferred FSA. As one old-timer saw it, "A lot of them, see, they wanted their own league down at Taney. The ones with problems, they left. They were not used to taking orders, or whatever it is they want for their kids—their girls to play on boys' teams. The ones that are staying here at FSA, they like the guys who run it all right. So they're okay."

A very common theme among newcomer professionals at Fairmount was their preference for the diversity of FSA over the class homogeneity of Taney. Common among the reasons for the loyalty to FSA was an affinity for the working-class style of the league as something emotionally familiar to many, either from their own parents or from their own childhoods. One newcomer, who actually lived in the Taney area but had spent a decade at FSA, explained his preference:

> I like the feel of it [FSA]. . . . In a time when the world has changed so drastically, it's a lot like when I played as a kid. . . . Some of the people's values are still in the '50s as well. But when Taney started, it was not even a consideration for us to go over there. I just felt like, where I grew up was fairly working-class, and I really appreciated that looking back. And this feels a lot like that. It was real people in a particular kind of way. And at a time where it's very easy to be in an environment where there is not a lot of diversity . . . Taney, it just didn't have quite the same feel at the time when it was being started. It was much more a very white, upper-middle-class organization. The people of Fairmount have their flaws. The people of Taney have their flaws. We all have our flaws. I was just more

comfortable with the people at Fairmount and their flaws. The people at Taney were just all too familiar to me. We felt that, for our kids, Fairmount was an opportunity to meet real Philadelphia kids who they would grow up with, and know, and, in some ways, sort of bond with. And should they decide that some day, as adults, that they are going to live in Philadelphia, these are probably kids they will come across.

A professor who knew many of the Taney people explained why he felt unsympathetic to their revolt:

> They felt like it [FSA] was a closed shop. They felt like there were sets of rules for the insiders of Fairmount, like their suggestions weren't considered. In fact, in certain instances, they felt that their efforts were being undermined. Things like miscommunication in terms of, say, the availability of times for the practice field. They basically felt persecuted. I would say they were a little paranoid. But I wouldn't say it was totally without merit. Though in some ways, I think it was an extreme reaction. And I happen to know some of the people. At least a couple of them were pretty high-powered people who basically weren't used to being told that you have to work your way up in this organization. You take a very high-powered businessperson or lawyer from a big law firm, he isn't going to want to hear, "Come on down at 6:30 or 7:00 Sunday morning, and pick up trash, and rake the field." They sort of saw themselves as executive decision-makers. And that was the part where I was much more sympathetic to the people of Fairmount who spent twenty-five or thirty years building this organization, and didn't need some fancy guy to come in and tell them, "This is the way you should be doing it."

Some newcomers at FSA had experienced both leagues and concluded that Taney had its own distinct set of problems, including serious internal political conflicts and a less than organic approach to baseball.

> My son had played at Taney before we came to FSA, a terrible experience. Everybody had said Taney was more low-key—but for us, a terrible experience. . . . Taney is run by a whole different group, people with graduate degrees and major business people. So I would say there's no improvement there—as many problems there as here. . . . My husband's view is that a lot of Taney people can't play sports, so they want a league where their kids can win. They can't easily win here. It's really critical for them. They don't look like they played sports, clearly weren't athletic. At least, in Fairmount you have people who played sports and know what baseball is. They really know how to play, may still be playing. I like that, even with its negative stuff—it's not fake baseball.

Others challenged the claim that Taney's middle-class league really offered a less competitive approach to baseball for its children. "These leagues are all the same. When they say Taney is more instructional, it's not true. I would stand up in court and say that. I've seen two attorneys up at Taney battle it out, rolling on the ground in the dirt."

Regardless of the truth value of these claims about Taney, the point is that many newcomers at FSA perceived themselves as making a conscious choice to be part of Fairmount and to work toward community understanding, despite its challenges. Over time, some even felt defensive on behalf of the Fairmounters, who were sometimes ruthlessly critiqued by the Taney people, even more so than by the professional discontents within FSA:

> What I don't like about Taney is the precious, special, upper-middle-class nature of the people there. I didn't really know about them until these people started coming back to Fairmount from there. They started at Fairmount and then went off when Taney was founded, a mass of them. First year, all they could do was bitch and moan about how terrible Fairmount was and how wonderful Taney had been, and now they had to come back and deal with lug heads in the clubhouse—just their lack of understanding of what Fairmount was about. . . . I thought the Taney people just kind of lacked a whole perspective about the class nature of their conflict, the rights and wrongs.

The sympathies that emerged across class and racial lines at FSA were especially apparent in encounters the ball club had with the outside world, such as in traveling team championships played in remote neighborhoods of the city and suburbs. Professional parents at FSA were sometimes surprised to learn that suburban teams viewed Fairmount in an undifferentiated way, as a low-class, inner-city team. The generalized apprehension of suburbanites for anything inside the city translated into nervousness about even neighborhoods as affluent as Spring Garden had become. This external judgment stimulated community loyalty. I remember feeling this acutely one year, as my son's twelve-and-under traveling team faced an extremely affluent suburban team. Our team was about one-third boys of color and their team was all white. Neighborhood men and women had driven more than an hour to see this important Fairmount game, many with no child on the team. After watching the Council Rock parents leave their BMWs and slick SUVs in the immense parking lot behind their practice field, I saw the Fairmounter adults line up behind our dugout. Seeing this crowd of adult Fairmounters outside our neighborhood, all of us looking particularly ragtag compared to the well-dressed suburban parents we faced, I could feel our "insider/newcomer" problem slip away. As the game proceeded, many Fairmounters shouted out nonstop encouraging comments to each of the Fairmount players. Although some were still strangers to me, they called to my son by name. They also called out the names of our black catcher and third baseman in a raucous, public testimony of solidarity for the community we sometimes achieved.

Although Fairmounters had many complaints about newcomers' individualism, some also recognized the importance of contributions made by professionals who were strategically placed in the city. Newcomers were sometimes generous in tapping their networks and resources to provide a different kind of financial support, one that was more lucrative than "booster day," where ballplayers knocked on neighborhood doors with FSA cups asking for donations. (My son calls this "kids' begging day.") As one FSA staffer acknowledged, "Yes, and they're [the newcomers] able to get us sponsored money, where in the past, we used to knock on doors. Now they just email each other, and it's here. That really helps. So it's less work for the twelve people most involved. It's less work because, they can call two friends and a check comes in the mail. It's beautiful." While receiving checks in the mail might produce more revenue, knocking on doors builds community support for the field and connects the baseball children with locals who might not have children in the league. It was this combination of both orientations, reaching inward to capitalize on community solidarity and reaching outward for inclusion and external support, that built on the strengths of the two worlds of Fairmounters and newcomer professionals.

A few strategic professionals also played an important behind-the-scenes role when FSA faced its most serious external threat in decades. Thirty years after Fairmount men defended their right to use the park ground as a baseball field with informal sit-ins, the field again came under threat from city agencies in the form of a Parkway development plan. The plan slated the baseball fields for mid-rise residential development. There was a sustained email campaign on the part of Fairmounters and newcomers in opposition to this plan. But significantly, Kyle, a professional who had coached at FSA for years, happened to work at the Philadelphia City Planning Commission, which formally responded to the Parkway plan of the Central Philadelphia Development Corporation. Although FSA leadership did not especially appreciate Kyle as a coach, Kyle was, nonetheless, a lover of the space and its history. He wrote the first draft of the Planning Commission's report:

> For many families in the Fairmount neighborhood, Fairmount Park's Von Colln Fields, known to those who use them as the Fairmount Fields, are the heart and soul of their closely knit community. The Center City District's concept to displace this neighborhood facility in order to reap a "higher, better and more profitable" use of city parkland is misguided for a number of reasons. For one, the idea of selling public parkland for commercial and residential development is an abhorrent precedent. The Von Colln Fields were created by the City for the neighborhood not on an

interim basis until a better deal came along, but as a long-term commitment to provide a much needed public amenity to a densely compacted
urban neighborhood. The recreational opportunities and visual openness of this wonderful piece of City parkland should not be for sale to the
highest bidder. The Fairmount Park Commission would *never consider
selling or building on Pastorius Park in Chestnut Hill or Rittenhouse
Square in Center City*, or any piece of its magnificent park system that
serves the City so well.

The Center City District's myopic suggestion that this site can simply
be replaced with a recreation facility somewhere to the south is a cynical
attempt to deflect the serious nature of its assault on the residents of the
Fairmount neighborhood. Moving the ball fields south of the Parkway
would mean that the many children who use the fields would have to
cross Parkway traffic to get to their baseball games and soccer practices.
Replacing the open space that affords a grand view of the skyline to all
who come to the fields with mid-rise apartment buildings would rob this
important City neighborhood of a tremendous and unique asset, one
that gives value to their properties and enjoyment to their lives. Is the
residential character and livability of the Fairmount neighborhood to be
sacrificed for the benefit of the hospitality industry in Center City?[26]
(italics mine)

Although this draft was toned down in the final report, it is striking that
part of Kyle's defense of the baseball space was class-based, namely equating
Fairmount's right to claim "its" park as a baseball field with the right of two of
the most affluent neighborhoods in the city to maintain the traditional use of
their prestigious parks. So while different cultural orientations divided some
Fairmounters from some newcomers within FSA, important cross-class ties of
solidarity coexisted, in the form of segmented understandings, more than the
organizational gatekeepers acknowledged.

The fact that many working-class people live in an obviously unequal social
world doesn't mean that they judge themselves, or others, in terms of the hierarchy of class or economic status. Michèle Lamont found that blue-collar workers and lower-status white-collar workers evaluated themselves and others
more in terms of the quality of their interpersonal relationships. They also often
articulated a moral critique of "people above" whom they judged as lacking
warmth, having domineering styles, and dedicated to a fast-track ambition that
impoverished social encounters. Something similar was behind the judgments
of Fairmounters about what was problematic in professional newcomers'
approach to the organization. But in the case of FSA we have a localized, neighborhood expression of this negative moral assessment of the more affluent. The
fact that the encounter occurred in a space historically nourished by Fair-

mounters, and on terrain where their baseball expertise should matter, even to professionals accustomed to ordering others around at work, further aggravated the general cultural grievance of these Middle Americans against the more educated upper middle class. The external hierarchy of work life was temporarily reversed in this space and hence maintaining locals' control over it was particularly important. Understandings were forged but control was non-negotiable.

IF YOU WERE a baseball coach and your team was in the field and faced a very close baseball game where any run scored mattered greatly, with a runner on third and less than two outs, you might opt to bring the infield in. Then on a ground ball you would have the chance to get an out at the plate and prevent the opposing team from scoring. It is a time-honored defensive strategy because it diminishes the chance of a ground ball becoming an RBI. But it also comes with a certain amount of risk, since the range of ground balls your team could field would be smaller than usual. You "bring the infield in" typically when you are winning or tied and the game is in the late innings. It is an aggressive defensive strategy to win the game. Fairmounter insiders who controlled FSA for decades did something like this in defending their baseball space as new professionals entered; they brought their infield in. They vigilantly and successfully protected their control of the organization, its leadership, and its social style. They monitored closely any newcomer moves that revealed a trace of autonomy or independence and made sure no unproven, inappropriately assertive types got any unnecessary runs.

How Parents Get on Base

From the very beginning there were problems. One evening after John, my husband the coach, came home from the draft, we were reviewing the list of kids on his new team. Some of the boys we knew from other years, some we had heard about, and some we knew nothing about, especially the younger ones coming up from the seven-to-nine division. John was pleased, because he had drafted three good players whose fathers he knew could help coach and run practices: Fritz, Paul, and Craig.

When a boy named Donald appeared on the list, Kate, John's assistant coach, said, "His father is very aggressive about where his kid plays." So, knowing only that Rickie, the father, was "a problem," John called him the first time to announce that Donald would be on the Expos, that John was the coach, and when practices would begin—a routine call for the beginning of the season. After listening to John's standard introduction, Rickie, the father, said, "I can help you out with coaching."

JOHN: Oh, thanks, but I already have plenty of people.

RICKIE: Well, I always helped out before, so I can help you.

JOHN: Thanks a lot, but I have more than I can use now, not sure we'll all fit in the dugout. Ha.

[Long pause.]

RICKIE: Donald's position is first base. He's an All-Star.

JOHN: Well, okay [knowing that the kid was just coming up from the seven-to-nine, that he was ranked "C" within that group, and that his chance of starting infield was almost zero]. We'll try him out and see how he is.

RICKIE: Superstar, man, real superstar.

JOHN: Well, okay then. See you next week.

Shortly after this call, I met Rickie myself at the Expos' first exhibition game. I was sitting alone on the bench waiting for the game, while our team was warming up. Rickie was (I later learned) a lower-middle-class Puerto Rican. He wore a sculptured beard, sunglasses, an "Expos" baseball cap turned backward, blue jeans, and a bright orange "Nautica" slick jacket with desert boots. He sat a few feet from me and pointed out his boy on the field, "That's my kid over there in the outfield. Donald. [So this is him, I thought.] He's quiet, real quiet. I call him the quiet superstar."

I watched Donald on the field for a few minutes. He was thin, and somewhat tall for his age, but with sharply slumped shoulders that diminished his height and gave him a lumbering look. The whole impression his body gave was one of submissiveness, like he was saying, "Don't notice me, just let me tiptoe by you. His fearful expression changed to a big bright smile when one of the coaches talked to him playfully. He'll be a handsome man, I thought to myself, if he grows out of his awkwardness. He looked interracial. Someone later told me that Donald is actually Rickie's stepson, the child of his longtime African American girlfriend. Perhaps because of the tenuousness of the tie, Rickie invokes the word "son" frequently in his public comments to Donald.

The quiet superstar, it turned out, was terrified of the ball. His batting stance resembled a cringing, wounded animal being forced to hold a stick up in the air as a defensive weapon. One Friday night, early in the season, the team went to the batting cages. Donald was the only kid, out of thirteen, who never hit the ball that evening, not one of the sixty machine-pitched balls. His father, who joined them, dismissed it as nothing, noting that "he was always a good hitter, must be in a slump."

Early on, Donald demonstrated a skill level consistent with his "C" ranking. In particular, he had major problems catching. John tried to work with Donald, but his father's presence aggravated Donald's terror of the ball. John and the other assistant coaches found it incredible that he had ever played first base in the seven-to-nine division, but then they realized that Donald's team had been one of the worst of that division. Something his father had obviously never focused on. It is extremely rare for a kid coming up from the seven-to-nine division to play anything but outfield his first year. John started playing Donald in right field. Donald had little success in this position, and it was compounded by the fact that he had a serious technical disadvantage. He had a peculiar problem with moving his glove to catch the ball. If a ball was thrown right at him, he could sometimes catch it. But if, for example, a ball was thrown a few feet to his right or left, Donald would reach his glove in front of him in a dream-like posture. As the ball passed, he wouldn't shift the glove even slightly in the ball's direction, but instead, would stand frozen, except for squeezing the glove as the ball whizzed by. This happened on many occasions. After a couple of these early games with Donald playing right field, Rickie called John at home one evening. Rickie speaks quickly, with an exaggerat-edly confident tone that belies an underlying anxious hunger. Even when pleading for something, he appears to be announcing a result.

JOHN: Hey, Rickie, what's up?

RICKIE: John, you should know that Donald is downstairs right now crying his heart out.

JOHN: Oh really, what's the problem?

RICKIE: He just feels marginalized on the team.

JOHN: Oh, really? [John initially thought Rickie meant that there was a social problem, with the kids perhaps excluding Donald] What's going on?

RICKIE: It's just that he is used to being an infielder, where the action is. He just feels marginalized out there in the outfield.

[Silence]

JOHN: Well, then, I guess your job is to tell him that the outfield *is* part of the team, that the outfield is important to the game. That's where we need him.

RICKIE: But he's used to more. He wants more action, crying his heart out.

JOHN: [Disgusted] I'm playing him where he should be playing. You tell him that. Rickie: You tell him that. Gotta go.

John told all this to our son, whose instant reaction was, "Donald's not down-stairs crying. He doesn't even wanna play. His Dad's crying."

After months of tension, misunderstanding, and resentment between father and coach over playing time and positions, their struggle came to a head in the final elimination game of the playoffs. I had been watching another game in the younger boys' league and arrived late, in the third inning. The Expos were down by only one run, but John, recovering from a fever of 102° the night before, was moving slowly around the dugout without much expression.

The rules are structured to make the playoffs a more competitive situation than usual. In a regular-season game, each team uses a continuous lineup so that all players get their regular at-bat, whether or not they are playing in the field. But in the playoffs, only ten players are allowed to bat, so some boys must be substituted. Moreover, once you take someone out of the game in the playoffs, he can't come back in. This rule change for the playoffs is not understood by many parents. Donald had played the first three innings. In the fourth inning, John took him out, along with another player, for two other players who had been on the bench. Rickie walked quickly to the dugout and asked loudly: "Hey! Why did you take Donald out?"

JOHN: He played three innings. I'm putting someone else in now.

RICKIE: Why don't you take some of those other guys out then? Donald comes to every practice, every game. Those guys don't come to all the practices, they miss. Take them out.

JOHN: Rickie, this is the playoffs. We're trying to win this game.

Rickie, exploding, moved toward the dugout entrance. "I WANNA WIN TOO! You think I don't wanna win? You think I'm a loser?" By that time, he was screaming. "Put Donald in and you CAN win!"

I was seated twenty feet away on the bleachers and could hear every word. I was certain they could hear also, up at the concession stand, two fields away. Rickie charged into the dugout and moved his body close to John's, in a threatening posture.

"What? Do you have to be the coach's son to play the whole game?"

John, in a loud but still pleading tone, responded: "Oh, come on. Stop this now. You know these are very hard decisions, Rickie. I really don't like making them. I worry a lot about these decisions before I make them. I would really appreciate your letting up now. I can't talk to you about this now. [more firmly] Now, leave the dugout."

Without moving, Rickie asked, "Are you gonna put him back in later?"

"No, I can't. In the playoffs after you take someone out, they can't come back in."

Moving in close to John's face, clenched fist waving in the air, Rickie shouted, "YOU CAN'T DO THIS. I PAY MY TAXES, I CAN'T BE TREATED LIKE THIS." John moved back, almost rearing, and then also erupted, "I'M NOT YOUR FUCKING MAYOR!"

Their two red faces were locked together, two inches apart.

RICKIE: [Hissing] Put him back in.

JOHN: I'm not your mayor! UMPIRE! I WANT THIS GUY THROWN OUT OF THE GAME!

The ump scrambled over and signaled Rickie to leave the dugout and, presumably, the game. Rickie braced himself, and for a long couple of seconds I was convinced he would pounce on John. The crowd had grown silent, so the words of the two men rang out even clearer. Then, unexpectedly, Rickie stomped out of the dugout still yelling something about rights, while John kept yelling, "I'm not your mayor! I'm not your mayor!"

Fritz, an assistant coach with a history of boxing and professional hockey umpiring, moved over to the bench and stood, trying to engage Rickie, who had begun to pace up and down frantically behind the dugout. I expected the umpire to come and remove Rickie, but perhaps his age—about twenty—prevented him from asserting himself further. Fritz is a white retired city worker, married to a black woman, with a highly athletic son on the team. He had expressed contempt for Rickie earlier in the season, when Rickie openly implied that black boys sat out more than white ones.

Pulling his arm, Fritz said, "Listen, Rickie, these are the playoffs, and this strategy gives us a chance to win."

Still yelling, Rickie pulled his arm away, "You think I don't wanna win? *I'm a winner, man!*"

Leaning forward, Fritz said what he had thought all season. "Listen, Rickie. I'm gonna tell you something now, so listen. Your kid can't hit, can't catch, and can't run. And after that, there's not a helluva lot left." Fritz walked away. For a full ten minutes more, Rickie stood alone behind the dugout, glaring at John's back.

Fortunately, during most of the scene, the Expos had been in the field, and Donald had been off, outside the dugout, playing catch with another boy. It was impossible, however, for him not to have heard the turbulence, or for him to have failed to realize that his father, and indirectly he, himself, were at the center of that dispute.

John did not recover for the rest of the game. Even when Rickie finally moved away from the dugout, he kept announcing in the dugout, and to no one in particular, "I'm having a hard time getting back into this. I'm still so upset." The confrontation cast a dark cloud over the rest of the game. In that inning, the Expos let in seven runs, and in the next inning they made a steady series of dramatic errors. They lost the game, 12-1, with the worst collective playing of the season. The season was over.

As the game ended, Rickie, obviously wanting to disassociate himself as fast as possible, came up calling, "Hey Donald, get your bat. Come on now, get your bat." A few parents came up personally and thanked John kindly. One professional couple remained seated at a distance on the grass. In contrast to Rickie, their own critique of how their son, who had missed one-third of the games and practices, had been utilized during the games had been articulated only indirectly, but nonetheless powerfully, during the season. They never approached the dugout at the end of the game to say anything. John, seeing me watching them, muttered, "They sit there with their silent yuppie critique. I wish they would just come up and yell also. Really cap it off."

For a full hour after the game, Rickie stood in the now abandoned ten-to-twelve field, alternating between pitching to Donald and having Donald pitch to him. Several boys lingered on the periphery, waiting for a chance to play also, but Rickie succeeded in controlling the field, keeping it for the two of them until the sun set. I wondered to myself about Donald's state of mind. Did they discuss it at all? Or had Rickie just immediately begun providing an alternative version of what he believed should have been Donald's game experience–the center of all action. They reminded me of a scene in the movie *The Great Santini*, where the father stayed in the family driveway, playing basketball in the rain until midnight, after his 16-year-old son had beaten him for the first time in their relationship–the father unable to see his son as separate from himself. I watched them both for a long time, feeling pained and saddened.

Later that night, I kept second-guessing everything that had happened, asking John about the range of opinions on definitions of "instructional league." Why did this substitution rule exist in the playoffs only? What could you have done differently? Why did Rickie need Donald to be something he was not? I had anxious nightmares about yelling fathers and crying boys. John didn't fall asleep until three A.M. The next morning, he woke up haggard and announced, "It's the epitome of yuppiedom, to keep worrying about this. I'm sick of it. I can't talk or think about any of it anymore. Next year, I draft parents, not kids."

4

===

The Dugout and the Masculinity Styles of Coaches

"Never Bail Out"

Because the encounter between newcomers and old-timers at Fairmount happened in the masculine realm of baseball, part of what was at stake was competing styles of masculinity. Baseball is a central site in American culture for the passing down, from one generation of men to another, of powerful lessons about what it means to be a man.[1] But if there is one thing well established in the literature on gender relations, it is that while certain gender styles are often dominant at particular historical moments, there are usually alternative versions floating nearby as well. Whatever we call the alternative versions of traditional masculinity, the range of actual male *behavior* is often far broader than our dominant *ideas* about how men should behave.[2] In the gentrifying neighborhood of Fairmount/Spring Garden, this encounter among men and boys from different backgrounds in the traditional realm of baseball, a central site where masculinity is played out and reconstructed, provides a unique opportunity to identify, dramatize, and explore the meanings behind the alternative ways in which men inherit and invent their styles of masculinity in a transformed and multicultural world.

As newcomers entered FSA, what was at stake for Fairmounters was not just control of the organization but the preservation of baseball itself—the game as it was meant to be played, and had been played in the neighborhood: adeptly, thoughtfully, strategically, and with discipline. For many in Fairmount, playing baseball well was a source of pride. Seeing local boys compete in city-wide competitions, representing the neighborhood at Philadelphia's Veterans Stadium, and following the championships of local teams were important neighborhood rituals. But essential to maintaining this respectable neighborhood baseball identity was the dedication of a cadre of coaches who both knew enough about the game and its intricacies, and had enough time, to train the next generation of players. Yet as time passed, there weren't enough old-timer coaches to do this job, and newcomers had to be brought in.

In many city leagues, neighborhood teams play only against other neighborhood teams at rotating sites. But Fairmount historically has had enough players to have both its own in-house league, where locals play locals, and a series of elite traveling teams, starting at age ten, that compete against other neighborhood teams in one of the city-wide leagues. Fairmounters see the in-house instructional teams as modeling the same hierarchical system as the minor leagues, with the traveling teams corresponding to the major leagues. In the seven-to-nine, ten-to-twelve, and thirteen-to-fifteen divisions, they stress instructional baseball. The traveling teams cull talent from these in-house instructional leagues for regional, more competitive leagues. As boys move up through the ranks of the instructional league and make it onto one of the traveling teams, the local expertise about baseball is gradually and carefully instilled. These teams are proof to many Fairmounters that tradition is being passed on. It is here that the game is played well. The traveling teams are the source of considerable local pride, evidence of a craft realized.

Fairmounter coaches deeply felt the importance of passing down the neighborhood tradition. In my interviews, one striking difference between them and newcomer coaches was the extent to which the Fairmounter coaches mentioned "paying back" what they had gotten from the neighborhood men who had coached them. They stressed their pride at seeing neighborhood boys compete successfully against boys from other neighborhoods. When asked about their own coaching strengths, the Fairmounter coaches often mentioned as fundamental contributions their knowledge of baseball, their sense of the game, and their effective strategies, a kind of masculine expertise unrelated to the workplace. This was especially the case among those who coached at the more advanced levels, where expertise played a bigger role. The central role Fairmounter coaches ascribed to the importance of equipping the next generation of baseball players, and to preparing neighborhood boys for city-wide competitions, was not well understood by newcomers in the organization. And as the newcomer coaches described themselves in interviews, these same concerns were not equally central to the agendas of many of them. Rather, newcomer coaches were more likely to stress their own interpersonal qualities, like coaching strength, patience, or humor in dealing with children, and spending time with their own sons, above the importance of developing children's baseball expertise or carrying on a neighborhood baseball tradition. But a distinctive emphasis on baseball knowledge versus social skills was only one dimension of the difference that emerged in the coaching styles.

In Philadelphia, FSA has a widespread reputation for being extremely competitive and for giving their weaker players a hard time. Coaches are central to this reputation. For example, in the early 1990s, a middle-class mother from an affluent downtown neighborhood, with a son of modest athletic ability, told me that she considered me "very brave indeed" for putting my son in FSA. She elaborated: "We just couldn't take the risk. We heard so many horror stories that we went for Taney [the predominantly middle-class league described in chapter 3] instead. There, he never sits on the bench and thinks of himself as a good player." Implicit in this mother's comment is the notion that FSA has a dominant style of masculinity that is excessively competitive and tough, a style from which her son needed to be protected. She shopped for an alternative, "softer" version in a league associated with more affluent professionals. But was her judgment full and accurate? Not really. Despite this mother's characterization of Fairmount coaches, developed from a distance, they are not uniformly tough or excessively competitive. From the inside, it looks different.

During the first few years I sat on the benches of Fairmount, I heard frequent mumblings about the "typical Fairmounter coaches" and the "yuppie coaches." When the mumblings were about the Fairmounter coaches, they usually referred to their yelling, or to their excessively high expectations about skills. I would hear things like, "Oh boy! He's a real neighborhood coach, screaming and terrifying the boys." When the mumblings referenced newcomer coaches, the implication was often that they had a less than complete knowledge of the game, used a more laid-back style, or were "one of those parent-coaches." One old-timer said bluntly, "There are two kinds of coaches at FSA, the screamers from the neighborhood and the fuzzies from outside." Yet, as I watched these coaches for more than a decade, I found notable differences among FSA coaches in their core attitudes toward the game, in their styles of coaching, and in their expectations for how boys should play the game. There was more to it than just being "yellers and fuzzies." I came to think of the coaching in terms of four key dimensions. Those key dimensions clustered in different ways to produce a range of distinct masculine styles.

First, the coaches differ widely in the degree of baseball expertise and training they apply to their coaching. Coaches range from those who have played their entire lives, either informally or formally, in competitive leagues, to those who have developed a more passive understanding of the game, mostly as spectators, but who want to support their sons as they learn the game. In many ways, coaches are like teachers, and every good teacher must, at least minimally, know the subject matter. It takes years of experience to competently master the techniques of batting, bunting, fielding, base-running, and pitching. The more years of expertise—or knowledge of the finer points of the game— coaches have, the more likely they are to place importance on developing a wider range of the essential skills than are coaches with a more casual level of baseball experience. For example, old-timer coaches will take the time to train their pitchers on how to keep runners on base, or how to execute pick-off moves without balking.

As another example, an experienced coach will teach his infielders how to execute a run-down play (involving the coordination of three, not two, defensive players) in the event that a runner is caught between bases. The coaches with this level of knowledge were concentrated among the old-timers. Especially with the older boys, expertise is clearly necessary in order to establish one's authority as legitimate. The younger the division, the less expertise is a factor in establishing a coach's authority. In the youngest divisions, mostly basic skills are at issue, like learning to get gloves down on ground balls, not overrunning a base, or stepping and shifting your weight forward on a swing. Younger boys often don't recognize who knows, and who doesn't know, baseball. Instead, they respond more to who is "nice" than to who is knowledgeable. Expertise is much more varied in the in-house teams. Coaching expertise tends to be concentrated in the coaches on the older teams, especially on the traveling teams, and coaches who do well with the younger boys often come under critical scrutiny when they take on the older teams.

Second, coaches also differ in their emphasis on individual skill building versus winning. What might help an individual player, especially a weak one, to advance his skills might actually be detrimental to the chances of the team winning a game; therefore, how far an individual coach might be willing to go to include weak players, on a non-meritocratic basis, varies widely. In the words of one little boy, "That coach never plays his scrubs, and that's not fair, 'cause we do." Less competitive coaches, and parents of less talented boys, often deeply resent the marginalization of weak players by some of the more competitive coaches. But it is not just instructional goals that conflict with competition. An emphasis on having fun, or tolerating play, can also be in opposition to competitive goals. When group malaise or boredom sets in among the younger boys, some coaches will abandon their competitive strategies. Others, as long as runs are steadily coming in, will not notice even extreme collective boredom. Coaches also differ in the degree to which they will ease up in a blowout game. Usually it is less knowledgeable and less skilled coaches who allow the score to run up because they see base-stealing, for example, as something that boys do or don't do, not as a trained skill commanded by the coach. Although expertise and competition are separate dimensions of coaching, they often hang together. In part, that is because the more you know about baseball, the greater the range of competitive moves available to you. The more competitive moves you know, the greater the temptation to use them and to include their use as part of your pedagogy.

Third, *how* coaches teach what they know—the type of reinforcement they use, positive or negative—distinguishes them. Because this feature of coaching is so salient, it is the one most commented upon by parents and children. Some coaches are remarkable for how consistently they find positive things to say about even the most botched plays, while others manage to be critical of anything short of heroic baseball and consistently yell and scream their negative evaluations. Illustrating the importance of this dimension, one eleven-year-old boy told me, "There are two kinds of coaches—the mean ones who yell all the time, and the nice ones who let you have fun." Knowing how to play baseball does not always translate into knowing *how* to impart expertise, into knowing techniques or drills for teaching that expertise. Whether or not a coach knows baseball well, whether he cares more about teaching or winning, it is the *way* he teaches, either with criticism or with affirmation, that sets the tone, or feel, of any game, for both the boys and the spectators. Individual coaches are not necessarily consistent in their use of positive or negative reinforcements. Typically, when interacting with their teams, most coaches mix both positive and negative comments, depending on the context and the player. Nevertheless, individual coaches do differ in their emphasis, or style, each being notably either more positive or negative in the frequency and intensity of both criticisms and their affirmations. Yet, their style distinctions are generally only noticed when they individually move to the "outer zones" of either negativity or praise in their interactions with the boys.

Fourth, coaches tolerate and manage their own and their players' emotions in different ways. Baseball is a game saturated with moments of individual failure—strikeouts, failed bunts, fielding errors, overthrows, humiliating rundowns, and moments of intense contingency—where a good play can save the game. Much of the emotional challenge of baseball for boys is about managing these potential and real failures. Some coaches denounce boys' emotions, some take them in stride, and a few actually embrace them. Coaches teach children what they consider to be adequate ways of responding emotionally to the challenges of the game.

At FSA, some coaches fully embrace the traditional emotional scripts of masculinity. Therefore, they expect boys to suppress their emotional vulnerabilities—crying, revealing fear, showing intimidation or anxiety—and to minimize their physical vulnerabilities by absorbing pain and injuries stoically. Additionally, they believe boys should downplay expressions of connectedness or emotional attachment to other boys. Also, an aversion for behaviors, mannerisms, or conversational styles construed as "feminine" often goes along with this emotional style. However, not all emotions are equally devalued and repressed. Anger, pride, and laughter are often tolerated as appropriately "male." I'll call this more emotionally withdrawn, sometimes angry style "tough masculinity." Joe DiMaggio comes to mind.

Other coaches rely on less traditional, "softer" emotional styles. These coaches not only tolerate, but acknowledge and work with boys' emotional sensitivities and reactions to physical pain, and are often more comfortable with emotional and physical gestures of tenderness between and toward the boys. I'll call this style of greater emotional expressiveness and tolerance for male emotional vulnerability "tender masculinity."[3] On many public occasions Lou Gehrig demonstrated a "tender" style of masculinity. Among FSA coaches, tough and tender styles of managing boys' feelings are combined in different ways. One of the sharpest reminders that the ballplayers, standing in their uniforms in highly stylized poses of readiness, are still little boys is when they suddenly and fitfully weep over an error. This happens regularly with the younger boys and semi-regularly with the older boys.

Beyond these four dimensions—degree of expertise, emphasis on skill building or winning, use of positive or negative reinforcement, and tough or tender style of masculinity—coaches also differ in terms of intensity and discipline. The sheer intensity of a coach's behavior toward the boys and the games can work at cross purposes with the coach's other behaviors. A coach can be very positive toward the boys and espouse a noncompetitive ideology. However, if he is breathlessly intense in all his interventions, or if he uses high-volume, nonstop chatter at a highly emotional pitch during close games, the content of his words can be overshadowed. Despite his noncompetitive rhetoric, the boys and their parents feel his intensity and his emotional involvement with winning. When a red-faced coach, with a trembling voice and clenched teeth, turns to his boys on the bench and says, "It's only a game. Perk up and go shake hands," it is not very convincing.

Coaches also differ in how disciplined they are in scheduling regular practices, starting them on time, organizing the practices to maximize the boys' involvement, and even in attending all of their own teams' games. Compared to the other four dimensions of coaching, intensity and discipline are unique in that, rather than defining a coaching style, they deepen its color. For example, a tough masculinity style can be further toughened by a very intense coach, or it can be softened by a less intense coach who delivers his harsh words less forcefully. Or a coach who may not know many of the intricacies of baseball, but who is disciplined and practices three times a week over the two months before the season starts, may succeed in teaching as many of the basics to young players as a more knowledgeable coach who shows up only occasionally.

Coaching Styles and the Power of Outliers

During the 1998 season, I decided to look more deeply into the issue of how different aspects of coaching match up with the coaches, to contrast Fairmounter coaches with newcomer coaches, in order to see whether the group stereotypes really apply. I categorized a group of coaches to see where they fell across a continuum of the dimensions—degree of expertise, emphasis on competition, type of reinforcement, and style of masculinity. I had watched these coaches closely over a number of years. I also collected a considerable body of testimony about their styles from parents and boys. This group of coaches was not selected to be representative of all FSA coaches, but was made up of those whom I had had the occasion to observe more than superficially. Table 4.1 presents, in schematic form, my positioning of twenty FSA coaches in terms of the dimensions of coaching. My placements hardly do justice to the complexity of each coach's efforts, but they do express general tendencies. It wasn't always easy to decide on the exact placement of any given coach. None of us are consistent in all of our behaviors. Some coaches are more inconsistent than others, and that made them particularly hard to place. Moreover, some coaches changed over time. My observations capture only these twenty coaches' styles, and only over a couple of seasons.[4]

Individual coaches combine the four dimensions of coaching in their behavior in various ways, but these combinations aren't just random. That is, the coaches are not evenly distributed across the cells. There is some clustering around different combinations of traits. For example, Table 4.1 shows one cluster of five coaches in the top right cell representing high expertise, a competitive game strategy, negative reinforcement, and a style of "tough masculinity." A second group of coaches cluster in the bottom left cell: low expertise, an instructional style, positive reinforcement, and a style of "tender masculinity." The top right cluster, the "expert disciplinarians," consists exclusively of five old-timers (labeled as "O"). The lower left cluster of four coaches, the "non-expert, positive reinforcers," are predominantly newcomers ("N"). Interestingly enough, these clusters do reflect the common depictions of "old-timer" versus "yuppie" coaches echoed in so many conversations with parents and coaches.

Let's begin with the first cluster, the "old-timers." The decades of involvement the Fairmounter coaches have with the league have consequences beyond mere possession of a deeper level of commitment to a neighborhood organization. There are also blatant payoffs for them in enhanced baseball knowledge. Many more Fairmounters lived and breathed baseball as children than did newcomers. When it comes to sheer expertise, or knowledge of the finer points of the game, many Fairmounters operate at a clear advantage over the newcomers.

Fairmounters are also more likely to adopt a more competitive game strategy with their teams, to employ a negative style of reinforcement in transmission of baseball knowledge, and to rely on a "tough" style of masculinity when dealing with boys' emotions. The fact that young boys' tears are a regular occurrence during games does not make them any more tolerable to many Fairmounter coaches, who find such displays anathema to acceptable masculinity. Beyond specific ball skills, these coaches also teach what they consider to be adequate emotional responses to the challenges of the game. Their more competitive approach often entitles them to coach one of the older, more selective

TABLE 4.1.

Dimensions of Coaching Styles and Placement of Twenty Coaches

Game Philosophy	Positive Reinforcement		Negative Reinforcement	
	High Expertise	Low Expertise	High Expertise	Low Expertise
Competitive				
Tough Masculinity		Timmie-O	Sandy-O **Billy**-O Robbie-O Norm-O Roy-O	**Kirk**-N
Tender Masculinity	**Shawn**-O	Jay-N John-N Howard-N Ryan-N		
Instructional				
Tough Masculinity			Nick-O	
Tender Masculinity	**Dan**-O Ron-N Will-N **Sal**-N	**Kyle**-N Victor-N Ben-O		

Source: Project Data, Grasmuck

Note: O = old-timer to FSA; N= newcomer to FSA. Coaches portrayed in chapter 4 are noted in bold type.

traveling teams that play against select teams from outside the neighborhood in city-wide competitions.

The second cluster of coaches, dominated by newcomers, enters FSA with considerably less baseball experience and technical expertise. They come predominantly as fathers, not as "neighborhood men," and are less invested in the organization, its external reputation, and any social benefits that come with organizational leadership. Although some of these men had spent eight or more years as coaches, by the late 1990s, they were still treated as outsiders by many of the Fairmounter coaches. College educated, often with professional degrees, the newcomer coaches emerge from work environments where they enjoy considerable autonomy and authority. They often pride themselves on their interpersonal skills and their nonconfrontational ways of getting what they want. The more tender emotional style of masculinity common among this cluster of men also contrasts sharply with that of many of the old-timers.

What I have described in terms of the two group clusters does not mean that there were not very knowledgeable newcomer coaches, or old-timer coaches who consistently treated their players with compassion and tenderness. These are only group tendencies. Nonetheless, they were tendencies widely recognized and commented upon by parents and insiders to the organization, by old-timers and newcomers alike. Comments about the newcomer coaches, like this one by an old-timer, were not uncommon: "They all want to be coaches, but they don't know jack shit!" Newcomer parents worried out loud on the benches that their kids were being scared and intimidated by Fairmounter coaches and that they might learn to dislike baseball. Newcomer parents also often complained about the amount of playing time allotted to their children. The salient and distinctive profiles of the two clusters of coaches congealed to inform the collective impression that there were indeed group differences between Fairmounter and newcomer coaches. But looking more closely at Table 4.1, we see that these group portraits really apply to only a minority of the coaches.

Less than half of the coaches actually conform to either the group stereotype of the "macho expert" or its antithesis, the "softy amateur." Just over half of the coaches fall into a category that combines the dimensions of coaching in ways that differ from the stereotypical, polar group images anecdotal evidence suggests.

Mapping out the coaches this way nicely illustrates the way group norms and stereotypes often work. While they generally highlight some real group differences (i.e., the clustering), they rarely account accurately for the behavior of most members of any given group. In fact, we see that most newcomers and most old-timers actually fall *outside* of either cluster, meaning that the dominant image of each group does not apply to most of its members. Therefore, the dual, stereotypical descriptions of old-timer coaches and newcomer coaches fail to account for the styles of most coaches, who instead scatter across the table. In reality, the group identifications are created by the fact that each group's outliers differ from one another in easily identifiable ways, despite the predominant similarities of the overlapping distributions of the two groups. The clustering means that some group differences do exist, and that these differences are easy for parents and coaches to focus on and point out, especially in moments of tension or conflict.[5] The clustering does not mean that all, or even most, of the coaches fit the stereotypes created and highlighted by the outliers. Most coaches are, in the mix of their personal styles, "social hybrids."

The best way of exploring the meanings of these masculinity styles is through the stories of various coaches from my field observations. The stories illustrate a range of positions along these dimensions of coaching and explore the complexities behind any of the neat placements on a sociological table. Two of the coaches fit, in many ways, the stereotypical portraits of Fairmounters and newcomers. But the others do not, and they represent the more typical "social hybrids" in the way they combine characteristics that do not hang together in the popular imagination of FSA. All of these explorations happen in the concrete moments of baseball. Since baseball is a game of contingency and strategy, it lends itself perfectly to seeing the way local culture and the game are both structured by the rules, but also finessed by personal judgments and choices.

The Old-timer, or Fairmounter, Coaches

Three coaches—Billy, Shawn, and Dan, all Fairmount old-timers in their forties—share a deep love of baseball and decades of involvement at FSA. For Billy and Shawn, baseball knowledge and intense competitiveness intricately hang together, but in different ways for each of them. The two cases illustrate the complexity of competition, its costs, its payoffs, and its implications for children of different sensibilities. Both Billy and Shawn score high on expertise and competition, as is typical of the "Fairmount cluster" in Table 4.1. Billy embodies the tough masculinity style combined with negative discipline that is associated with the stereotypical Fairmount coach. On the other hand, Shawn's distinct emotional style and affirming approach makes him more of a hybrid, separating him from the cluster. Dan, the third Fairmount coach, also knows the game well. But he uses his expertise noncompetitively and places the developmental needs of young boys at the center of his game strategy, making him one of the most successful of the "Fairmount hybrids."

Billy the Expert Disciplinarian: No Tears and No Mental Mistakes

Widely known to hundreds of parents whose boys have played for him over the twenty years he has coached, Billy has a deep understanding of baseball and a keen sense of strategy. For years, as a single man in his early forties, he coached one of the high-status traveling teams that compete with the best teams from other neighborhoods in the city's Devlin League. It was difficult, if not impossible, to escape his influence, if one desired to rise in the hierarchy. Not only did he serve on the organization's board; he also served for years as one of the commissioners, with all the attendant headaches and thankless hours devoted to scheduling games and assigning late players to teams entailed by that position. He has family ties to one of the deepest insiders in the organization, and he has younger relatives who play regularly on FSA elite teams.

Billy's imposing physical presence—he stands about six foot three, with broad shoulders that arch slightly to one side—underscores his authority. Widely regarded by knowledgeable parents as one of the more expert "chess players" of the game, he regularly leads traveling teams to regional playoffs. He is especially adept at evaluating game situations and making appropriate offensive and defensive adjustments. In particular, he is brilliantly precise and quick at coaching while the ball is in play. For example, he always sees a runner trying to take an extra base, or taking too big a lead, and he uses his booming voice to direct the play appropriately. While this is standard baseball, Billy demonstrates remarkable skill and intelligence in sizing up the multiple contingencies of a game and making rapid-fire, analytical decisions, often way ahead of his fielders and other baseball aficionados on the sidelines.

Toward the end of one season, when it was becoming clear that the ten-and-under traveling team coached by Billy had a chance at winning the city-wide championship, a number of his buddies, other old-timer coaches, began showing up at practices and giving supplemental coaching tips to the boys. This is an example of how the neighborhood's expertise is imparted to the boys. Billy decided his pitchers needed practice with pick-off plays. So he had another of the Fairmounter traveling team coaches, Sandy, take two starting pitchers and two relief pitchers aside to work on different pick-off moves. As Sandy demonstrated various moves, the four boys paid rapt attention to his subtle insights and his smooth execution of the footwork of each of the techniques. Sandy said he had been watching them and that their pick-off moves to second weren't fast, or deceptive, enough to catch runners off guard. He showed them "the Dominican," a pick-off move to second, demonstrating as he explained: "Here's how you do it, guys. Your back foot is on the rubber and your front leg moves up into balance position. At this point, the runner is likely to lean or step toward third, thinking that you're going to throw home. *But* instead of shifting forward and pitching, you're going to continue moving the leg backward toward second base as you pivot on the other foot and [growing excited] *throw him out!*" Significantly, when this team did go to the out-of-state regional championship, the ability of the pitching staff to execute successful pick-off moves proved a notable advantage. The pitchers did not need to think hard to appreciate the wisdom of the old-timer's instructions. Nor did Sandy let them forget. Even though he was not their coach, he traveled with them to the regional championship in New York, and when one of the relief pitchers smoothly picked off a runner leading off from third base, the old-timer jumped up, screaming, "I taught him that move! I love him! See that, he listens! I love him. I taught him that!" The players and parents laughed. Playing for Billy provided important experiences, including his utilization of other Fairmount coaches.

Playing for Billy also meant winning games and championships, something he cared deeply about. He used his considerable expertise in an aggressively competitive manner. And the fact that he coached a traveling team, and not an officially defined "instructional" or in-house team, legitimized his competitive approach. Billy decided who the most strategically talented players were for different positions and played them almost exclusively, regularly leaving a good section of the team on the bench. Occasionally, in a blow-out game, he would bring in the backup players. At times, if a critical play needed to be made, he might move a very strong player from his regular position to substitute for a weaker player at another position. He made decisions based on a meritocracy, always with the goal of benefiting the team *and* its chances of winning. For example, if he perceived a player to be an inconsistent batter, he regularly signaled him to bunt, maximizing his advantage to the team, even if lessening the boy's chances of improving his swing. Traveling team parents usually tolerate highly competitive approaches better than other parents, as such approaches often advantage their own highly-skilled sons. In addition, there is no claim of instructional democracy at the traveling-team level, and most parents of traveling players accept this. However, sometimes Billy went too far, even for these parents.

Such was the case when Fairmount made the city-wide playoffs in 1998. The first playoff game went eleven torturous innings. The weather added drama to the game. In about the fourth inning, it began to drizzle, and black ominous clouds descended with winds so high they inverted my umbrella. The whole thing felt like Dorothy's house in the twister, as if at any moment the field might be carried off to Oz. At one point, Billy sent the Fairmount boys scrambling up to the shelter of the field house while the opposition, an all-white, affluent team from the suburbs, bolted for their cars. But soon the winds died down, and the game resumed.

That storm punctuated one of the most contentious games I ever witnessed at FSA. Relatively early in the game, Fairmount had runners on first and third with one out when the umpire called catcher's interference on a three-two pitch. Meanwhile, the runner from third base scored. Billy maintained that the run counted and that the batter should advance to first. The other team's coach screamed in an imperial voice, "Ump, it is either a dead ball and the batter advances to first, or it is not dead and the run counts, but the batter is out." The team demanded that the home plate umpire consult with the first base umpire and review the decision, which stalled the game for quite a while. The umps decided in Fairmount's favor: the ball was not dead, the runner scored, and the batter was advanced to first. At that point, the other team decided to register an official protest, further delaying the very tense game. The umps documented the protest in the score book and then had the coaches sign in a book their agreement about how the play was described. Billy paced around the dugout, calling out to no one in particular, "They can protest all they want. I know what the outcome will be. I lost a game in Veteran's stadium over this call. I know what it is. This game is won right now!"

In the top of the third inning, the opposing team scored two runs. The score remained tied through the seventh inning (the normal limit), sending the game into extra innings. It was in this context of a very important game that Billy's competitive tendencies took over. He left our star pitcher, Gary, in through eleven innings—despite the fact that Gary could no longer keep his pitches down and had lost his velocity. Given the risk of permanent injury to his shoulder, pitching a ten-year-old boy for the entire game is questionable enough, but this game went for four extra innings. This upset several parents. Still, no one raised the issue directly with Billy. In the sixth inning, a father named Mateo began proclaiming loudly to other parents, "He needs to start warming up Kevin [the second pitcher]. Gary can't keep this up. It's not worth it. You can't sacrifice the kid's arm. Why isn't he warming him up?"

Billy's decision reflects both his competitiveness and the masculine ethos of "toughing it out." From Billy's point of view, this decision was justified, because winning this game was so important, and because Gary wasn't complaining. To my amazement, Gary's father and mother didn't say anything either. Why? Because given the looming power of the "tough it out" mentality, even Gary's father didn't want to be seen—or to have his son seen—in this context as a "pussy" or a yuppie "wimp." Instead, they (we) tacitly opted instead for the potential outcome of a permanently injured boy.

In the top of the eleventh inning, with the tension mounting, Gary's fatigue peaked, and to his obvious devastation, the opposing team succeeded in scoring two more runs. It was late and growing dark. League rules stipulate that, if a game is called because of darkness, the score reverts to what it was at the end of the last completed inning. Thus, if this game were to be called because of darkness, the two runs scored in the top of the eleventh would not count, and the game would have to be resumed on another day. It was implausible, given the strength of the opposing team's pitching, that we would take back the two runs in our final at bat. I assumed the game was over. But Billy decided to engage in the only competitive strategy left—stall the game and have it resumed with a tie score on another day. Billy did this by suddenly removing Gary and sequentially calling in three relief pitchers. Each new relief pitcher required a trip to the mound and ten warm-up pitches. The coaches on the other team were incensed, and soon began to yell out in disbelief at the obviousness of his strategy, "He's intentionally stalling, Ump. We protest!" In a threatening tone, Billy screamed back, "If you hadn't protested so much earlier, we'd be finished by now!" and then looked back at his team parents for supportive nods. Next, our catcher made a great tag at home plate, the third out of the inning. Players and parents screamed and danced with delight, most not fully aware that Billy was trying to stall rather than to finish the inning. Annoyed, Billy turned to the crowd of parents standing behind the dugout and said firmly, "I didn't want that out." Aware of his tactic, I felt disgust but avoided eye contact. Some Fairmount parents began to grumble under their breath that this was not a fair way to win the game, that the boys couldn't feel good about such a win. But no one confronted Billy. The confidence with which Billy had fixed his eyes on the parents, demanding their tacit approval, was telling. Behind it lay the implicit assumption that everyone shared his ethic of competition, the key dimension of high competitiveness (and tough masculinity) that says "whatever it takes" to shut them down is justified. It was true that as a group, in the context of the sport, we "hated" this team, both because they were the rich suburban team and because they had protested a call. We relished this chance to beat them. But there was more at stake than just competition. The authority behind Billy's tough masculinity characterized, and carried, the moment. His command of team parent approval depended on the inability of others to step up to him in this tense situation and take the risk that insisting on a code of fair conduct would have implied, that of being perceived as a "limp-wristed wimp." At that moment, any challenge to his traditional, tough masculinity would have been very hard to make. In the "maleness" of this context, a mother just wouldn't have the authority. No father dared. It was the authority of his style of masculinity and the masculine ethos of competition that enabled Billy to do things on the ball field that, in other contexts, would have produced more than a few parental grumblings.

Billy's competitive strategy worked. The game was called for darkness, the inning didn't count, and the score was restored to a tie. The next day, the game was resumed, and Fairmount eventually won. There was a lot of discussion among parents about the previous evening's dramatic events—especially about how many innings Billy had pitched Gary. Mateo, the father of one of the most talented players at FSA, whispered to me, "Whenever Billy says anything to me about Ramón pitching, I always say, 'Oh, you know, Ramón isn't a pitcher.' But it's not that I think that. I think he can pitch. But I want him to pitch when he's strong, say fifteen, pitch like his cousin [who pitches seventy-five miles an hour], not blow himself out down here. It ain't worth it, man." This father has sized up the competitive climate, and the masculine ethic of having to be tough, and has decided there is only one way to protect his son from injuring his arm at such a young age: to keep him off the pitcher's mound. Such a strategy of resistance works to protect his son from harm, but it also leaves the reigning ideology of competition unchallenged.

Due to his inability to control his temper and frustration at what he considered to be mental errors, Billy's expertise and competitive strategies were often tragically wasted. Errors, pure and simple, he handled calmly. But repeated mental errors triggered explosive reactions. Although many highly skilled boys, including my son, admired Billy and expressed their loyalty by remaining with him over years of coaching, he was also known as one of the meanest coaches in the league because of his temper. During an early game one season, he had stressed to his players that they had to take a first strike before they could swing, because the opposing pitcher was throwing particularly hard.

He wanted both for his players to get used to the pitcher's heat and to make the opposing pitcher throw strikes. When Adam became the second batter in a row to forget his instructions and swing at the first pitch, Billy took off his hat, threw it at the boys, and shouted, "Adam, that's just ignorant! I told you not to swing at the first pitch! [Tense pause] I ought to send you home." The silence built as Billy stood frozen. Then he stomped over, grabbed the score book out of the scorekeeper's hands, and threw it high in the air, up and over the top of the dugout fence and into the trees beyond. Lamely, his assistant coach tried to calm him. "Ahh, come on, Billy." But Billy just shouted, "NO! That's just ignorant!" Having now struck out, Adam slouched into the dugout. The adults sat in stunned silence, staring at the ground. One parent quietly retrieved the score book. The group slowly refocused on the next batter. We lost the game by a couple of runs, and the team sat waiting on the bench. In his evaluation of the game, Billy neither apologized for the outburst nor included a single positive comment. Indeed, most of what he had to say after every game included a series of negative comments about errors and a rebuke about the need to "keep your head in the game." In his debriefing after another game in which the team had lost to a relatively weak team from across town, Billy gathered the boys together in the dugout and said, "You know why you lost?" He waited. Most of the boys stared at their feet. One boy stared angrily out into the field, as if Billy weren't there. Billy continued, "Because baseball is about mental toughness. You have to have the right mental attitude." Then, as if released from his own punishment, he lightly added, "Okay. Be here on Thursday, at 5:30, for practice."

At the end of one season, after a very difficult home game with one of the better ranked teams from across town, Billy made another series of comments that illustrated his use of negative reinforcement. His team had been behind by five runs in the second inning, had had several rallies, and had finally ended the game with a one-run victory. Because a number of excellent plays had been made in the last few minutes, and the pregame predictions of a blowout had not materialized, most of the parents and players were approaching the dugout smiling. The evening was beautiful. There was a blazing red sky, and clear signs of summer warming were everywhere. Billy crouched to his knees in front of the players and their parents and waited for silence. He began, "There are eighteen outs in a baseball game. [These games are six innings] Today, eight of those outs were called-third strikes. [Silence.] Now that's what I call pathetic. Really pathetic." As I watched my son's smile fade, I felt angry. The crowd of parents and players were no longer smiling. One father, who had already overtly identified himself to parents in the bleachers as hostile to Billy's style, began shaking his head and moved away from the group. Billy continued, "Now, I want to see some improvement on this. You got to do what I tell you to do. You got to listen. That's all. Is there anyone who can't make practice on Thursday? If so, you need to tell me now. [Silence] OKAY. Then, be here at 5:30."

The annual opening-day ceremony parade winds through the historically white working-class row home community adjacent to the playing fields.

The sports association's opening-day parade starts in front of McKenna's bar, in the heart of the Fairmount neighborhood.

Over the years, Fairmounters successfully fought to locate and preserve the fields on public park land less than a mile from city hall.

An influx of new professionals into the neighborhood and the increasing integration of the local Catholic school were factors in the changing demographic on the field.

Uniforms, expensive equipment, and field upkeep are funded by players' fees, local sponsors, and contributions solicited door-to-door in the neighborhood.

"A mother told me she dreaded when her son reached fifteen and she would no longer have an excuse to come to the field. 'This gives me something to look forward to...I talk to people.'"

—A parent

"The people who helped him with losing the most were the Puerto Ricans. I love their approach. A guy strikes out, comes into the dugout and the coach says to his teammates, 'Show him some love.' Oh man, they love the sport, make it fun, they play with their hearts, they don't dwell on mistakes."

—A parent

"These parents wouldn't even know each other if they weren't playing baseball. Even though not everybody playing lives next door, we have community here."

—A parent

"At that time baseball was something that everybody played; we knew it, almost like it was bred into you. If you lived in the neighborhood, in the summer time you played ball. Baseball is all we had."

—A parent

"Old-timers" often watch the game from a shady spot near the clubhouse, monitoring plays closely from a distance. More than a hundred adults donate approximately 2,400 hours of unpaid time each season, a contribution worth more than $320,000 per year.

Many coaches participate for more than a decade—long before or after their own children are on a team. Despite clubhouse socializing, any man who agrees to coach a team has agreed to spend more time with children than with adults.

"When somebody is nice to your kid, you tend to like them, you know. They were all fair with my kids. Not huggie-huggie all the time. Not honey this, honey that. But they were very fair and helped kids feel good about themselves."

—A parent

"The moment I like best is when we all walk out onto the field from the dug-out with our uniforms on, like heroes."

—A player

"I just want to stand out on that field, make the play, and hear Shawn do that 'BEAUUTIFUUUL!'"
—A player

"I absolutely love baseball. It's a thinking person's game, so strategic. I like watching the very skilled make their moves. I love the surprise on boys' faces when they see a woman who knows baseball."
—A female coach

Teams with positive emotional workers (i.e., boys who circulate saying "That's okay" or "You can do it next time") have more fun. On these teams, the weaker players tend to be more resilient.

"I grew up at that baseball field. All the highs and lows of my childhood happened right there, on the field, on the bench, or under the trees."

—A parent

A girls' softball league shares the smaller field of the 7–9 boys' division. The girls who watch boys' games in Fairmount tend to be baseball players themselves.

"Come on Benji, keep it going. Keep us alive. If you get on base, I'll stop calling you Benji. Yeah, if you get a hit, I'll call you Ben. Keep us alive, Benji."

—A player

Billy does have moments when he tries to be positive, but they are usually *not* during a game. And they are often minimalist. After another game where Fairmount won by a large margin over a much weaker team, Billy settled the boys down on the bench. He began speaking in a quiet voice, "A lot of mistakes early. OKAY? A lot of stupid mistakes early. Then you guys started to play your game. Once you played your game, you were fine. But you can't come into a game like that. We've all been there before, and we all know what it's about. You can't come out and make stupid, stupid mistakes early. And that's what a lot of it was—stupid mistakes. [Pause] All right? Our next game is Tuesday. Home. Be down at the field at 4:30. [Then more gently] OKAY? Tuesday. Field at 4:30." He repeated the time again, softly. In a departure from his usual demeanor, this entire speech was delivered without a trace of anger. This time, he was genuinely trying to be nice. But his positive reinforcements, like "your kind of game," were not explicit. He seemed unable to elaborate on them, unable to say something more like, "Errors early on make it hard to recover and exhibit your considerable talent. Good plays." He elaborated and focused on errors, while the positive in his words was only implied. And because he used, and emphasized, the word "stupid" four times, its overall impact was quite negative—even in the context of an important win that gave us home-field advantage for the playoffs.

As a coach, one of the biggest challenges for Billy is handling the emotional outbursts of his players. During an in-house game of the ten-and-under traveling team during the 1997 season, two different boys cried, one over a second strikeout and another over a significant fielding error. One of the boys has an especially hard time stopping himself from sobbing. In a somewhat more restrained manner than in earlier games when similar things had happened, Billy approached him and told him to snap out of it. But when the boy, unable to hold back, continued sniffling, Billy walked away, calling out, in an exasperated tone to the rest of the team, "No tears! I hate that!" The message was unmistakable. Anger, tantrums, even ruthless criticisms are acceptable displays of masculinity. Tears, remorse, and vulnerability are not.

Also during the 1998 season, when he did not perform according to his own high expectations, one of the most talented players on Billy's team regularly erupted into tears. This display from one of the higher-status players seemed to unnerve not only Billy, but other assistant coaches and adults standing by. There was a particularly big crowd of Fairmount supporters at one of the traveling team's home games. The same boy hit a dribbler to second and was thrown out at first. As he turned to face all of us in, and behind, the dugout, his face was contorted. He fought to contain his tears, but the anguish flooded out of him, tears pouring down his red face. Standing behind the dugout, Larry, a loud Fairmounter who coaches another team, called out in a foghorn voice: "Hey, next time we're gonna give you a rattle, [if] you keep that up." The boy's mother, standing a few feet away, looked furious. Larry noticed and moved over to justify himself. "These guys just don't want to get even one out. That reminds me," he said, "of that kid who used to play with Ben. He used to cry every game. Pete. Remember him?" Refusing to acknowledge him, the boy's mother stared straight ahead. Despite his initial discomfort with her son's tears, Larry genuinely liked the boy. He attempted to reframe his comments: "I think some guys are like that when they are super-aggressive. Like, they think they can't even get one out, and they're just too aggressive about it." Larry translated her son's vulnerability and emotional expressiveness into hypermasculinity—the only way he could tolerate it. Nevertheless, the boy's mother continued to refuse to look at him and said nothing in response.

Several games later, Larry once again lent his booming voice of support to Fairmount. He stood behind the dugout, firing a rapid series of mostly positive comments to Kevin as he pitched, "Fire it away, Kevin! Throw 'em some heat, buddy. Show 'em your stuff. Get it over now." But that afternoon, Kevin was having a hard time getting the ball over the plate. Larry called out, "Hey, you're throwin' like a sissy! Let's see your stuff, Kevin." He chuckled to someone next to him and added, "That always gets 'em going." I wondered to myself what his ball-playing daughter thought, standing next to him behind the dugout.

An inning later, on a close play, Kevin was called out at first again. This happened right after an inning in which his pitching had not been as stellar as usual. Again he left first base with an anguished expression, fighting back tears. As Kevin walked toward the dugout, Billy's assistant coach, standing off first base, said to him loudly, and with a harsh tone of disgust, "Shake it off!"

The display of hostility toward Kevin's grief continued to build; they couldn't seem to leave him alone. Sitting next to me on the benches, Craig, a parent of a star pitcher, added to the chorus of disapproval showering down on Kevin. "Get that guy in boot camp!" he yelled.

I wanted to take Kevin aside and whisper to him, to redefine his emotional reactions as strength rather than liability. I wanted to say, "Kevin, they don't understand. You have a talent. You still know how you feel. You feel pain and disappointment at a loss. This emotion, these tears you shed openly, your ability to hold onto these feelings is the ingredient you need to develop one of the finest of human characteristics: compassion. We only know compassion by recognizing the pain of others. And we can never do that if we lose our own ability to feel. There are many voices around you, telling you to forget those feelings, to put them aside in favor of a form of inexpressive manhood, of a manhood that has become disconnected from admission of hurt or loss. But if you listen to them, you run the risk of no longer knowing what your feelings are. And when you need them, when they are appropriate, when someone you love longs to hear them, when your chance to attach yourself in a profoundly human way to a stranger depends on your ability to connect their weakness, or difference, to your own emotions, they'll be lost. Hold on to those 'unmanly' tears, Kevin. Your humanity may depend on it." But, like all of the other spectators, I said nothing.

After the game, a parent from the team expressed to me his opposition to Kevin's treatment. "Why can't they let him come back from first base feeling anything? Kevin is a great player. What does it matter if he cries when disappointed? Craig is a guy that cares deeply about the game, worries about its technicalities. But what is it that bothers him? An error? A weak defense? No, he can't stand to see Kevin cry." True, I think, but this can only be said in whispers on the sideline.

Billy's case illustrates something else important about masculinity styles—their instability over time.[6] Sometime around 1996, when Billy had reached his late thirties, he married the divorced newcomer mother of one of his players. Because she was a professional, old-timers teased that he was now part of a "mixed marriage." After the couple had a baby girl, the boys often joked among themselves that a good game was when Billy's wife would turn up with their newborn baby, because he tended to yell less when they were present. He even spoke sweet baby talk to her in the dugout. This made the boys in the dugout stare at each other in amazement. Many of the boys recognized that Billy had good intentions but seemed to lose control during the games. For example, despite my son's shyness, and the fact that he did not grow up in a household with a style of tough masculinity, he learned over the years to care deeply for Billy, because, between the explosions of anger, he came to believe that Billy earnestly cared about the boys and, within his code of competition, was extremely fair to individuals. My son, for example, said of Billy, "He doesn't yell if you stink or just can't do something. He yells when he knows you can do something but don't. With Billy, you know where you stand. Not like the yuppies, who pretend to love everybody but stab you in the back." For boys, part of the lesson of tough masculinity is learning to read between the lines, learning to see tenderness in highly understated gestures. As another of Billy's ten-year-old players told me one afternoon, "He's not always mean. He does try to be nice sometimes. But he can't really do it. When you make a good play and he wants to be nice, all he does is tug at your hat or put his hand on your head when he's talking. That's when he's being *really* nice. But he can't really *say* anything nice."

The boys on Billy's team were right when they noticed that Billy changed in the presence of his wife and daughter. Evidently, the change deepened over time. When his daughter reached the age of eligibility for T-ball, Billy, a centerpiece of the high-status teams of FSA baseball for more than twenty years, announced his retirement as a *boys'* baseball coach. The next year, he signed up to coach his daughter's T-ball team, where mental errors, complex strategy, and tears would take on very different meanings. He would finally become a "father coach." Interestingly enough, in the context of the very young children, where he abandoned his harsh reactions to tears and errors and looked the other way as his daughter left the field after each at bat and headed for the hot-dog stand, his masculinity style was transformed.

Shawn the Trickster: Fierce Competition, Expertise, and Soft Masculinity

Like Billy, Shawn is a maestro of baseball and is known throughout the league as one of the most competitive coaches. But Shawn mixes his competitive stance with more positive teaching. Besides, Shawn is a baseball trickster, and his fun is contagious. Like Billy, Shawn is a longtime Fairmount resident. He is also a father, with children in the same local Catholic school as many other old-timers. Shawn has decades of involvement with FSA and holds a formal organizational position, but he maintains an unusual social distance from the organizational leadership—he is an "outsider-insider." A wide range of parents and kids would vote for Shawn as one of the most knowledgeable of FSA coaches, and also one of the most, if not the most, competitive coaches in the organization. Somehow, he manages to combine his fiercely competitive approach with a tender masculinity style that relies mostly on positive reinforcements.

As a highly skilled player on his Catholic high school team, Shawn is reputed to have thrown in the mid-eighty-mile-per-hour range. At one point, he tried out for a minor league team in the Phillies organization. Although he had not been able to afford college, he always struck me as someone with CEO potential. He ran draft meetings in a highly efficient and authoritative manner. He was comfortable with a wide range of people. And he delighted all with his witty and authoritative conversational style. Skinny, with lanky legs and a ruddy complexion, he would have had a hard time passing as anything other than Irish. Quick-witted, crafty, and always upbeat, he was the Huck Finn of the ballpark. And like Huck Finn, he had traces of the "cross-over" about him, moving adeptly between the old-timers and the newcomers.

Shawn practically lives at the field. He had coached the older, competitive traveling teams, served as commissioner of one of the divisions, and umped countless games throughout the age divisions, often filling in when others failed to show. On any given Saturday one was almost certain to find him at the ball field, although usually not inside the field house. On one occasion he brought his newborn son, less than a week old, to the field to show him off. When another coach knelt down momentarily to play with the baby, Shawn whispered to him, "Now, this one is gonna hit." A parent, passing by, called to Shawn, "You got another one? You're gonna be down here forever!" Shawn smiled broadly, and said, "That's okay with me!"

Shawn is passionate about the aesthetics of baseball. He had no trouble finding the means to regularly spice his comments about boys' efforts with positive observations, because he sees so much beauty in mundane plays. Most of the boys like Shawn a lot. My son longed for years to get him as a coach. "I just want to stand out in that field, make the play, and hear Shawn do that 'BEAUUU-TIFUUUUL,'" he said, imitating Shawn's trademark call. There are other artistic dimensions to Shawn's coaching—for instance, his love for the theatrical play. He loves to insert psychological drama into the games he coaches, and he tries to maximize his wins by taking advantage of the mistakenly taken-for-granted. One of his favorite tricks is to stand on third base coaching and adopt an active "stooge" role. For example, during a game in the 1998 season, right before a strong hitter on the opposing team came up to bat, with runners on second and third, Shawn called a time-out and summoned his infield onto the mound and held a ridiculously long session with them. It appeared to be a strategy session for a pick-off play. However, Shawn then returned to third base, and, in order to confuse the opposing players, quickly yelled out to his well-prepped pitcher, "Anthony, don't worry about the runner, just get the batter." It was usually a pretty effective strategy. Even though the more sophisticated runners on the opposing team might have predicted a pick-off attempt, it is hard for an eleven-year-old boy to lose his sense of trust in an adult coach and switch to thinking of him instead as a con artist. A lot of opposing coaches and parents are wise to Shawn's tricks and have grumbled about them. However, even their warnings to stay focused and expect anything from the Diamond Backs often fail to pre-pare the boys to see through Shawn's masquerades.

Yet Shawn's poetry never overwhelms his hunger to win. Although Shawn regularly coaches in the ten-to-twelve in-house teams, many claim his compet-itive drive does not fit with the instructional goals of the in-house division. For example, when confronted with weak opposing pitchers, Shawn frequently tells his batters not to swing at balls. Yet this is the age division in which boys begin to pitch, and many teams have very weak pitching. Teams are both learning to bat fast-pitched balls and developing pitchers who can throw and get balls over the plate at reasonably fast speeds. It is fairly easy in this context to get a walk by doing nothing, a strategy often adopted by boys who are afraid of the ball and by competitive coaches like Shawn who want to gain runs off a weak pitcher. But it is not a strategy that teaches boys to bat or that builds the confidence of new pitchers. During one game in the 1998 season, following a game Shawn's team had won with a very high number of walks, the same pattern of walks developed again. Recognizing this, one of the coaches on the other team began to scream, "Hey, Shawn, what are you doing? Having them practice walking?" Shawn didn't reply to the coach, but instead walked around the dugout with arms widely extended in a dramatic shrug, saying loudly to his manager, "If they had anyone who could throw a strike, we would swing."

In the playoffs, Shawn's competitive impulses (like those of many coaches) are especially intense. During one such game, he began resorting to some of the coaching tricks he is renowned for. One of his players got on first base, which was coached by Alex, a rather timid coach. Alex's job was to direct the runner.

Shawn called out, "Alex, talk to him." Howard, another assistant coach, also yelled from the dugout, "Alex, talk to him." Shawn, unable to contain himself, bypassed Alex and yelled directly to the runner, "Take a lead, Michael. Take a bigger lead." One more step and then, just as the pitcher lifted his lead foot, a bellowing, "NOW!" rang out, to indicate the moment that he wanted him to break for second. I noticed that Shawn's cries occurred seconds before the pitch, timed to rattle the pitcher. This happened many times over the next few minutes. Rosetta, a knowledgeable baseball mother from the opposing team, watched Shawn carefully, eyes squinted. After a relatively weak batter on Shawn's team came up to bat and quickly earned a couple of strikes, Shawn started in again. Just *before* the next pitch left the pitcher's hand, Shawn suddenly erupted, "That's IT, Anthony!" His batting tip had preceded the swing. Unable to pull this interference off two times in a row, Shawn directed his cries during the next pitch back to the runner on first base. Again, seconds before the pitch, Shawn shouted to the first base runner, "NOW, Gabe!" The mother on the bench jumped up screaming at Shawn, "Hey! That's mean to the pitcher, man!" Then to the crowd, "He's doing that on purpose. It stinks." Hearing this, Shawn's first base coach turned and said to her in a serious and condescending tone, "No, it's not mean. He has to direct the runner." "Oh *really?*" she replied, "And what is your job, my little friend?" He ignored her, because by now Gabe, the runner, was already on second. The pitcher, who had by then walked two batters, stood downcast on the mound.

Shawn has an answer for parents who claim that he is too competitive. He argues that getting used to distractions, learning to focus, is a big part of the game. Nor does he complain if other coaches do the same to him. He merely talks to his boys about the need to concentrate, about learning to focus. If other coaches use a similar walk strategy in the face of his weaker pitchers, he merely drills them more, to insure that every pitcher he uses can, at least minimally, get it over. Once, when confronted with a team that could successfully lay down numerous bunts, Shawn welcomed the challenge and simply played his shortstop at third.

Shawn's jovial and often tender manner with the boys tempers his fierce competitiveness. Relying predominantly on positive reinforcement helps him to establish rapport with even the surliest adolescents. He very successfully uses humor to instruct and encourage the boys. Over several practice sessions, Shawn drilled the boys about always swinging on a close ball if it followed two strikes. During the very next game, Shawn stood on third base coaching, while his son came up to bat, only to commit the cardinal sin. A called third strike was a pretty big "no-no" for the son of a commissioner. His son walked quickly back to the bench and sat down without speaking. A few minutes later, Shawn wandered into the dugout and made a point to lean into his son and ask, "Did you see that third strike?" Fearlessly, his son looked up and smiled broadly. "Yep, sure did." Shawn, smiling back, said, "Well good, 'cuz the ump did too!" His son then squirted him in the face with his water jar. As they both chuckled about this, all the other boys on the bench responded with smiles. Shawn often succeeds in creating these little playful moments while reinforcing an instructional point.

Nor is Shawn repulsed by his boys' expressions of vulnerability, weakness, or tears. After a series of batting mishaps in one of the early playoff games, his team collapsed after a strong player struck out looking at the ball. Several sat in the dugout, weeping openly in despair. But in the next inning, they got three quick outs. They rallied again and ended up squeezing out a 5–4 win. During these sobbing breakdowns among his players, Shawn never expressed abhorrence or contempt for their emotions. And after the game, he had other things to criticize. "That was too close, you guys. You scared the crap out of me. You guys have to have faith. You have to be a team. That was one hell of a game. You guys were in here, scared and crying, but the game's not over 'til it's over, 'til the fat lady sings. You can't give up. If you don't have it today, you have to trust your teammates to have it. You can't be sittin' on the bench cryin' because you think you lost, when we have another inning to go. . . . " There was not a trace of scorn in his voice when he spoke of their tears. His only rebuke was directed to their having given up.

For one entire season Shawn struggled with a very temperamental boy named Bobby, who had a difficult home life and problems with anger control. Bobby also believed he was a stronger player than he was and often sulked when he didn't get his way. When Shawn announced, in the first inning, that Bobby would play right-center field rather than his normal position of first base, Bobby was visibly upset. He didn't head for the field like the other players. Shawn moved right in. "Bobby, I need you in the outfield, so you can back up the infield." Bobby looked skeptical. "I'm serious. Last game, two runs could have been avoided if the right play had been made in the field." I think he invented this fact. Bobby didn't seem convinced, but he took the position. In the second inning Bobby made an excellent stop in the field and almost threw the runner out at first. "Didn't I tell you, man, I needed you in center? See that great play. Don't think I don't know what I'm doin'. Man, that was a great play." Bobby beamed and played hard the rest of the game. This approach did not always work with Bobby, who tended toward conflict with coaches and fellow players alike during much of the season. But when there were positive breakthroughs with him, such as in this game, it was usually Shawn driving them.

During the season, Shawn works hard with his boys on pick-off plays, and he teaches and uses bunts more than any other coach in this age division. Identifying with the highly competitive tendency of many of the highly skilled players, he appeals to their drive for individual distinction (over team wins) by always pointing out, "Remember. A bunt is as good as triple, when it comes to batting averages." His meticulous coaching paid off during one playoff game, in which his boys laid down several well-placed bunts and executed a successful pick-off play. "BEAUUUUUTIFUL!" Shawn sang out after each one.

Before the second championship game of the same season, Shawn resorted to spiritual humor to calm the boys' nerves. While the Diamond Backs were sitting on the benches waiting to play, Shawn walked up and down the line, sprinkling water on each boy as he passed, "This is the holy water. Blessings, my son. Blessings, my son. Gabe [the only Jewish boy on the team], come over here. Even people who aren't Catholic are getting blessed today." Gabe smiled but ducked quickly to miss the water.

After watching Shawn coach in the ten-to-twelve division for several years, a newcomer mother of a boy who had played at FSA for almost a decade, took him aside to say, "Shawn, you gotta get out of here. Your competition is over the top, way over the top for the in-house teams." The following season, he heeded this advice and left to become the head coach for the more competitively oriented traveling team. Despite the fierce competition that drives his participation, Shawn consistently manages to affirm his players, to embrace their passions positively, whether expressed in joy or tears, and to pass on to subsequent coaches hundreds of boys closely tutored in the finer, more aesthetic possibilities of baseball. He is a poet-hybrid who rejects the tougher style of masculinity of some of the old-timers and adds unique features from his own personality to the game in remarkably successful ways.

The kinds of moves made by coaches like Billy and Shawn—teaching bunts and multiple pick-off moves, playing weak players minimally (even in unimportant games), making excessive use of a young pitcher in a highly competitive moment, rattling opposing pitchers during tight games with a variety of maneuvers like verbal interference and slow-up strategies—place these coaches at the far end of the expertise, and the competitive–instructional, continuum. But adopting a harshly competitive approach to the game is not an inevitable outcome of knowing a great deal about baseball and its strategies. It is also a choice that operates independently. There are coaches who know a great deal about the game and its intricacies but who, nevertheless stress individual skills, teamwork, and the importance of "heart" over winning. Dan, another Fairmounter coach, specialized in this.

Dan the Pleasure King: Expertise, Tenderness, and Fun

The way Dan, an old-timer who had coached in the seven-to-nine division for more than ten years, usually approached the draft illustrates his easygoing, less competitive approach to the game. Dan has owned a small construction business in the neighborhood for decades and is about fifty years old, one of the older FSA coaches. His older children played in the league years ago, and in years past he regularly served as a board member of FSA. He knows the ins and outs of decades of organizational intrigues but has grown weary of them. Dan is of average height and weight and often wears an impish expression. His long, wavy hair and graying beard give him a slightly hip look, unusual for an old-timer. His coaching prioritizes fun and play first, instruction second, and competition third.

During the draft meeting of 1998, a particularly intense coach whom Dan especially likes to tease came in armed with game statistics for every player who had played in the seven-to-nine division the year before. After this coach returned from the bathroom, Dan turned to him and said, "Say, Timmie, every year we take a vote to see who is the coach we all want to beat the most, and you just won. Hee. Hee." Timmie looked worried. In contrast to Timmie's feverish attempts to get the highest-ranked players, Dan often prioritizes boys who have played on his team before, placing loyalty over skill. This means that the Marlins come to be associated not just with Dan, but with particular groups of boys over several years, which adds cohesion to his teams. At the beginning of the 1999 season, one parent, who had been with the Marlins for two years, was talking to a former Marlins parent whose son had just moved up to the older age division. "Yeah, Dan got most of the same boys back again who are still eligible. [Laughing] He even picked Ralph again. Can you believe it?" With an expression of disbelief, the other parent answered, "You're kidding! Ralph?" "Yes, Ralph," the first parent responded. "Now that's compassion."

Coaches also differ in how they select the three players from their teams who go to the "All-Star" game at the end of the season. Some simply make executive decisions: the manager/coach decides. But Dan's approach is radically democratic. He lets the boys, as well as all assistant coaches, vote. Every year during the team picnic, he takes each boy aside and says, "Now, you need to give me your three votes for the All-Stars, and it's OK for you to vote for yourself." After one such picnic, I asked him, "Does anybody not vote for himself?" Dan responded, "Oh, we haven't seen that yet! Hee, hee, hee."

One year, the son of one of the officer's of FSA was one of the younger players on Dan's team. Neither Dan nor his coaches had voted for him for the All-Stars, believing that, although he was talented, he would have opportunities for several years, unlike a couple of the older players. He laughed as he told how, as a result, the FSA officer had refused to speak to him for the next five years. Dan maintains that, in the end, the boys always make "the right decision" anyway. But letting the boys decide introduces an instructional element into the decision, causing the boys to think about individual merit and its criteria, even as it makes them own the decision. For example, some boys on his team told me that they "didn't vote for any 'big shots' who don't come to practice." Over time, Dan's approach to selecting All-Stars was influential in the league and came to be adopted by many other less competitive coaches.

Dan could often be remarkably tender with his boys. In one of the last games of the 1998 season, he allowed one of his weakest players, Ralph, who had been hounding him, to catch. After one inning, a low pitch hit Ralph on the tip of his big toe. He fell back into the fence, crying loudly and shaking his foot in the air. Dan came over, with several other adults, to try to determine the extent of the damage and to comfort him. They removed his headgear to find an extra-red face (he always is a little flushed) smeared with dripping, dirty tears. Then, as if to protect him from the gaze of the crowd, Dan pulled Ralph's head into his stomach, lifted his own clean shirt out of his shorts, and slowly wiped Ralph's entire face with it. Ralph didn't move away, but stood close, slowly taking in the comfort. "Now doesn't that feel better?" Dan asked. When the gesture was complete, Ralph looked up briefly at Dan, slightly restored. Dan then called to another boy to have a go at catching, and reentered the dugout with Ralph still under his arm, Ralph's red dirt smeared across the front of his white shirt.

One boy on the 1998 Marlins, Alvaro, has beautiful brown eyes with thick eyelashes and extremely long hair that he wears in a ponytail. His professional parents had recently emigrated from Argentina, so it was Alvaro's first season ever to play baseball. His mother told me that several of the boys on the team had teased him and consistently referred to him only as "she." But Dan took it all in stride. One very hot afternoon, when the boys were coming in from fielding, I noticed Dan trying to arrange Alvaro's long hair. When Dan entered the dugout, he leaned over to the boy's mother and said, "Now, I have to tell you. In all my years of baseball, that was the first time anyone ever said to me, 'Could you please fix my ponytail?' His mother smiled and answered, "Well, it won't be the last." Dan's comfort with the unorthodox, or non-American, gender style of this family set the tone for the rest of the team.

Over the decade I spent at FSA, I learned a lot from watching Dan. He is a competitor who understands the excitement and group fun associated with competition, but he also understands its dangers and navigates it carefully as he balances its benefits and costs. I don't know if he always understood these things, or if he learned them along the way during his decade or more of coaching. Competitive drives are especially problematic with younger boys, whose developmental needs are more in conflict with what it takes to sustain a winning strategy. Probably the most remarkable feature of Dan's coaching is the way he accepts the developmental stage of the boys not as something to overcome, but as something to be embraced. His involvement with his team, the Marlins, in the 1998 playoffs best demonstrates Dan's restrained style of competition.

A season of children's baseball is like an ocean wave rolling toward shore. Every season, like every wave, has its own rhythm. Teams, like surfers, have to position themselves along the wave to be in the optimal position as the wave breaks. Coaches do a lot of the positioning. Being ready too soon, with too much intensity, can make one end up in choppy water. By playoff time, the boys have heard it all before. But sheer escalation is not always the solution. There are limits to how revved up a coach can get before he unnerves the players. They need only a modest increase from the usual style to get stimulated but still hold onto their centers of gravity. For example, during the 1998 season, two coaches on one team were in an almost-playoff mode from the beginning of the season on—both of them ranting and chanting in high gear from the very first game. They played themselves out early and literally fizzled, never making it to the playoffs and forfeiting the final game with only four players left. Coaches for two other teams, the Senators and the Blue Jays, started out in a more laid-back fashion and were able to stay there throughout the playoffs—steady, even-keeled, with no strong peaks, and no large dips either. Dan, the most experienced of the group, the one who always seemed to be enjoying himself the most, peaked at exactly the right moment, in a way that his boys could respond to and take pleasure from, somewhere in the middle of the first playoff game.

Dan's early season pregame chats with the boys consisted of a few general suggestions he called out as they were entering and/or leaving the dugout. He said things like, "Now let's get out there and get some outs," or "Okay, guys, now we need some hits." These comments were scattered throughout the games, and in their tone and delivery they never conveyed a trace of his own needs or desires. In the first game of the playoffs, however, I noticed a change. He gathered his team together in a little circle out on the field. As he knelt down and talked to them at eye level, the moment had a very private feel. So private that I could not hear its content. However, I could hear the second such "cabinet" speech, which occurred one inning later in the dugout. He knelt again, gathered the boys around him in a little circle, and spoke to them softly. "Okay, guys. Now that's the way to play baseball—by getting these guys out. Now I want you to just step up to the plate, put the ball in play, and good things will happen. He waited. Then he changed the cadence of his voice to signal the beginning of a chant between them. "You guys still want to win this game?" he asked at a rapid, staccato pace. "Yeah!" they softly called out. "That doesn't sound very loud!" he responded. Then, speeding the rhythm of his voice again, in an upward lilt he repeated, "You guys wanna win this game?" "YEAH!" they screamed, catching his enthusiasm.

One inning later, they again came in to bat with the score tied. Drawing the same small circle around him, Dan began, "Now that's the way to show 'em how baseball is done! Now you need to hit 'em good—just like last time. Make contact, and good things will happen. [Pause] You need to step up to the plate and make contact. You have to *want* to win this game more than they do, and they're not givin' up. You guys still have to want this game." Raising his voice, he sang out what became his mantra to them for the rest of the game. "STILL WANNA WIN THIS GAME?"

"YEAH!!!" they shouted back, louder each time, each time getting closer to the pitch he invited them to join. After the Marlins gave up a run, for the fourth time he said, "Okay guys, don't worry about that. Now, that's what happens in baseball. You don't have to make every play. Listen up. You got to want this more than they do, 'cause they're not givin' up. You gotta want it more and show it on the field. [Singing now] YOU STILL WANT TO WIN THIS GAME?" "YEAH!" his team shouted.

In the course of that one game, Dan delivered about eight of these little "cabinet" speeches, peppering them with more intensity and excitement than he had in earlier games. His challenge to them always took the form of that simple question: "You wanna win this game?" The context was less important than the fact that something had changed. He had spoken to them softly and respectfully, at their age level, and every time he had emphasized the importance of their desire. In so doing, he had delicately positioned them for the challenge. He turned up the steam, slightly, but explicitly, offering them a choice. Dan seems to view his team as actors, temporarily on his stage, and himself as the director, curious about how their talents will unfold. *His challenge involves little of his own ego.* They knew he wanted to win, even as they did. But he had stressed their own desire—winning not to please him, but to please themselves. Whether or not they won depended on their own ability to balance on this building wave of excitement, before a growing number of gathered strangers. It also depended on a million other technical combinations and flat-out accidents. The Marlins won that playoff game, and one more, with the boys all the while enthusiastically shouting, "Yeah," in unison to their coach's repeated inquiry about their own intensity of desire.

In the third playoff game of that season, Dan's opening speech to his Marlins as they huddled together, separate from the spectators, was similar to those he used in the other playoff games. The Marlins needed to get in front of the ball in the outfield, to want the game, to want it more than the other team. But the first inning cast a shadow—two of the three best players struck out right away, and the third player was put out on first. The team walked despondently onto the field, while Dan called out to them to get the outs in the field. Instead, they let in several runs. A short time later, Julio, their talented shortstop, ignoring the call of "mine" by third baseman Mike, nabbed the ball and made the out on third. Mike's fury at being ignored by Julio lasted two more innings. Dan continued with his upbeat comments, but after a few more errors, the boys grew despondent again. After the next at bat, Dan began, "All right, guys, you got a couple of those runs back. OKAY, looks like you're starting to play baseball again. Now you gotta go out there and play defense. OKAY? You gotta make the plays you can make. You guys still want this game?' ""Yeah!" they called out weakly. Dan replied, "What? That's not very loud." They tried again, but it was really only one little voice that called out, "YEAH!" Dan responded anyway,

"That's a little better. Let's go!" He watched them with a concerned look. The weakness of their response turned out to be foreshadowing, almost an announcement that the boys had made a decision—"Not today, thank you."

Dan noticed, and several innings later he issued one last challenge to them, mentioning that winning was at stake—something he rarely referenced. But the fielding disasters continued. In the outfield, Jake hurt his finger during a catch and danced around, waving his finger in the air. Dan leniently let him milk it. A short time later, in a fit of anger, two outfielders hurled each other to the ground. Then after the team got up to bat, one of their strongest hitters, Evan, struck out and sat crying gently on the bench.

At some point, Dan seemed to decide that they didn't want it, that they had made their choice, and he changed his expectations. He accepted this long before I did. Dan began talking to them about having fun. But I was so caught up in the desire for them to win, I felt frustrated by his shift. In truth, I felt desperate and perturbed that the boys had screwed up so many things they knew how to do. After a tumultuous inning, in which the opposing team moved ahead by five runs, Dan calmly delivered the understatement of the season, "OKAY guys, they got some runs back. They did, this time, what we're trying to do." One player asked, "Dan, are we tied now?" I thought, "WHAT? WHERE HAVE YOU BEEN?" Unruffled, Dan answered, "No, it's not a tie game. Just keep your bat on the ball and have fun. Just relax. Have fun. Take a big breath and let's go."

Where did he find the reserve of calm to answer so patiently? Even without a child on the team, I was so attached to the boys' fate my insides were knotted. As he had all season, in the next and final inning, one of the weaker runners, Andy, insisted on sliding into first base which resulted in a predictable out. Dan called out to him, "Good running—almost beat him."

Again, feeling my Texas blood surge, I thought, "WHAT?" The Marlins had one last chance to bat, but the bottom of the lineup came up, and with three quick strikeouts the season was over. Dan's final words to the players were low-key and brief. "All right, number one, no hot dogs, because the kitchen is closed." The boys groaned, "Oh nooo." "I think we had a great season. I know I had a lot of fun. You guys deserve a round of applause." The parents all joined in. Dan continued, "You worked hard all year and it was fun. OKAY, that's it then." Lucas called out, "And it was goofy!" Dan answered, "Goofy? OKAY. Maybe. But you guys got into the championship. So it was a good year all round."

Two of the boys, who were having a spitting contest on the bench, ran out of the dugout to continue it on the field. One of the younger boys seemed to be trying to decide if he wanted to cry but then just picked up his glove and strolled out. As the rest of the boys ran off, Dan called out to his two cocky infielders, who will move up to the older age division the next year to play with the bigger boys, "Now remember, Julio and Roland, next year you're gonna be playing outfield! Hee hee hee."

So the Marlins ended the season on a calm note, with no great trauma over their defeat. Dan had offered them a choice in the playoffs. He had urged them on and offered them a challenge that was not scary. But they had opted for a low-key, not too concerned approach. Dan sensed this at the end, before I did, and pulled back from his pumped up challenge of the early playoffs games. This worked well for the boys because the coach's disappointment didn't magnify their own. They didn't seem to want it terrifically nor to feel excessive adult pressure to deliver. In the end, the boys and Dan took it all in stride. Before this season, Dan had won plenty of championships, and he had dealt with them gracefully. But it is how coaches handle losing, not winning, that reveals the most about their core attitudes toward the game.

Dan embodies what I came to think of as "caring competition." He mixes elements that do not always hang together in boys' sports. Adult baseball might be about talent, game understanding, discipline, and will—a complex chessboard of contingencies where spontaneity gets in the way. But little boys' baseball works only when coaches can ignore the weight of some of these contingencies to embrace the inevitable eruptions of spontaneity and random needs that fragment children's worlds. Younger boys' baseball is closer to play than sport, and this is why Dan prefers it. Like many other Fairmounters, Dan possesses a keen sense of baseball fundamentals. But he also, uniquely, succeeds in combining his acumen with fun and only as much competition as he judges the young boys can tolerate and still be at play. This makes him another Fairmount hybrid, outside of the "old-timers cluster." His kind of caring competition permits the excitement and striving associated with goal-seeking but balances it with attending to the developmental needs of children, by pulling back when the levels of tension are too high for the children to manage. His boys played baseball, organized by adults, but still had fun. Sometimes, balancing these needs with teaching the fundamentals of baseball produced a championship win. It often did so for Dan. But to Dan a winning season was something other than merely winning.

The Newcomer Coaches

Three portraits of newcomer coaches—Kyle, Sal, and Kirk—provide an even sharper contrast in coaching styles than among the Fairmounters just described. Just as Billy represents what many had in mind when they talked of "Fairmounter coaches," Kyle fits the role of the stereotypical "father newcomer coach." Sal's story is important for its illustration of the way tender masculinity is not just about reactions to vulnerable moments but is sometimes expressed more dramatically in the simple inclusion of the most vulnerable of boys and in modeling acceptance of their imperfections. The way Kirk, the third newcomer coach, uniquely combines some of the most negative elements of all coaching styles as an extreme reaction to, and attempt to manage, his outsider status offers broader lessons about the cultural scripting of masculinity.

Kyle the Earnest Rookie: Hypnosis, Low Expertise, and Democracy

Kyle, an urban planner from outside of Fairmount, is typical of the cluster of relatively noncompetitive coaches we saw in Table 4.1, newcomers whose enthusiasm for boys' baseball is not matched by their expertise. These are the coaches relied on, but resented, by many old-timers of FSA. Kyle managed a team at FSA for four years, always a team on which his son played: three years in the seven-to-nine division, and one year in the ten-to-twelve division after his son moved up. Of average height, Kyle wears a thick brown beard, is balding, and doesn't look particularly athletic. He slumps slightly when he walks and speaks quietly. Like other newcomer fathers, Kyle also coached outdoor soccer.

Although Kyle had played some baseball as a boy and knew the fundamentals of the game, his practices rarely stressed the nuances of baseball skills. For example, he never taught his ten-to-twelve team, the Rangers, the signs for stealing bases. He simply let them decide, or called them out openly to them, considerably reducing their chances of success. His assistant coach, who was highly knowledgeable about the game, complained that Kyle didn't seem to know how to work with their pitchers, all of whom were weak, to improve their deliveries. Nor did Kyle teach or use bunts. Since boys who move from the seven-to-nine to the ten-to-twelve division are facing pitched balls for the first time, it takes many of them a full season to lose their terror of the ball, never mind to hit consistently. Too many of these fearful players can doom a team, unless a coach teaches at least a couple of the faster runners to put the ball in play by executing bunts. With one exception, not one of Kyle's players laid down a bunt during the entire 1999 season; but the exception actually confirms the overall point. In this one game, when the Rangers had a man on second and third with two outs, Kyle's clean-up hitter, Matt, who is an exceptionally slow runner, came up to bat. Whimsically, Matt asked Kyle if he could bunt. "Sure," Kyle responded, in his typical, laid-back fashion. Matt laid it down and moved in slow motion to first, where he was out, ending the inning and stranding the two players standing on second and third. In another game, at the beginning of an inning, Kyle's first base coach told him that she was going to have all the runners who made it to first steal on the first pitch, until they had one out against them. Therefore, she wanted Kyle to make sure to tell the batters coming up not to swing on the first pitch (while the steal was happening). Kyle said, "Oh, I don't really like to do that, because some of them are not good hitters, and I don't like to waste one of their pitches for them." The assistant coach told me later, "Wow, I was dumbfounded. That's precisely why you do want them to take it, because you can't have one of these little pop-ups to the infield on their first effort and get a double play. But what are ya gonna do? He's the coach."

While he was less concerned with, and less knowledgeable about, the nuances of the game, Kyle did consistently use more positive affirmations as compared with some of the old-timers. He often took pains to focus his comments more on the players' *approach* to the game than on the *results* of particular plays. Kyle seemed to focus more on general attitudes, like being ready for the play, paying attention, and showing effort. For example, in one seven-to-nine game, Kyle asked each of his players in the field to put his hands on his knees before each swing of the bat to indicate readiness. His comments were always about trying hard and not quitting, rather than about whether they got a hit or not. Interestingly, Kyle's interventions did not change much whether the kids were winning or losing, because he focused more on the abstract qualities of playing (i.e., being ready). Kyle almost never criticized his players if they struck out or made an error, and he focused his comments on effort, attitude, and the "breaks of the game." Even the example above, about not wanting weak batters to take first pitches, reflects more than just weak baseball strategy. Kyle genuinely desired to maximize the positive experience for the individual boy who might be struggling to gain confidence at the plate. Parents whose sons lost sleep over strikeouts appreciated this approach, regardless of the implications for the game.

Kyle was passionately hostile to the highly competitive approach, not only as it was used by many of the old-timer coaches, but also as it influenced the highly competitive way the entire FSA was structured. If his team's lead was more than eight or so, he would typically slow up stealing or let boys play new positions. He also fiercely opposed the way the organization often changed rules to favor the needs and schedules of the competitive, high-status traveling teams over the instructional, in-house teams. The traveling teams were usually coached by Fairmounters who often got their way simply because they had more organizational clout. "They just rob the talent from the neighborhood, all for the glory of a handfull of coaches who want city-wide reputations. This season, traveling team players can't even play on their age-appropriate, in-house teams. Weaker players in the in-house lose the chance of building up their skills with the more talented kids. When they do let them play, they freeze our pitchers for their teams, which demoralizes our whole team, when we do nothing but walk."

It is not that Kyle didn't care about winning. But he did have his own, almost "new-age" way of going about it. For example, during one of his early years as a seven-to-nine coach of the Senators, he had been dating a psychologist who worked with athletes at a local university. She used various techniques to help players create images of games in positive ways, even using quasi-hypnotic states to induce positive associations with the games. He considered having her work with his team of boys, and even went so far as to suggest it to the parents of his boys that season. He told me this story not as an example of his unorthodox approach to the game, but as an example of how obnoxious some "uninformed" parents could be. "I mean, well, it's not really hypnosis. It's not really taking them under. It's just more like imaging, in a calm way. I thought, (a) this might be fun for the guys to just sit under a tree in a relaxed way and use images of winning. Not that I wouldn't have done anything to beat Howard, mind you [laughter], but I really suggested it to the team, mostly 'cause I thought it would be a hoot, and (b) I was getting to know her and wanted to kind of see what kind of stuff she did. Well, anyway, I suggested it to the parents, and this one mother, a total case, went berserk, 'Hey, no way, what is this? Kyle, this is going too far. These kids are eight years old, and you want to do this—just to win. That's too far.' Maybe. But it beats humiliating them."

While he spoke I imagined him, not winning, but sitting under a tree with his boys, lying face up and gazing toward the sky, as this woman cooed soothingly to them while old-timers strolled by to take in one more outlandish newcomer innovation to coaching. I said to him, "Kyle, I can't believe you are telling me this story, when you know I am writing a book about the league." He only laughed.

Like other newcomer fathers, Kyle coached an FSA baseball team up to the time when his son no longer wanted to play. Because his son grew to prefer soccer, Kyle intensified his involvement in soccer coaching and retired from FSA. Despite his somewhat marginal acceptance by FSA insiders, even after leaving it Kyle remains deeply loyal to the organization. It was Kyle, in fact, who in his capacity as urban planner shadow-authored the defense of FSA's access to city park land described in chapter 3, when FSA's use of the field was challenged in 2000 by new, "unenlightened" (Kyle's words) development initiatives. And though Kyle passed through FSA along with his son, he brought to the organization an important source of social capital—networks to strategic city planning officials—and cashed it in, even after his coaching days were over, for the organization's benefit.

As an "instructional rookie" who used a positive, noncompetitive approach with his players, Kyle used a coaching style that corresponded to the stereotypical image of newcomers at FSA. Another newcomer, Sal, shared Kyle's noncompetitive approach but combined it in a unique way with greater baseball experience and coaching skill. Sal was unique among newcomer coaches in another way. He coached a younger team for more than six years after his son moved up, as a way of "paying back" FSA for his son's positive experience there over more than a decade.

Sal: Low Drama, Expertise, and Compassionate Masculinity

One of the most revealing moments for tapping into a coach's degree of competition is at the draft. Some coaches approach the draft as if it were a crucial affair of state, selecting only the highest-ranked players available with each opportunity. Others think of their teams as extensions of their family and seek out familiar boys regardless of skill level. Some coaches have worked hard at gathering information about the boys prior to the draft, in order to feel that they will pick well. The meeting at the beginning of the season in which coaches draft their players often produces controversial results that are widely commented on for the rest of the season. Drafts rarely result in teams that are equally balanced. Some teams are stacked by the fact that fathers of highly talented players often choose assistant coaches who have similarly talented sons, a method of front-loading that occurs even before the draft. And unknown (and therefore unranked) players often join the league after the draft, introducing a variable that can unfairly advantage or disadvantage teams. But it is usually insider Fairmounters who are present when the new kid comes in and are able to ask a few questions about his experience. Then, there is also the "car-pool" trick, where a coach claims that a particular kid, often with talent, must be on his team for transportation or family reasons. Finally, sometimes a ten-year-old who moves up in the league is so paralyzed by fear of the pitched ball that he is permitted to move back down and play another year with a seven-to-nine team. Every season, there is a great deal of grumbling among the coaches meant to point out their recognition of specific draft injustices—like when a seven-to-nine coach commented, "Great hit, for a ten-year-old!" Some teams also end up with a disproportionate number of boys coming up from T-ball, tiny guys with no experience at hitting a moving ball. The more competitive coaches often approach the draft more tensely.

In contrast, an old-timer Fairmounter coach named Nick, whose team my research assistant described as "the family team" (his wife was his assistant coach and his two boys played on the team), took perhaps the least competitive approach to the draft I ever observed at FSA. Each year, he came to the draft with a list of five names of somewhat weak players he described as "my obligations." These were boys who lived close to him, or whose parents he knew, and who he "wanted to take care of." This approach differs radically from that of Timmie, a coach who is reputed to have skipped over his son's best friend because he was a "B" ranked player, and reveals core differences concerning what the whole season's enterprise is about. Nick's team rarely advances very far in the standings, but their games are densely attended by groups of parents and extended relatives who stand around behind the dugouts, joking and socializing around the game.

The way a coach organizes his practices also tells a lot about his philosophy of the game, his approach to the boys, and his own creative ability to communicate the expertise he may or may not have. One practice of the Blue Jays early in the 1998 season illustrates well the way Sal, a newcomer coach from outside Fairmount, translated his considerable baseball expertise into highly effective practice drills that were fun and took into account the diversity of talent and character of his players. Sal is college educated and had owned his own business before his current job as a building inspector. He sees himself as someone who has lived in both the newcomers' and old-timers' worlds. Wearing a baseball cap and sunglasses and sporting his trademark large mustache, Sal carries himself with an understated athleticism. Like Nick, Sal favors boys who have played with him before over unknown boys who might be ranked higher. But Sal's loyalty to vulnerable boys did not mean that he ever stopped working hard to improve upon what any particular boy could do. His practices illustrate how Sal translated his acceptance of players' widely divergent skill levels, personalities, and capacity to focus into a series of well-crafted activities designed to impart baseball fundamentals while including enough play to make it fun. Sal never ceased to model a tolerance for difference while stressing the importance of the "baseball lesson of the moment."

As I stroll up to the "triangle" practice field, I see six men scattered among a larger group of boys. With the exception of Sal, all of them are fathers of boys on the team. Roy, Sal's grey-bearded, thin assistant coach is working one-on-one with Gene, a dark-haired, serious boy. Lennie, a boy with obvious emotional problems, is alone and running in place in fast motion. There are about three or four other clusters of kids working with one or two adults. On the far end there are five boys all lined up in a row opposite an assistant coach who is throwing grounders at them. Another two parents are throwing pop-ups to a small circle of others. All the fathers appear easy-going, but perhaps that is because they defer to the tone set by Sal.

While Sal is arranging equipment and greeting parents and boys, he directs Roy to set up the boys in two lines to play a fielding game. "We decided to work on fundamentals. You need to pick a partner." Roy demonstrates how fielding a grounder consists of three separate steps. "Do what I do. Ready?" They squat down with gloves open in front of them. "Break!" They turn on their pivot foot and swing their lead foot ninety degrees in front of them to get into the throwing position. "Throw!" Kevin, the youngest of the boys, beams at the end of each change, thrilled to be in the position, doing the action, being a player. He eventually falls down when waiting for the "throw" command. Robert bursts out laughing—a surprise to me, coming from this otherwise serious lad. Roy says, "Hey, this is not that complicated; you stay relaxed. You don't need to tense up to the point of passing out!" They laugh. Every single step of the instruction is new to me. I realize that, along with the boys, I am a virgin listener. I feel an impulse to stand up and practice along side the boys. A familiar wave of instructional envy overwhelms me. During my childhood I almost never got this kind of close attention to my athleticism. I rarely have the impulse to jump up and help the coaches, as some fathers do; I just want to get in line and get my footwork corrected.

After about ten minutes of the fielding game, Sal calls everybody together. The boys gather around and watch him eagerly. "Now what I want us to do is get in a small circle. Gene, come here and help me demonstrate." He bends down with a yellow tennis ball. "Now stand there with your feet apart and bend down with your hands on the ground. I'm going to throw the ball and you have to keep it from going through your legs. As soon as it comes, hit it back with both of your hands." He demonstrates how they are to scoop it back to the legs of someone else in the circle. They all start bouncing around: "Let me try it!" "Oh, I can do that!" Sal interrupts, "Okay, I'm going to give you each a number." He starts counting down the line and pointing to each one in turn, "One, two, one, two, one, two, Lennie, you're one, two, one, two," and so on. "Now I want you in two groups; the ones go over there and the. . . . " "But I don't know my number! You were pointing to both of us." Another kid answers, "You're two." Another one counters, "No, he's one." At this point Lennie's big brother says, "Okay. Let's do it again. You're one, two, one, two." Sal complains, "But now you're giv- ing 'em different numbers than I did! Oh well. Just move now, guys." Most of them get the plan right away, but a few keep asking where to go. Finally the two circles form. Sal assigns himself one and Pete, one of the father assistant coaches, takes another.

The exercise requires that the adult bend down for a long period of time. The boys are delighted with the game. Sal tosses the ball and it goes through the legs of several. "Oh heck!" "Wait, try it again, I wasn't ready." They finally catch on to what he wants, and they begin to be able to stop the ball quickly and slap it back to another kid. Often when a kid receives the ball from another kid (rather than from Sal) and misses it, he will say, "Hey, you threw that bad." Every few minutes, one of them hits one to Sal. Once in a while he too lets one through his legs. Whenever this happens, they explode with cheers and cries: "I got him! I got him!" or "Yay for our side!" He always laughs and seems genuinely to have a good time, although the bending gets to his back. Whenever a kid isn't down far enough he says, "Hey, if I can do this, you can do it. Get down here." After about fifteen minutes the other parent asks Lennie's brother to relieve him and walks away rubbing his back. Sal keeps his group for the whole time. His group cheers and laughs the most. The boys' faces are intently concentrat- ing, broken up with bursts of frustration when the ball gets though. In this drill, as in many others, Sal discreetly and adeptly increases the pace of the toss to the few who catch on right away in order to sustain the challenge to them as they wait for the others.

Sal's fine-tuned instruction, tailored discreetly to accommodate differences in ability, was also apparent in the final drill of this practice. "Okay, guys," Sal calls out to signal the transition, "Everybody come over here and get in a single line." Sal then positions himself in front of the boys' line at an imaginary home plate. Two other parents, Roy and Pete, position themselves at short and first. Sal explains the drill: "I'll cry out 'go' and then throw the ball to Roy at short who will then throw it to Craig's dad who is the first baseman. The idea was that the kid would run at "go" and try to get to first base before Roy, at short, could throw it to Pete at first base. "Now I want you to run as fast as you can, and run though first *without looking at the ball or the fielder*. Don't look to see where the ball is. That wastes time. Just run right through the bag without stopping or slowing. Whoever gets there without stopping or looking is safe, and gets a point for your side. Whoever doesn't is out and gives me a point." The boys start jumping up and down, some pushing and shoving to express delight at this challenge.

"Okay. Everybody ready? GO!" Sal throws the ball to short and the first boy takes off. He runs pretty fast but looks toward short just before getting there. Pete, standing on first base, shouts, "You looked. You owe me five dollars."

"Oh geez," answers the boy.

"Okay," Sal yells. "You're out." Craig, the second boy, takes off. He runs quickly, and never looks, but just before he arrives at first he slows down considerably.

"You slowed up. Don't slow up, Craig. Out." As Sal shouts his third "Go!" the third boy anticipates the cry, takes off a bit early, and runs at full speed. He looks once and then looks again. By the time he arrives at first, he has looked four times. Three parents call out together, "You looked! Out." Sal turns calmly to the line of boys and repeats, "Guys, don't look behind you, keep running, and listen to the first base coach."

The fourth boy takes off. He runs quickly and never looks. He arrives at first base just as the ball hits the ground and scoots under the first baseman's glove. He keeps running as he should and then turns around to witness the parent scrambling to get the ball. He throws his hands up and struts back punching the air like a world champion. Sal smiles, "One point for your side."

The fifth player runs swiftly but at the last second glances over his shoulder. "OUT!" cries Pete at first base. The next runner, Lee, who recently has been dramatically improving his ball skills, runs right through the base at full speed. Perfect execution. He whirls, his face beaming sheer joy: "HA, HA, HA." He keeps this up all the way back to Sal. A full belly laugh from the sheer fun of it.

After every boy has a turn, Sal announces, "Okay. We're starting over now. Now it's real. We keep score." Kevin, the smallest boy on the team, who wears a short crew cut and bounces about almost constantly, comes up. After Sal's "Go!," Kevin runs fiercely down the line. He gets to first in due time but as he runs back toward Sal, he announces proudly, "I missed the bag." Pete then yells out, "Hey! He missed the bag. Tag him, Sal." Kevin's freckled face is beaming as he runs up close to Sal, who is already occupied with getting the next boy set to run, challenging him to tag him. Sal pretends not to notice until Kevin gets close, then grabs his leg while yelling, "You're out!" The boy collapses on the ground in giggles.

Finally, it is Lennie's turn. One of the first indications to me early in the season that Lennie was a boy with special needs was how many times he would make oppositional statements to either Sal or other boys but always deliver them with a big smile. If Sal said, "Let's all get in a circle," Lennie would answer, "No, I don't want to join you," but with a weirdly affirming smile. He is always moving at a frenetic pace when the coaches are asking for concentration or focus. Now, when the appropriate moment comes to run at full speed, Lennie sprints off the plate but then slows to a snail's pace as if someone has turned his switch to "slow motion." His competing thoughts overwhelm him. Right before the base he comes to a full stop. It is startlingly weird. No one makes a big deal of it or mentions his speed. Sal only gently calls out, "Lennie, don't stop before getting there." The moment captures a lot about Sal's coaching; he both attends to teaching skills and accepts Lennie as Lennie.

During the third round, when it is Kevin's turn again, he charges in his usual rapid, tiny steps, on the balls of his feet. If there were music accompanying him it would sound like, "Tot, tot, tot, tot," His manner makes the adults chuckle, and even the other boys are forced to smile at his unintended charm, the little crew cut and perfectly round head with freckles. Sal, who has been studying him carefully, suddenly has a revelation—"Oh! He's ice skating!!!" (Kevin plays hockey on a team at the Rizzo rink.) I laugh because it makes perfect sense; I can easily imagine him hunched down, driving the skates forward with the balls of his feet. Roy at short calls out, "Bet you're really fast on the ice."

Watching the line of boys waiting their turn is like watching an insulated society, disconnected from the adult world a few feet beyond them. Only the first two or three actually watch what the runners are doing, as they anticipate their turns. The rest are in pairs or triangles turned inward, jumping, swatting, and bouncing. In fact, if you concentrate just on their formation and look at them in a visually unfocused way, they look like a rippling rope that is being rhythmically jerked by a giant hand. The wave of movement goes up and down the line, sometimes rapidly, sometimes slowly, no body ever coming to rest for more than a second at a time. Sal just continues pitching out to his adult helpers, recruiting one runner at a time while the rippling wave of creatures keep up their hullabaloo behind him.

After about ten more minutes of this drill, Sal gathers the group together around the equipment. He keeps motioning for them to circle in closer and they do. Briefly, the boys give him their full attention. He begins, "Do you know what we were doing out there?"

"Yeah—running past the base without stopping."

"That's right, and learning not to watch the ball and trust the base coach. But what about the other part with the tennis balls?" Lee, the constantly smiling black boy, standing on the outside of the circle, turns to his buddy and says, "That was FUN!" His friend gives a half smile. Several boys talk at once.

"Hey, I can't hear. Yeah, it was fun, and it was learning to get your glove on the ground, to be ready to field those surprises." When it becomes clear that Sal's tone is turning pedagogical, about a third of them tune out. Sal recognizes this instantly; he cuts short the verbal lesson, satisfied that the drills have done enough, and announces the times of the next practice and next game. "Who are we playing?" Sal answers, "The Grays." Grumbling. One of the parents proclaims loudly, "And this game we are going to win." The Blue Jays are the only team that has not yet won a game this season, a fact that is beginning to trouble a few of the more skilled players. Sal only casually answers, "We'll see; we certainly have the talent to beat them."

About two months later, toward the end of the season, I see a repetition of the first-base drill at another Blue Jays practice. When I arrive at the "Dairy," all the boys and assistant coaches are out in the field except for Sal, who is working alone with Marcos on his batting stance. I once asked Sal if Marcos had ever spoken to him, since I had never seen Marcos utter a word to any boy for the entire season. "Well, he does speak to me because he had to at the very beginning of the season. But I think I'm the only one. I'm not sure how much English he speaks, really. I know his grandmother only speaks Greek to him." Sal continues to work quietly with Marcos for another ten minutes. Then he calls everybody in and arranges a repeat of the first-base-running drill. The temptation to look for the ball on the way to first base still torments a few Blue Jay players during games. After several rounds of this drill, with Craig and Lee, two of the three top players, still biting the bait and looking over their shoulders, Marcos, who always sits alone on the bench and has still not hit in any game this season, comes up. Sal hits the ball toward first and Marcos takes off. He runs slowly but there is much more feeling in his run than usual. The whole way, he maintains a steady gaze on Pete at first. As Marcos arrives at the plate, Sal yells dramatically, "SAFE! Marcos is SAFE!" Marcos turns and trots, almost skipping, back to the line of boys. I've never seen him display a trace of animation before this moment. On his next turn, he repeats the perfect execution. This time almost everyone calls out, "SAFE!" This causes a half-smile to cross Marcos's face and he runs friskily back to the community of other boys. It is only a half-smile, only a tiny skip, and merely for a direct run to first. It might never happen again in a real game. But Sal's smile and affirming nod to Marcos, who dares to meet Sal's eyes as he passes, Sal's ability to wait for Marcos to feel enough trust to emote, communicate to this deeply self-protected boy that once in a while there might be reason to lay down his shield after all.

That season, the Blue Jays ended up next to last in the standings. Some parents complained that Sal was "too laid back," or "not hungry enough." Perhaps. But his drills and practices were among the best crafted that I observed at FSA. Sal understood baseball and cared, like many expert coaches, about imparting skills. But his human skills went deeper. After watching Sal for a season, I had the sense that he had a deeper understanding of the complexities of the emerging character of each boy on his team than most FSA coaches had. He saw his boys as more than players on his stage. Sal knew how to accommodate Lennie's extreme outbursts and withdrawals while minimize their damaging effects on the group; he recognized that Marcos deeply depended on his quiet guidance and occasional touch but could never be forced, or even directly coaxed, to utter a word to the other boys; he understood the need to reign in the harshness of two of his more talented, but insecure, players; and he succeeded in creating collective fun over Kevin's desire to be teased and his ability to give as good as he got. Sal's season was laced, like Marcos's skip, with tiny moments of grace that revealed his capacity to offer dignity to the most vulnerable of boys, to teach effectively baseball fundamentals, and to engage with the complexity of the personalities of all the children who came briefly under his patient tutelage.

But not all of the hybrid coaching styles (Sal combined considerable baseball knowledge with his compassionate masculinity) translated into positive experiences for the boys in FSA. Kirk, another newcomer, managed to combine almost all of the most problematic features of coaching, from both newcomer and old-timer stereotypes, including low baseball expertise, high competitiveness, negative reinforcement, a tough style of masculinity, and an emphasis on negative discipline.

Kirk the Wannabe Old-Timer: Masculinity as Tantrum

Rather than critiquing the negative style of coaching that many (erroneously) saw as the specialty of old-timers in the organization, Kirk, a newcomer, in an attempt to fit in, coped with his outsider status by appropriating the harshest aspects of the style of tough masculinity. To that end, he adopted an exaggerated style of raucous, showy language and ostentatious beer-drinking. Indeed, though a newcomer professional, Kirk applied one of the more brutal coaching styles I witnessed at Fairmount.

Kirk usually parked his red sports car in front of one of the towering apartment buildings that grace the area. When they played against Kirk's team, the boys who knew this would shout, "Hit the red Mustang!" Involved in corporate finance and international banking, Kirk embodies class confidence. Of average height, with a head of longer, thick, black hair, he usually wears polo shirts and shorts to show off his year-round tan. He walks with an urbane swagger, smiles a lot, and frequently offers loud public commentary to informally assembled audiences around the ball field.

In 1998 Kirk was coaching the Expos in the ten-to-twelve division for the second year in a row. His A-ranked son played on his team. Unfortunately for his team, and his son, despite his social confidence, Kirk knows relatively little about baseball instruction. He compensates for this by focusing obsessively on rigid notions of proper technique, which he applies regardless of the situation.

This was demonstrated repeatedly in his interventions with his pitchers, who lacked the magical "freeze technique" that Kirk deemed essential to the wind-up.

Early in the season, Kirk stressed to his pitchers that, during the windup, they needed to freeze one leg in the air for several seconds at the balance position. However, holding the balance position too long in a windup is likely to encourage steals. But Kirk insisted on it. This obsession was evident in the first two innings of an early 1998 game. When the Expos' starting pitcher, Ben, started his first windup, Kirk began to yell, "Hold your leg! Two seconds. Hold it on top. *Freeze the leg.*" I wondered, "What the heck does that mean?" For two straight innings, Kirk repeated this demand. When his second pitcher came in, he continued, "Step forward. Right at the batter. Step to the batter. Hold your leg. *Freeze it on top.* Make sure you follow through." His out-of-order instructions were confusing and seemed designed not for the pitcher, but for the audience of adults observing. Several innings later, after a third relief pitcher walked a couple of players, Kirk stared harshly in his direction from inside the dugout. After the first pitch to the next batter, Kirk's loud voice, with its particularly unappealing, nasal whine, preceded him as he burst from the dugout. "I don't want to waste my breath again, Mike. Freeze the leg!" I thought, "Is this guy for real? Even I know this is irrelevant." On the second pitch, Kirk exploded, "FREEZE the LEG!" On the third pitch, "I SAID, FREEZE IT!" Kirk then demonstrated by violently planting his own leg in the ground and grinding it.

Kirk's obsessive, misplaced instruction continued as his team came up to bat. His first batter took a strike. "CHRIS! Look at your feet! What did I tell you? FOUR INCHES. Exactly four inches apart!" Even through his dark tan, the purple veins on his forehead stood out. I watched over several games, but none of the pitchers he subjected to the freeze grill ever improved their ratio of strikes. Lacking the compensatory baseball expertise of Fairmounters like Billy, Shawn, and Dan, Kirk combined his low level of game command and knowledge not with positive emotional support for the boys as Kyle did, but with highly negative reinforcements and even harsher individual critiques when the boys failed. My research assistant, Dylan, who over one season watched several of his games, always referred to him as the "wannabe old-timer." Kirk took pleasure in being outrageous. Once, I met another coach leaving the kitchen area, shaking his head about a comment that Kirk had just made. Apparently, as a description of why kitchen duty was important, Kirk had loudly volunteered, "It's like fucking an ugly woman; somebody's got to do it."

Kirk's class cockiness added a particularly devastating quality to his negative reinforcements. In a game against the Bisons, when an outfielder overthrew to the third baseman, Kirk walked out toward the field and called out, "What are you doin'? Now that's just STUPID!" A few minutes later, a weird foul ball was hit just off the first base line. The first baseman spontaneously threw his foot out to his left to block the ball, and then danced around from the pain. Kirk leapt from the dugout and cried out with disgust, "HEY! You already hurt your arm! You want to crawl out of here on that foot? Listen, we're not good enough to play around like that!" In another game, his boys were fielding in a particularly despondent manner. His son, Otto, was caught sitting on his glove in the outfield when a ball was hit near him. He scrambled for it but overthrew the ball to the third baseman. Kirk came out of the dugout, lifted his hands in the air, and cried to the entire team, "WHAT are we DOING? There is no reason for this. There were two outs." Then he turned to reenter the dugout but, reconsidering, whirled around in rage and shouted at his son, "Otto, get out there! Is this a fucking tea party? Guys, *get your heads out of your asses!*"

In relation to the boys' egos, one of the down sides of baseball is how the game spotlights individual mistakes. Not only did Kirk seem incapable of converting individual mistakes into teachable moments; his interventions often further enhanced the pain of error. During a game against one of the better teams, Shawn's Diamond Backs, Kirk's second batter swung at a very high ball on the first pitch. Kirk bellowed from his third base coaching position, loud enough for the entire community to hear, "If you are just going to hurt the team, don't come. Just stay home. You're more help to us there than here."

Although Kirk is often especially harsh with his own son, he reserved his most hostile comments for a chubby, Andean-looking boy named Craig who was somewhat scared of the ball. During one early May game, this hostility bordered on open abuse. I was standing beside two mothers chatting with each other behind the opposing team's dugout, where a large crowd of parents and younger children had gathered, as Craig came up to bat. Standing in the dugout directly beside Craig, separated from us in the crowd only by the fence, Kirk began berating the second Craig took his stance: "Get your feet together." Craig shifted his feet slightly. "Craig, I said get your feet together!" Craig complied, but stood away from the plate. In a vicious tone, Kirk called out, "GET THAT BAT UP TO THE PLATE." A good pitch went by, but Craig did not swing. Kirk came out of the dugout and bent down, with his hands dramatically turned out, as if pleading with Craig, "Hey! What are you waiting for? Divine Intervention?" he asked. Then, after a long pause, he commanded, "GET UP THERE!"

The woman standing next to me was, I realized, Craig's mother. She stood looking down at the ground, her hand covering her face, pretending to scratch her forehead. Reflecting her association of this kind of screaming behavior with old-timer Fairmounters, her friend asked, "Wow, who *is* that guy? Is he Mr. Big at Fairmount baseball or something?" Craig's mother, still cupping her face, whispered, "I'll tell you who he is. He is my son's coach. And he is out there, just shrieking at my son, and I can't take it." But she did take it, and consequently so did her son.

Kirk called time out, left the dugout, and stood right behind the tormented

Craig. With his hands squeezing Craig's shoulders, Kirk shoved him toward the plate. "This is where you stand. YOU COVER THE PLATE."

Kirk's coaching was not without positive moments when he praised his players and found constructive things to say. Just after the incident with Craig, Paul, one of the smallest boys on a team with a lot of large players, came up to bat. As he stood at the plate, his right leg trembled. Looking at his strange-looking stance, my legs began to tremble also. Paul struck out quickly. Kirk, calmer now, perhaps purged of his rage, watched him enter the dugout. He patted him on the head in a friendly way and said, "It's okay, Paul." This positive reinforcement happened with the next batter as well. Two strikeouts and two head pats. But Kirk's high-volume rage is made worse by its unpredictability. He would turn on players who showed signs of fear, or mediocrity, but with little foreseeable reason—the perfect recipe for creating a state of constant anxiety in the players (and the parents).

Typically, the limited use he did make of positive reinforcement happened when his players delivered winning results. He rewarded success, not effort (the opposite of Billy), but he often punished failure with humiliation. And his rewards and punishments were not systematic. Kirk did not exhibit respect for his players. He often seemed more involved with the surrounding adults than with the boys. He chatted to them as they stood behind the dugout and made joking comments to passing coaches about his boys being "a bunch of little assholes."

Kirk's case is particularly remarkable, because he becomes notably more obnoxious when there are more Fairmounters observing him. In this sense his rough style is produced and performed *for* the adult audience of Fairmounters. This is interesting, because it shows not only how group cultural differences become stereotypes, but how they can play an active role in structuring behavior, in this case Kirk's. In turn, this cultural scripting has to do with deep-set masculinity issues: the chief way for Kirk to have his masculinity affirmed in the FSA context was to have the Fairmounters accept or admire him. In contrast, if the Fairmounters turned on a coach, it diminished his masculinity and put his baseball knowledge in question.

Billy, the Fairmounter coach with the heavy disciplinarian style and the fear of tears and mistakes, seemed genuinely trapped in his style of tough masculinity and struggled, often unsuccessfully, with his armor when he wanted to be gentle. In part, that is why he was often forgiven by boys and their parents, Fairmounters and newcomers alike. Despite his way of throwing a fit, there were always boys who thought of Billy as fair. But Kirk's yelling had an air of arbitrary cruelty. As an outsider, Kirk aspired to be like Billy, to have a "Fairmounter" style on the key dimensions—to display expertise, be highly competitive, use negative reinforcement, and be tough—but he exaggerated these traits, and he did so in a way that was inappropriate to the context: he coached a less competitive, non-traveling team. Also, it was apparent that his level of expertise did not back up his self-presentation. So, instead of being perceived as a tough insider coach, he became a kind of class clown. Kirk sees discipline as a form of masculinity more than as a way to further baseball instruction. Kirk sees and imitates the outward form of discipline, not its purpose. He behaves the way he does in order to embody masculinity for his imagined audience, a stereotypically macho group of Fairmounter men. Precisely because he does not have baseball expertise, he resorts to a rather clumsy and ugly performance of negative training. Because he does not understand the connection between baseball strategy and his approach, his efforts become cruel as well as foolish.

Balancing Coaching Goals While Not Bailing Out

FSA is a place where diverse local subcultures are brought together around baseball. Competing versions of the meaning of sports in boys' lives are reflected in diverse coaching styles as well as in parental expectations. The different styles of the coaches were highly visible, and widely commented upon, by large groups of spectators who came together ritualistically to watch the results of coaches' and boys' efforts. Though there were some salient group differences, as represented in the clustering of Fairmount old-timers among the more knowledgeable, more competitive, and emotionally harsher coaches, and the clustering of newcomers among the less knowledgeable, more instructional, and gentler coaches, in reality most coaches fell outside the stereotypical portraits of either group. But cultural memory and cultural images are biased toward the salient extremes, or what Barrie Thorne calls the "dominant outliers."[7] So, it is often the sharp contrasts that crystallize in people's minds and thereby influence their behaviors and their expectations about "the other."

Because, for example, men with tougher styles of masculinity often yell and dramatically censor boys' emotional behavior as unacceptable, they get noticed and commented on more than the gentler men. This is why Fairmount has the reputation it does on the outside. Because more Fairmounters could be found among the outliers with tougher masculinity styles, and more newcomers could be found among the outlying "softies" with the more tender masculinity styles, the belief that the two groups had radically different styles of masculinity took hold, despite the fact that the majority of both groups hovered somewhere in between, along a continuum of styles and key dimensions. Additionally, the two groups, Fairmounters and newcomers, were both invested in thinking about each other in stereotypical ways. On the Fairmounters' side, this investment had to do with the fear, as we saw in chapter 3, that the newcomers were trying to take over. Hence, emphasizing newcomers' baseball "incompetence" was a defensive response on the part of Fairmounters to their fear of takeover, and it expressed an oppositional stance to newcomers' pushiness. In contrast, as newcomers often felt powerless in the face of all kinds of decisions that affected their children, their teams, and the league, and as their social influence in other spheres made this relative powerlessness hard to take, newcomers cast Fairmounters in the role of abusive, beer-drinking tyrants.

Relatively few coaches engaged in consistently abusive treatment of the boys. At the same time, however, relatively few openly embraced the gentlest styles of masculinity. Rather than accept boys' tears and vulnerabilities directly, with physical or verbal comfort, even the coaches with the most openly tender styles of masculinity (generally) merely tolerated public displays of emotion. More importantly, they also often tolerated, by the complicity of their silence, the harsher styles of other coaches. For example, a coach named Ben, who was personally very tender with his players, tolerated an abusive assistant coach on his team who physically threatened other coaches when his team lost and talked threateningly to the twelve-year-old runners he coached on third base. Despite one coach and one parent's protest, and their threat to leave the organization unless Ben's assistant coach was immediately removed, both Ben and the FSA leadership permitted the assistant to remain. It proved to be one thing to embody a soft, caring style toward the boys, but another to challenge the oppressive behaviors of other men. Why is that?

The masculinity styles, tough and tender, that we observed at FSA occur in the broader social context of the changing gender norms that are a fundamental part of contemporary American society. All of the men at Fairmount have witnessed transformations in their own workplaces and homes, as larger and larger numbers of women with children take up full-time work outside the home. This broader social context has challenged many assumptions behind the traditional, tough style of masculinity, and has left many men unclear about what is expected of them. The connection between a more traditional masculinity, and the working-class Fairmounters is clear, but it is not universally true. A lot of the Fairmounters who don't practice tough masculinity would still have a hard time criticizing it, because it represents a time-honored "protest ideology"[8] deeply connected with class identity.

On the other side, the newcomer men, whose social experiences and families put them in positions where women often have more real power[9] and where there is more expectation that they do things like take care of their own children, are "softer" or more tender men, but this is not universal either. To critique macho, rough behavior toward boys opens a man up to the epithet of "wimp," or "yuppie," or worse. That is, in part, why Kirk is so interesting. He can do what he does without seeming as foolish as he really is because he is imitating the "norm." The traditional narrative of masculinity has a hold on men that exceeds its correspondence to their lived experience. This may also explain the reluctance of those with more tender styles of masculinity to challenge the periodic cruelties of coaches like Billy and Kirk.[10]

During my fieldwork, and during my experiences as a baseball mother, I came to feel especially passionate about the masculinity dimension of coaching. One day in 1998, after witnessing a particularly harsh denunciation of a pitcher who cried at a FSA game, I walked home to discover on television that the final game of the Soccer World Cup was being played in France, between Brazil and France. France won, an outcome unusual in and of itself. Because the announcers are so dramatic, my husband and son watch these games on the Spanish channel. The end of the game was a sea of tears. The Brazilians sobbed and fell into each other's arms in open displays of anguish about their defeat, giving themselves over to the release of the end of the World Cup games. One of the French players also gave way to his emotions, distinguishing himself from the other French players with a flood of tears, sobbing over their victory. Witnessing the Frenchman weeping openly, the already spasmodic Argentinean announcer began screaming something like, "There is at least one with Latin blood! One who feels as deeply as we do!"

There are alternative models available, of men with athletic prowess who emote, who feel, who cry, and who see it as natural male behavior. But somehow, in this limited little space, and FSA is not unique in this regard, the dominant lesson of masculinity is still that tears are shameful. The message is clearly articulated and rarely resisted. Not once did I ever hear one parent stand up and say, "Let my son cry." As a culture, we need to find ways to invest men with the emotional skills to tend to boys' feelings, and we need to come to see the teaching of these skills as being at least on a par with the teaching of pick-off moves. We also need to entitle ourselves, even oblige ourselves, to stand up to adults who ridicule and emotionally abuse boys for expressing their normal vulnerabilities.

Though this chapter has stressed the differences among the FSA coaches, they also share important similarities. They are all men who live in an era that has been described as devoid of community involvement, obsessed with work, and lacking in fathers' involvement. Yet they devote hundreds of hours of voluntary labor to a community organization that produces the annual spring rituals of children's baseball, and that draw hundreds of parents and neighborhood spectators into its community. These coaches watch each other make these sacrifices and learn something about each other, and about masculine involvement, in the encounter. Over time, the boys also watch the differences in their styles and develop their own vocabularies for discussing those differences: for recognizing at young ages that there are diversities of social style among the adults outside of their homes and schools. Through these encounters, some coaches also come to change their styles over time, presumably drawing from the competing versions of masculinity around them and learning from their own mistakes. Parents do the same. And there are emerging generational changes apparent in these neighborhoods and in FSA. In fact, some of the youngest Fairmounter coaches, representing the emergent fourth generation of Fairmount insiders, reject the harsher gender styles of their fathers and model themselves on the more tender styles made available by the changing landscape.

IN BASEBALL, one of the hardest things for most boys to learn is to overcome their fear of a hard ball thrown toward them by an often inaccurate pitcher—or learning not to "bail out" of the batter's box. This is also one of the central challenges of coaching: teaching boys to cope with this fear while learning to hit. Bailing out is a batter's physical expression of the fear he feels as the ball is released from the pitcher's hand and comes hurtling toward him. Because it is an expression of fear, bailing out is particularly loathsome to coaches who are threatened by boys' vulnerabilities. These coaches tend to treat bailing out as either a moral weakness or a personal insult, and they scream at and ridicule the boys who do it. Often, bailing out is feminized by these coaches, given a symbolic significance in the emotional economy of masculinity. The use of humiliation tactics in coaching increases boys' levels of fear, and bailing out becomes something unnatural, something feminine, and adds the burden of shame to a boy's already complicated task of learning to bat. To be scared or give way to emotion is the worst thing of all—it is to be like "a girl." To be scared is to be banished from the male kingdom. These tactics make a boy's journey unnecessarily lonely. On the basis of years of observation of boys' baseball, and also on the basis of my conversations with boys and men about their experiences learning to hit, it is evident to me that boys learn to hit *despite* the tactics of humiliation. One highly skilled fifteen-year-old player described the process of learning to hit in this way: "When I was ten, I was terrified. It was a gradual process where I had to build up confidence. I finally learned to hit enough to take the ball before it took me. I knew it was bad to bail out. I quit showing that I was scared for about two years before I really didn't feel scared. That's when I became a hitter."

In terms of baseball skills, what is really at stake in learning how not to bail out is to be able to develop enough confidence to successfully apply the already learned mechanics of batting to a live pitching situation. For those boys who are scared of the pitch, and who bail out of the box, this confidence is only gained over time, as they acquire more experience, learn to cope with their fears, and gain some success. Humiliation and the stigmatization of fear as "feminine" do not contribute in the slightest to the process of acquiring confidence. The boys who cannot overcome these fears, who continue to bail out, usually drop out of Fairmount baseball by the time they reach the thirteen-to-fifteen year-old league. And there are plenty who do. They do this because baseball isn't fun anymore, and because they are emotionally exhausted from the continual assault on their male identity. It should be a simple thing for a coach to say to a boy, "I know you're scared. It *is* scary, but you'll lose this fear as you learn to hit." But the uneasiness toward male vulnerability associated with traditional masculinity makes this very hard to do. Bailing out remains a powerful symbol of two fundamental aspects of coaching: the approach to the game and the approach to the boys. Good coaches, found among the Fairmounters as well as among the newcomers, recognize that fearlessness is an impossible human goal, impossible for all of us. They work creatively with the boys' emotions, including their fears, as they teach them how to stay in the batter's box.

Making Room for Lennie

Competition isn't just about winning games. A less recognized, but important dimension of competition is the extent to which a coach is willing to take on kids who are known by all to be somehow problematic. Some children have emotional or learning difficulties of such magnitude that their inclusion on a team is a sure headache for a coach, in terms of regular tantrums or breakdowns, guaranteed outs on every play, consistent lack of attention, hostility from other children, or the amount of time and patience required to integrate the child into routine team activities. These kids are usually the last considered; they are the problem kids, or the kids of problem parents, that coaches prefer to avoid. The commitment of a coach named Sal to a boy named Lennie illustrates the way caretaking of all children, even the distressed ones, can produce profound results in teaching of children about community nurturance, even if it gets in the way of game wins.

Sal, a newcomer from outside Fairmount, coaches the seven-to-nine Blue Jays. Although a college-educated former restaurant owner, he now works as a building inspector in Fairmount. Sal looks like the Marlboro Man with dimples, and for several years he assisted Nick, the old-timer coach who ran the "family team" and who perhaps socialized him into the importance of community caretaking. When Sal announced to his boys early in the season, "I told you guys. I don't give the score. It's not important," I knew instantly that Sal leaned more toward instruction than toward competition as a key dimension. I thought, "Oh no. Not this again. Now the boys will just run around constantly and whisper to each other nonstop about the score." The logic (a noncompetitive one) is that not knowing the score will free the younger boys up to have fun and to not feel overly pressured, for example, when

143

batting in a tied-up game. This practice became rather widespread, especially among the more noncompetitive newcomers, but was openly snickered at by some parents, especially old-timers (and, I confess, by me as well).

One of the most troubled kids in the league was a little boy named Lennie. From the first Blue Jay game I attended, he stood out. He exhibited signs of extreme behavioral problems that seemed to border on autism. Lennie's family lives in Fairmount and is well known among the community for their active involvement in the Catholic Church. Both Lennie's older brother and his father have serious physical health problems. Lennie rarely makes eye contact. Over the course of one season, I witnessed more than fifty occasions when Lennie moved outside the group of his teammates, appearing to be involved in a fantasy life that paralleled or incorporated elements of the "real conversation." He would often make loud proclamations of incomprehensible or grandiose phrases, exclaiming things like "You're gonna have to clean up all that garbage," or "Hey, guys, listen up. I'm a hero," or "I took care of the garbage. There were some bad banners," or "Hey, who's gonna tell me to shut up? Just let somebody tell me to shut up, and I'm gonna bust 'em." Even when he was sitting on the bench, his body never stopped moving. He gave me the sense of an object in perpetual, high-velocity motion. However, despite his dissociative behavior, he never wanted to miss his turn at bat. Whenever it was his turn at an activity, he would shoot through the group to participate. And at bat, the rapidity of his body movements would vanish; he would swing in slow motion after the ball was already in the catcher's glove. Even then, his movements were out of synchronization with the others. When Sal would gather the kids together, Lennie, sitting alone at the extreme end of the bench, would ignore him. But Sal would coax him to join the team. When Sal was trying to call out instructions to his runners, Lennie would frequently interrupt. And with patience, Sal would respond, "No Lennie, remember what we talked about? Remember our talk? Settle down now." And when Sal would turn back toward the field, Lennie would sit still—for about fifteen seconds. I was astonished to learn that Sal had requested Lennie in the draft. Lennie had been on Sal's team twice before, and Sal had picked him up again because he worried that the other coaches would not be patient enough with him.

About mid-season, after having failed, because of his slow-motion swings, to make any contact with the ball, Lennie finally publicly registered his pain. After strikeouts, he usually ended by screaming belligerently at the umpire or at an imaginary character unrelated to the game. Other times, he seemed to forget instantly, and would instead, on entering the dugout, smile and clap for himself. In this game, his usual pattern of swinging at the ball as if time had stopped produced his third strikeout. He was furious as he walked away from the plate and slammed the bat down, perpendicular to the ground, like he was drilling. So the umpire would not be forced to respond, Sal moved in quickly to defuse the situation. He patted Lennie's shoulder, saying, "Hey Lennie, those are the breaks. You got some cuts in there. You can try again." With extreme intensity, Lennie yelled, "I quit. I'm never gonna play this game again! I'm going home." I thought, "Someone should block the dugout, because he looks ready to run into the street." Lennie's older brother, who helps Sal with the team, whispered to Lennie, "You tell Dad that." Lennie threw himself on the bench, covered his face with his hand, and let out a profoundly woeful series of moans—the kind of cry you might expect from an adult upon the sudden death of a child. I remember wanting to lie down, so unbearable was the wail. Then Lennie leapt up and ran toward the concession stand. His brother pursued him. When they returned a few minutes later, his brother was rubbing his back. Gently, Sal simply said, "Good. Now get ready to field."

As I watched Sal handle Lennie, I imagined the incredible loneliness of Lennie's life and thought about how his condition must affect his family, and I realized the incredible gift Sal was giving to Lennie and his family, and to the spectators and FSA as a whole. By welcoming Lennie onto his team and accommodating his special needs, even to the almost certain detriment of his team's standing, he set an example of patience and love. For players and adults alike, he modeled a more compassionate style of masculinity. And I wondered how able the more competitive coaches were to recognize and appreciate the value of his gift. Sal doesn't win many championships, but he makes me think of a line from a Robert Creeley poem: "Must humanness be its only reward? / Is this happiness?"

Ultimately, Sal and the Blue Jays did receive a payback for accommodating Lennie's considerable needs. Toward the end of the season, Lennie engineered one of the richer and more memorable moments of the Blue Jays' season. Toward the middle of one particular game, Lennie came up to bat with two runners on base and the usual low expectations. As usual, he stood with one of his knees cocked weirdly, too high up. But on the first swing his timing was reasonable, not his usual slow motion cut. Then, by some miracle, the second swing made contact. A dribbler of a ball landed right in front of the pitching machine. Lennie ran at his usual snail's pace and was out at first by a mile. But, helped by a fumble, he drove in the two runners. The crowd went berserk. I threw my notebook down and jumped into the air, screaming in unison with the crowd. Next to me, a parent was so overcome that he unwittingly stomped up and down on my notebook. If an alien from another planet had arrived at that moment knowing nothing of baseball, from that scene he would have had to conclude that the object of the game is to get thrown out at first. Lennie entered the dugout to a chorus of pats on the back and cries of "Way to go, Lennie," and "Great hit, Doctor Perry!" (his name for himself). He stood basking, taking it all in, and finally, accepting the triumph and glory of victory, he held both fists in the air, and cried, "OKAY! That's for Doctor Perry!" Even Timmie, the umpire, broke out in laughter and clapping. Gene, one of the scoring runners, entered the dugout, huffing and puffing and smiling, saying, "I almost fainted on base!" A father leaned over to Lennie's father, congratulating him. "Good hit. If he'd a run, it would have worked." Lennie's father just nodded, with a slight smile, in a moment of unusual acclaim for his son. Discussing it later, two of the boys said, "OKAY. Now Lennie can hit!" then added, "If only we could attach a rocket to him and get him to base."

Lennie's moment was one of the highlights of the season, and though his inclusion on the team was only one of the many factors that contributed to the Blue Jays' low position in the final standings, this coach's contribution to Lennie's life— by *choosing him* and patiently waiting for that moment—was a supreme testimony to the importance of balancing the individual needs of even the most troubled of children against the pleasures (and need) of winning. Not just Lennie and his family, but the team, and the league as a whole, were the beneficiaries of that moment.

5

==

The Bench and Boys' Culture

"The Heart of the Lineup"

What mattered to the boys? How did the background context shape their experiences? Did the changes in the neighborhood, the encounters with parents from different backgrounds, the organizational challenges and tensions, and the range of coaching styles filter down to them in meaningful ways? For one thing, because baseball is a highly structured encounter between competing teams, the social chemistry of a team matters greatly to any boy's experiences. Many parents and coaches mention that teams have personalities. We have seen how the divergent styles of adult coaches give rise to very different environments for their players. But a coach's influence only counts for so much. A coach who acts in a very similar way over three seasons will often have three very different teams, not just in terms of their standings but in the feel and character of the team. Curiously, the internal dynamics among players are mostly ignored by coaches. They may be aware of certain tensions between a few players, but they usually address them only when serious conflicts flare up. Yet coaches often scratch their heads about what happened to their team or to other teams during a season. They will say things like, "With all that talent, they should have done something. But they just gave up."[1]

There is a great deal happening in any baseball game. In the seven-to-nine league, which is the subject of this chapter, coaches have many considerations to balance: who to play where and for how long, the batting order, adjusting the pitching machine, what plays to call in a game. It is not surprising that they rarely get around to addressing the group dynamic on the bench. Their obliviousness is in part because that dynamic remains hidden to them. This is because it is an unfolding, ever-changing dynamic, one being constantly constructed and contested by the boys themselves. Boys take the structure of the game, and the adult messages, rewards, and punishments, as they gradually come to understand them over time, and blend them together to create their own meanings and practices. The boys' space operates semi-autonomously from the adults around them. They create their own social order on the bench. This social order, or bench culture, is enormously important in defining and creating meanings of baseball for the boys and for the success or failure of a team.

The Social Order of the Bench

One theme that cuts across all the teams and leagues in Fairmount baseball is the gradual winning out of purpose over play. The teams with the largest number of young players are the most playful, while the teams stacked with older players are more focused and goal-driven. Also, the seven-to-nine league in general is more playful, while the ten-to-twelve and thirteen-to-fifteen leagues are more competitive and hard-nosed. While this might be thought of as simply the result of "maturity," it is more than that. In any given league context, the loss of playfulness happens unevenly; typically it happens most quickly with the more talented boys on teams, who are not always the oldest players. As they cope with the weight of adult expectations and with challenges to their top-dog status from weaker players, they disconnect from play more readily. This early sobering of the "top dogs" sets a commanding tone over the season for the other younger boys and carries over more uniformly to all the boys as they move up to older divisions. Some boys struggle against the weight of seriousness longer than others—they specialize in bench disruptions, or they simply quit. It is not only the boys who never master a good batting stance or base running who drop out of baseball. Some experience the entire sport as tedious or negative. Parents and coaches offer many interpretations for why boys sometimes vote with their feet. But strangely, "not having fun" is rarely among the explanations. Partly, this is because from the purposeful world of adults, it all looks extremely playful.

A second feature common to the boys' culture of the bench is the way the status order is dictated by the hierarchy of athleticism. In the seven-to-nine league, boys who are at the top of the lineup, who play shortstop or first base, even when individually disliked, receive more honor or deference than weaker players. I was often surprised at how frequently and frankly they discussed each other's relative abilities and monitored each other's achievements and failures. The team hierarchy, once created, is actively maintained, challenged, and reorganized by struggles and pacts among the boys.

Beyond these two common dynamics—the steady reigning in of play and the obsession with skill hierarchy—found in most teams, I observed four other features that lent distinctive character to seven-to-nine teams. First, the range of athletic ability on a team matters. Huge gaps in skills among teammates challenge even the most generous of boys. Second, the "posture of talent," or the way superior players respond to their own failures and to those of their weaker teammates, conditions the feel of a team. Third, the emotional resilience of underdogs can be important for counteracting the negative vibes of top dogs if they exist. Fourth, the presence of positive emotional workers strongly flavors teams.[2] Teams with players who move around doing "female work" have more fun. "That's okay." "You can do it next time." It just takes a few to make the team tolerable for a weak player. Emotional workers, who often are leaders of chants, permit weaker players to define top dogs as "meanies" and to hold on to pleasure without excelling at the game. These four features of a team—the range of skill, the posture of talent, the presence of emotional workers, and the resilience of underdogs—can reinforce each other or counteract each other on any given team. They carry weight in differing degrees at different moments in the season. It is impossible to see them clearly operating simultaneously at any given moment. But the way these features play out over the course of a season matters centrally to boys' experience.

Capturing the patterns that result from these dimensions of teams as they unfold over the course of the season is no easy matter. The internal dynamics are only part of the story. There is also the weight of the larger forces identified in earlier chapters, the class and race dynamics of parents, the masculinity styles of coaches, and the autonomous contributions of boys as they conform to, resist, and challenge the expectations of adults. Any given moment in a game is a combination of countless influences. Even if it were possible to recount every interaction that occurred among the boys in just one game, we would not see all the multiple influences that contribute over time to the "feel" of a team. Some elements surface only occasionally, such as a coach's tantrum or the meltdown of a strategic player. That meltdown might only happen once, but it leaves its imprint on the boys' collective memory and can invisibly condition behavior in many subsequent games. Hence selecting one game to represent these dynamics, even selecting several real games, proves to be an unsatisfactory solution. The more common sociological approach to this dilemma, selecting numerous decontextualized moments from many different encounters to illustrate each feature, also does not work. That is because it is not possible to see the workings of these features outside the logic of a specific game, since the structure of a game, its rules and frame of innings, operates as the plot behind most encounters in this space. The plot line of the game is the ubiquitous point of reference, even for those who tune in only occasionally. The goal then must be to see how the various dimensions touch down over time in concrete baseball moments. My solution to this conundrum is to develop a series of exemplary games that combine strategic elements from real games recorded in field notes in condensed form.

In order to show how these processes unfold in practice, I will rely on "typifications" of games drawn from field notes taken from two teams that differ in terms of these features. By typification I mean a composite of actual plays, events, and conversations that occurred over time but are here truncated into one or two vignettes, in this case games, in order to represent the broader patterns efficiently. These are not fictions. They represent actual occurrences, but they are condensed to provide a sharper image. These constructed practices, or typifications, enable us to see the juncture or gap between what sociologists call "structures of constraint" and human agency. How boys draw upon their own resources, the contours of the game, and the mix of temperaments of their teammates, as they conform to and resist adult expectations, is often unpredictable and mysterious.[3] The goal here is, if nothing else, to capture the feel of these dense two-hour rituals around which all the actors of this little neighborhood baseball world focus their attention. We'll see the above themes only as they touch down in fleeting encounters in several condensed games drawn from two teams.

Both of the selected teams, the Marlins and the Blue Jays, are from the seven-to-nine division, but they occupy different places in the hierarchy of wins and losses. The Marlins ended up in the middle of the pile and the Blue Jays next to the bottom. Although the styles of their coaches were not radically different—both were knowledgeable coaches with fairly laid-back coaching styles and soft styles of masculinity—the feel of each team was very different. For one thing, on the Marlins there was less of a gap in ability between the best and the weakest players than there was on the Blue Jays. The posture of the talented players on the Marlins toward the weaker players was also more neutral, even benevolent, than on the Blue Jays. The weaker Marlins players were also more resilient and engaged than were their counterparts on the Blue Jays. The more benign feel of the Marlins was further underscored by two very affirming players who led chants, consoled their teammates, and wove playful, quirky tones into Marlins games. The Blue Jays were troubled by insecure talent, more vulnerable and withdrawn weak players, and the presence of almost no one doing sustained emotional work to build group spirit. We will see these dynamics unfold in two "truncated" games of the Marlins followed by two games from the Blue Jays.

The Marlins began the season with two A-ranked players, four C-ranked players, and six unranked boys coming up from T-ball. The two "A" players were playing their last year in the division. Although coached by Dan, an old-timer Fairmounter, the team was heavy with newcomer boys. Only three Marlins players had parents who had grown up in the area, two of whom were Puerto Rican. Most of the other boys who lived in Fairmount had newcomer professional parents. While the team was ethnically diverse, with one black and four Hispanic players, it was dominated by boys with professional parents, both black and white.

The Marlins

May, Mid-Season. Marlins versus Padres: Friday, 5:30 P.M.

It's cool, maybe seventy degrees, without the humidity of the past few days. A great night for baseball. The two coaches, Dan and Ben, have arrived early. The Padres' coach, Ben, with his usual zeal, sets out the Padres' equipment in the dugout: batting helmets face down on the ground, catcher's equipment—mask and helmet, chest protector and shin guards—on the bench, bats hanging neatly from the chain-link fence like levers in a row of slot machines. He wears khaki shorts, a plain blue T-shirt, and his customary maroon-colored hat with the Fairmount Sports logo on the front. Most coaches wear a hat with their team name, but as an insider, Ben owns one of the cloth Fairmount hats, with an elastic band, and he wears it proudly. As his boys arrive in their black and tan uniforms, he greets each one with a slap on the back or an emphatic hand-shake. "Hey, buddy," he says, "you ready to play some ball tonight?" Some shake their heads, smiling. Others say things like, "Coach Ben, can I play second base tonight?" Ben just laughs. "Are we home team?" asks another. In fact, the Padres are home team tonight. By convention, home team takes the dugout with their backs to the trees that block the view of the Art Museum, while the visiting team has their backs to Benjamin Franklin Boulevard, now swarming with Friday evening rush-hour traffic.

In contrast to Ben, Dan, the Marlins coach, has left his two equipment bags unopened, leaning against the dugout fence. Since he is visiting manager tonight, he doesn't have to worry about setting up the pitching machine or installing the bases. He chats with Kate, his trusty assistant coach, laughing occasionally. They are good buddies. As his boys arrive, he is low-key, even distracted. "Grab a ball," he says as they arrive, "and warm up." Some follow his instructions and go to the bottom of the short incline behind the bench and throw to each other. Others, notably Julio, ignore him. Julio, a small-boned Puerto Rican boy with beautiful eyes, is the star of the team. Once his mom fully appreciates that I'm not another parent in this division who might feel competitive, she shares with me her pride about his talent. "One of the other coaches told me last week that Julio is the best player in the whole seven-to-nine league!" Julio now enters the dugout and, despite the request to warm up, spends ten minutes carefully opening his baseball bag, putting on his cleats, inspecting his batting gloves, and making other inscrutable but seemingly serious preparations. He is, after all, the star. Dan pretends not to notice but is, I suppose, both bemused and annoyed. "I guess some of us don't need warm-ups," he says, giving Kate a conspiratorial grin. Some battles aren't worth fighting, and this is one of them.

Followed by three boys carrying bases and inserts, Ben walks down from the clubhouse pushing the pitching machine like a wheelbarrow. When the machine is in place on the mound, the large rubber wheel on which it now rolls spins at the receiving end of a small channel, through which the ball is inserted, and which grabs it and shoots it towards the plate at about forty miles per hour—slow enough to hit, but fast enough to travel in a relatively straight line from point to point. Ben brushes away the dirt from a spot behind the mound until he finds the buried electrical outlet, lifts the cover, and plugs the pitching machine in. Now comes the difficult and seemingly endless struggle to set the speed correctly and to adjust the placing of the tripod footing and the angle of the pitching armature so that the ball crosses the plate at a height more or less hittable for a group of boys who range from under four feet to over five feet tall. Not an easy task. Some of the very experienced coaches are skilled at making slight adjustments to the machine during the game in order to serve up consistently hittable pitches to their boys. Bad luck with the pitching machine can dampen even a good offense.

Meanwhile, the boys scoop out dirt from the square receptacles at each of the bases, insert the pads, and square the rubber bases on top. Earlier, one of the Fairmounters had dragged a screen over the infield dirt with a four-wheeler, so everything looks sharp: brown dirt, white bases, green grass, blue sky. This is why some arrive early. It always takes a few minutes to drink in the beauty of these evenings before the roar of the game begins.

Just at 6:00, Steve strides down from the clubhouse with a mask in one hand and an umpire's counter in the other. Time to play ball. Because it's still early in the season, he gives a short instructional speech to the boys in each clubhouse. Some of the seven-to-nine rules are a bit arcane.

"Yo, guys, listen up. First, no throwin' the equipment. You do it, and I'm taking you outta the game. Next, no leavin' the base before the ball is pitched, you understand? First time it happens, it's a warning, second time you're out. Everybody got it? Also, infielders, to call time you need to raise the ball above your head and yell loud enough for me to hear, okay? Also, the play ain't dead until the runners've stopped, you know what I mean? And third, remember, on the bases, it's slide or surrender. You got that?"

Silence. Blank stares.

Kate quickly interprets. "You know what he means, right, guys? He means you have to slide or stop, you can't run the guy over."

"All right, have a good game, fellas."

With my note pad, sunglasses, and water bottle in hand, I take my place behind the Marlins' dugout to watch the game. On the other side of the backstop, behind the home team's dugout, there are two bleachers. Usually team parents sit together on one or the other of the bleachers. I see a small group of Marlins' parents on the far bleachers. But I'm not ready to sit down yet. I like being closer to the game, especially at the beginning. With me, behind the bench, is one boy's teenaged sister. She sweetly leans over the short fence behind the bench, and playfully adjusts her little brother's hat. He doesn't even look up. Dan, wearing blue jeans, T-shirt, and his red and black Marlins hat, trots out to the mound to work the pitching machine. Kate gets the lineups squared away and is ready to keep score.

"Batter up."

Aaron, batting lead-off, squares into the batter's box. Each hitter gets a maximum of five pitches from the machine. On the fifth pitch, if you don't hit it, you're out. Another arcane rule of the seven-to-nine league, but it's necessary to speed up the game. He takes the first pitch, as he always likes to do. On the bench, Jeff, Ralph, and Con are already distracted from the game. Jeff spits a piece of red candy on the dusty ground. "See how far it goes," he says proudly, "See that!" It's a red Lifesaver. Aaron hits a hard line drive foul over the third base on the second pitch. "All right now, Aaron, straighten it out," Dan says, encouraging him. He holds up the ball for the third pitch, inserts it into the machine, and Aaron hits a disappointingly weak ground ball to the right side. It should be an easy out. The second baseman comes up with it cleanly but then gives a nervous low toss and, as so often happens in the seven-to-nine league, the ball squirts under the first baseman's glove. I hear some of the parent's exclaiming, "Oh, no." They must be Braves' parents. I also hear Ralph ask Jeff, almost at the same time, "What flavor was it?" All three are staring at the dust-covered Lifesaver, absolutely unaware of the action on the field. "It was cherry," Jeff says. "Cool." Aaron takes his place at first, left foot planted on the bag and right foot spread toward second base, ready to run. I think, since I've been studying how to keep score, that Kate will have marked E–4 into her scorebook.

Roland, the second most talented player on the Marlins, is a peppy, confident little guy. This is his fourth year in the seven-to-nine division. Roland always seems happy during the game, like he's really having fun. Unlike the less experienced players, he displays very little anxiety when the spotlight is on him. He comes up to bat now and blasts a hit to left field, a high arc, way beyond anyone's reach. As soon as the ball is hit, Roland's father, standing next to me and engaged in a conversation, suddenly titters, almost as if someone had tickled him under the arms. As Roland runs full speed around the bases, he titters more. Roland enters the dugout, beaming, and slaps his teammates' hands. His father sees him, and the titters turn into full laughter, as if there were some amazing joke that had just unfolded. Roland asks him, "Dad, did that hit the sidewalk?" It wasn't really even close, but his Dad answers, "Almost!" The uncontrollable laugher, an unusual expression of parental pride, continues to ring in the air.

Julio watches the two of them neutrally. In contrast to Roland, Julio doesn't easily share his emotions with the other boys and rarely expresses pleasure at his own success, which makes it hard for the other boys to cheer him enthusiastically. He doesn't attack or openly criticize any of the weaker players, but he avoids much contact with them. He is the alpha male, alone in front of the pack. On his first pitch, he strokes a grounder into left, and challenges the defense for an easy double. Two batters later, he scores on a ground out to second, enters the dugout without expression, sits down on his throne at the far end of the bench without speaking to anyone, slowly removing his batting gloves and placing them into his bag.

Later in the inning, with four runs in and two outs, and the bottom four batters in the lineup coming up, Kate urges the boys to cheer for their teammates. "Let's hear it, guys. Talk it up, Marlins!" They don't really need much of a reminder. While most of the boys add their voice at some point to the ritual chants, a couple distinguish themselves as the emotional cheerleaders of the team. The Marlins are blessed with two brothers, Alvaro and Diego, children of immigrants, who developed this specialty early in the season. Alvaro now arches backward and then leans in slightly as he screams out the first cue and paces himself so that the others can easily join in: "Single, single, just a little single. s-I-N-G-L-E, single, single, single. Double, double, just a little double. D-O-U-B-L-E, double, double, double. Triple, triple, just a little triple. . . . " When this ends, Alvaro leads them into the next chant: "Extra, extra, read all about it. Diego's gonna' hit it, no doubt about it." Julio, wrapped in an invisible bubble, looks solemnly towards an abstract point on the field, the only boy not participating in the fun and exuberance. Diego hits a weak grounder toward first and is tagged on the basepath by the incoming first baseman for the last out; Julio and the rest of the boys then grab their gloves and head for the field. The bottom of the first is fairly uneventful: even with the top of their lineup, the Padres only score one run on two hits. Two of their three outs are on strikes. They are, in fact, the weakest team in the division, so it looks like it'll be an easy day for the Marlins.

Ralph, a freckle-faced boy with bright red hair and one of the weaker players on the team, leads off the top of the second. In the seven-to-nine league, all the players on the team bat, so innings can be either very long or very short depending on who is batting. Surprisingly, Ralph hits a roller to second, but the play is made easily, and he's out by five steps at first. He runs back to the dugout with a victorious look on his face and sits down next to Joey, one of the strike-out victims in the first inning. "You always say Ralph doesn't hit. Oh, Ralph doesn't hit. So what do you say now?" he says, beaming. Joey glances at him briefly and then looks away without commenting, disgusted, as if even the slimmest response would have compromised his integrity. "Didn't I get a hit, Kate?" Kate saunters over and, accepting his utopian interpretation of the word "hit," pats him on the head and says, "You sure did, sure you did. You hit it all the way to second." "SEE!" Ralph says triumphantly, looking back at Joey, who pretends not to hear him, his gaze fixed forward. But, as is often the case on the Marlins, the unfriendliness of the moment passes quickly. Several minutes later, I watch Ralph demonstrate to a smiling Joey how to execute an elaborate "cool handshake."

Alvaro, who rarely hits, even during practices, is after Ralph. With his thick eyelashes and dimples, he is a boy of breathtaking beauty and is still unaware of it. Alvaro and his brother, Diego, recent immigrants from Chile, have never played baseball before this season, putting them considerably behind many of the boys in experience and skill. Both have exceptionally long hair. Alvaro wears his in a thick ponytail that reaches the middle of his back. From time to time, some of the other boys wonder out loud about their gender. Especially about Alvaro, whose name, as well as his hair, confuses their expectations. Seemingly without malice, they say things like: "Are you a girl? Why do you have your hair like that?" His professional mother takes it all in stride. She says, "He wants long hair. So he'll just have to deal with it if that's what he wants." Flat-footed, Alvaro chops at the first pitch for strike one. Amazingly, he gets a piece of the ball on the second pitch, fouling it into the backstop. Dan calmly encourages him. "You got a little piece of it, pal, now see if you can get this one in play." Alvaro smiles, as if relieved to have made a little progress, but then swings way over the third pitch for strike three. He comes into the dugout with a neutral expression on his face, removes the batting helmet, and sits down. One sharp difference between this age group and the older boys in the ten-to-twelve and thirteen-to-fifteen leagues is that there isn't as much humiliation associated with a strikeout, at least for the less skilled boys. The older boys have live pitching, and so a strikeout amounts to a batter losing his duel with the pitcher, and thus is met with cheers and groans from both sides. The batter, depending on his age and on the circumstances, will often respond with disgust, dismay, anger, and sometimes tears. But here, Alvaro's strikeout is met with silence from both teams, and Alvaro seems unfazed.

Con, a lefty, is up after Alvaro. He's only seven, just up from T-Ball, and he looks frozen at the plate. He often swings after the pitch has crossed the plate, making his at-bat look like an exercise in slow-motion stimulus-response. He waves at the first three pitches, but then continues to stand at the plate with his bat cocked over his left shoulder, waiting. Gently, Dan reminds him: "That's it, Con. You only get three swings." Bewildered, he returns to the dugout and complains: "But I thought I had *two* swings left!" "Geez," Ira says emphatically, quickly rising in solidarity in the face of this injustice. Ira often pays even less attention to the game than Con. As the boys are taking the field for the bottom of the second, Dan comments wryly to Kate, "It looks like we might have a pitchers' duel today." "Yep, could be," Kate says, smiling.

During the bottom of the second, I decide to go over to the bleachers, sit down for a while, and hang out with the parents. After seeing so many early season practices, with most players present without their parents, it is always surprising to see the parents appear and form themselves into groups. The social and ethnic differences between them are more salient than among the boys. The boys, in comparison, flow in and out of each other's conversations more effortlessly, focused on the here and now. When I see the parents, I immediately wonder about how the boys will be in ten years, how they will relate to each other then.

There are two sets of bleachers behind the home dugout, each normally occupied by the parents of one team. On the Padres' bleachers, six black parents sit clustered on the top two rows, five women and one man. The women are talking and laughing, while the man seems to be correcting a typewritten paper with a red pen. There are several pairs, or clusters, of white parents, and two individual parents who sit alone.

The Marlins' bleacher is dominated by Puerto Rican parents, mostly Julio's relatives. I sit down with them, as I often do, because I enjoy their company and the opportunity to speak Spanish. Julio's mom wears large gold earrings and a tight ponytail and attends every game. She almost always comes with her sister, Julio's aunt, who wears a thick braid that hangs to her waist. Also, of course, there is Carlos, Julio's dad. They speak Caribbean Spanish at lightning speed, talking mostly about the plays as they happen. Carlos is knowledgeable and passionate about the game, having played first base on a semi-pro team in Puerto Rico. They are joined by four other Puerto Rican parents, who stand behind them talking, purportedly on their way to the bigger boys' field. Julio's mom and dad participate in the conversation, while also monitoring the game closely. Carlos is worried about how far off the line Jeff is playing at third. "*Está fuera de tercera de nuevo*," he mumbles to Carmen.

One Fairmounter, a white woman, is seated slightly apart from us, talking to two other white women who are seated below her. When she finishes her conversation with them, she turns to the Hispanic group and says jovially, "Hey, they're gonna say I'm prejudiced against Puerto Ricans," then slides over on the bench closer to the group. Julio's mom and aunt smile at her, but the conversation continues in Spanish. The bleachers are a hybrid, contradictory place, a place of marked ethnic and racial clustering, but at the same time a close, sometimes intimate place of contact and exchange.[4] Above all, these are the Marlins' bleachers, and we are cheering together.

On the very bottom bench, Aaron's mother, a professional woman who lives in an affluent Center City area, sits alone, holding on to the leash of her enormous black dog—a Bouvier, I am told. She rarely follows the game, beyond monitoring her son's at-bats. At one point, she walks towards the Padres bleachers to let her dog greet a reddish retriever led by a passing woman. "Is he friendly?" The dogs pull the two owners together right in front of the Padres' parents. They stand there letting the dogs sniff each other and chatting about their dispositions. Willa, a no-nonsense, heavyset woman, who speaks from the side of her mouth in a wonderful Mae West style, and follows the game closely, is unable to see the game. Annoyed, she says loudly, "Excuse me, ladies." Unaware of their transgression, they continue their conversation until the Bouvier mounts the retriever who, deeply offended, snaps back, barking. Aaron's mother bends down and wags her finger at her dog saying, "You are being so fresh." She looks up at the Padres' parents on the bleachers for their amused approval, but Willa gives her a cold stare, and then dramatically stretches to one side to see the game. Finding no audience, Aaron's mom retreats to her original position on the Marlins' bleachers. She regularly scans the crowd for a conversational buddy who might take her away from the monotony of the game. A baseball fan she is not. Ten minutes later I spy her sitting on the grass beyond the bleachers on a neatly arranged blanket with the dog, her husband, and a middle-class black mother wearing a stylish straw hat. For most of the remainder of the game they are engaged deeply in conversation. Occasional conversational fragments float over: I hear one of them say, emphatically, "Oh, he is THE most gifted teacher I have ever known in my life."

I tune into the sound of the Braves' assistant coach, Mario, a Hispanic man with a booming voice. He is at the pitching machine, encouraging his batters as he always does with rapid-fire chatter. Miraculously, the Padres have managed to score two runs with the middle and bottom of their lineup, with a combination of muddled defensive plays and several slow rollers in the infield that nobody could field. There are two outs with runners at first and second. Improbably, the score is 4–3 Marlins, and Mario, smelling an upset, is pumped: "Okay, Rashaan. Who's the man, who's the man? We need a hit, just a little contact, relax now and watch the ball, pal. Just a little contact. Level swing. Hands together. Come on, buddy. You can do it." Rashaan almost never makes contact. He swings late at the first pitch, and the force of the swing tilts the loose-fitting helmet over his eyes. "Nice swing, pal. All right now. You're ready. You can do it. Let's go now. You're set, buddy." Rashaan pushes the helmet up off of his eyes and, predictably, swings late at the second pitch. Strike two. "Now listen to me, Rashaan. You gotta get this one, pal. Look at the pitch all the way. Give it a whack now. We need ya, buddy. Okay, here we go." Strike three. What a contrast Mario is to Ben, the head coach, and to the other assistant coach, a skinny Jethro Tull type with scraggly, long, blondish hair, who wears funky canvas tennis shoes and rarely speaks to the boys. The nonstop, one-man chorus from Mario means that the Padres never develop a specialized cheerleader, like Alvaro on the Marlins. Who could compete with Mario?

Top of the third. Marlins 4, Padres 3. Tight game. Carlos, Julio's father, decides to leave the bleachers and position himself behind the dugout, his preferred spot for watching the game, especially when the Marlins are batting. I go with him. Since he does solitary work as a janitor and lives in a Spanish-speaking household, his English is thickly accented and uneven. His natural gregariousness and passion for baseball often overwhelm his linguistic limitations, both when he is speaking to the boys and when he is speaking to other parents. He leans over the fence and whispers something to Jackson, an upper-middle-class black boy, who is one of the youngest of the Marlins players. I developed a soft spot for Jackson early in the season, owing to his exuberance and contagious smile. There is something simultaneously boyish and manlike about him. Now Jackson looks up at Carlos, trying but not understanding his message. "When you get the bat, you have to look the ball all da way and swing like this," Carlos repeats, bringing his hands together and swinging an invisible bat through the air. Jackson smiles, as if he gets the point (does he?), and graciously reassures him: "OK, I'll try." Julio, Carlos's son, on the far end of the bench, has been watching their interaction closely.

Jackson finishes putting on his batting gloves and helmet, grabs a bat, and heads for the plate. He's the last batter in the lineup. As usual, he strikes out, and he returns to the bench dejected. Jackson wants badly to be a stronger player. Carlos pats him on the shoulder and says, tenderly, "That's okay, *muchacho*. You'll hit it next time." Diego, the Chilean boy, also comes over to Jackson and gently pats his head, saying, "Nice try." Jackson tolerates this but never looks up at him. Diego regularly offers this kind of direct emotional support to the players who need it. He has a gift. Along with his brother Alvaro, he has carved out for himself an unusual and significant niche on the team, that of nurturer. There are very few boys who have the internal resources to do this. Yet the role of nurturer, if someone can perform it, becomes especially important on a team such as the Marlins with a competitive alpha male leader (Julio) who sets a tone in which success and dominance are the most important sources of prestige and recognition. Through their cheers, and their compassion, Diego and Alvaro supply something vital to the team. As community builders, they contribute tremendously to the overall positive feel of the Marlins' bench. In baseball, which is such a psychological game, teams whose only language is that of harsh, hierarchical masculinity often implode. Over the years, I've seen a number of good teams choke in the playoffs due to excessive bickering and bad feelings on the bench.

One down, top of the lineup. Aaron and Roland both get on base, setting up Julio for the big hit. He struts to the plate, but the boys remain quiet. Kate turns back to them and says, "Okay guys, let's hear it. Let's hear it!" One of the boys cautions her, "He doesn't like it, Kate." She considers this. "Oh, he doesn't? Okay then. Never mind." The boys are often more attuned to the unique emotional needs of star players than are the coaches. This is both because other boys monitor more closely what their team leaders want but also because the "top dogs" feel more entitled to assert their preferences. With the bench quiet, on the second pitch Julio hammers a line drive to left. The ball skips past the left fielder and with his speed, Julio scores easily. Home run, three RBIs. Aaron and Roland are all smiles, giving high fives as they re-enter to the dugout. Julio walks in behind them, helmet already in hand, a solemn expression on his face. When the other players move toward him to celebrate, he looks almost irked and slides past them to tend to business: removing the batting gloves, drinking some Gatorade, and waiting for the next responsibility. The boys disband quickly and head back to their seats, except for Aaron who, in his joy, presses further. He wants to celebrate and congratulate. He goes over and puts his hand out for five, but Julio wants no part of it and stares at him blankly. Aaron shrugs and timidly moves away. But once he sits down his face turns angry. Why does Julio have to assert his dominance so aggressively, just at the moment that he's hit a home run? He has nothing to defend. His position as the star of the team is indisputable. So, why does he work so hard at building, monitoring, and reinforcing a hierarchy in which he sees his teammates as rivals? His indifference, his occasional cruelties, and his isolation are bound together with the joy he gets from playing well and from his sense of identity and self-worth on the team.

Still only one out, and the Marlins have now opened up a 7–3 lead. Vic, who plays second base, is up. He's a decent hitter, and a very competitive player who straddles the border between the three top dogs (Aaron, Roland, and Julio) and the middle of the pack. He swings extremely hard at the first pitch, perhaps imagining a home run to follow Julio's, and hits a high pop-up. Ranging back several steps, and waiting patiently, the Braves' shortstop pulls it in easily, perhaps the only player on the field that could have made the play. Two outs. Little Pete is the next batter. I watch him take the first pitch and then, suddenly, I see Kate walking across the dugout saying, "Vic. Vic. Hey, hey." Vic is slumped over on the far end of the bench, sobbing uncontrollably. "Vic, hey, hey, sometimes they CATCH 'em. Sometimes they just catch them. It's no biggie." She pats him on the shoulder, but he is inconsolable and continues to weep, with his face in his hands. His mother walks over from the bleachers and is talking to him as well. Kate continues to pat him, though she turns her attention to Pete who is set for his fifth and final pitch. Something inside Vic has snapped, and he cries even harder. Probably the sheer shame of the crying has pushed him even further. Miraculously, Pete hits a roller to the right side that gets past the second baseman for a weak single. Vic continues to shake with tears, huddled over. The other boys say nothing, and pretend not to notice. Ironically, this may be a kind of masculine caretaking. By ignoring him, they minimize his shame. Since there's no crying in baseball, to console him or to recognize his pain would only make it worse. Diego strikes out for the third out, and Kate gives Vic a final pat and says, "Okay, Vic. We need you out there at second. Okay? You'll get 'em next time." Vic walks out to his position, head slumped on his chest.

It's the bottom of the third. The Marlins get an easy first out, but the second batter hits a fly ball that rolls between outfielders in left center field. An almost certain home run in this league. But, then again, nothing is certain with this age group. Julio runs quickly into the outfield, almost falls down catching an awkward cut-off throw, recovers, whirls around, and throws a high looping toss towards the plate. Roland has come in from first base to get the throw, which lands, amazingly, in his glove (the "catchers" in seven-to-nine normally can't catch), just in time for him to tag the runner barreling into home plate. Simultaneously, I can hear wild cheers from the Marlins' bleachers, and audible groans from the Braves' parents. Dan and Kate and the boys in the field are all cheering as well. It was a great hit, the Padres had sorely needed this run, and yet it just goes in the book as another out. I admire Ben's composure as he stuffs his disappointment, and greets his runner with affirmation. "TREMENDOUS HIT, Tyrone. UNBELIEVABLE! Great hit." Where does he get these resources? I wonder.

The fourth inning opens with high drama. In his at-bat, Diego swings hard at the first pitch and catches the ball on his fists. Amazingly, the ball rolls into right, and he runs out a double. But then he sits down on the base, holding his hand and grimacing. He sees blood all over his fingers, and lets out several blood curdling screams. Within seconds several men, including Dan, Carlos—who has just taken over as first base coach—and Diego's father are out there to tend to him. Someone else runs up to the clubhouse for ice. It looks bad, and his father carries him off the field. As he rushes off, he yells back to Carlos, "*Carlos, cuida a Alvaro y dile a su mamá que fuimos a la sala de emergencia con Diego*" ("Take care of Alvaro. Tell his mom that we've gone to the emergency room.") They drive away with Diego crying in agony, as he holds the ice pack on his fingers. The rest of the inning is uneventful, both teams coming up with goose eggs.

Finally, in the top of the fifth, the Marlins break the game wide open with seven runs. Dan tells the base coaches to slow the runners up and not to take any extra bases. Roland, however, is feeling cocky and tries to run to third from first base on a grounder to the right side. It ends up being a 4–3–5 double play to end the inning, with the first baseman easily throwing Roland out at third. Kate cheers for the Brave's defense.

In the sixth, the Marlins score another two runs, making it 16–4. Julio opens the inning with a triple but stretches it into a home run despite the stop sign from the third base coach. Both Dan and Kate are annoyed by the aggressive base-running of their top dogs, but they don't say much about it to the boys. Is it because, at this age, as the boys are learning and rehearsing their masculinity, no one really expects them to be able to forgo their aggressiveness for the sake of community? The next batter is Vic, who hits a shot to center but is thrown out on third, trying, like Roland and Julio before him, to take advantage of the comfortable lead by engaging in hyperaggressive base running. Julio, having just pulled off some successful macho base running, is interested in how Vic will take this. Also, because Vic had sobbed uncontrollably over a humiliation earlier in the game, Julio can't resist the urge to scrutinize him. Vic sits down, and Julio stands and walks around in front of him to look at his face, almost stalking him for a sign of tears. Satisfied that Vic is taking it neutrally, Julio returns to his seat on the bench without comment. In the bottom of the inning, Dan pulls the entire outfield into infield positions, and sends the infielders out. Even Alvaro, who is afraid of the ball, gets to play second. Despite the easy defense, the Padres only manage one run, and the game ends 16–5, Marlins win.

Just as the game ends, the Padres' coach gathers his boys into the dugout and kneels down as he talks to them. "Look at me. Look at me," he urges as they gradually quiet down. "Look at my eyes," he says, pointing to his face. "Look at my eyes. Guys, you should hold your chests up." He dramatizes holding his chest up and out. "Hold your chest up. You played great out there today. We had a fantastic game. So you go over there and shake hands with the Marlins and know that you done great." They move toward the lineup, and consistent with their upbeat approach to most games, the Padres' boys walk through the line slapping hands, not proudly, but with no one sobbing or being bitter-faced either. As far as I can tell almost every one of them says "good game" as they slap. This is unusual, especially for a losing team. The Marlins, as victors, collectively beam as they make contact. The opposing sets of coaches are even friendlier to each other, several back pats. The hardiness of the hand slapping is moving down the line and the sunset is warm and reassuring.

Dan's speech to his boys happens after the lineup, so I can hear as well. His speeches are always minimal. He gets the Marlins to settle down on the bench. One of the players asks him about the final score. Despite their constant obsessing among themselves during the game, they aren't allowed to know the score. "It was 16 to 5," Dan answers. The boys all exclaim in awe, "AHHHHH!" "And you know why?" Dan asks. "Because you guys played a great game. You got hits. You fielded. And you got hits! That's all I want. Okay. Tomorrow is picture day. Be here at 2:00. Now, after hot dogs and sodas, because it's Alvaro's birthday, his parents are treating you to birthday cake over on the picnic tables." The boys all cheer even more, and Alvaro flashes his dimples. "And another thing, guys. You have got to stop these one run leads. I'm gonna have a heart attack." The parents smile, but most of the boys have already scrambled away to the concession stand.

Most of the parents also immediately leave the dugout area to escape to the sun. Jackson's dad, a lawyer, still standing behind the dugout fence, reaches over for Jackson's glove, expecting his son to run out with the other boys. "Here, I'll take your glove." Jackson, one of the youngest players on the team, says in a slightly whiny way, "Noooo." "Well," his father asks, "aren't you going to get a hot dog?" "Yeah," Jackson replies. "Well, I'll hold it for you," his father repeats. Jackson stares at him and holds onto the glove, then says, "No, I don't think so." The father looks baffled, but allows him to have his way, saying, "Well, okay." Jackson takes off to get his soda and hot dog, waving his glove in the air. Having only just come up from T-ball and being the youngest boy on the team, he is still not casual about the glory of it all and needs his prop (as if the uniform weren't enough). Jackson's passion takes me back to the first season my son played at Fairmount. I once asked him what part of the game he liked the most, and he answered, "When we all walk out onto the field from the dugout with our uniforms on, like heroes."

As Dan finishes, Jorge's father immediately leans over the dugout fence to whisper to his son, who is looking for his glove, asking eagerly, "You wanna go now?" Jorge answers, "Okay." And his father continues, "Cuz we might . . . " then whispers something. Jorge hesitates but again answers, "Okay. I'll go." His father motions for him to jump over the fence, which would bypass any further group contact. They seem to be stealing away. A strong statement. They are here for the game and want nothing to do with these purely social moments.

May, Mid-Season. Marlins versus Angels: Saturday 1:00 P.M.

This is the first fully sunny weekend day we have had this season, and it's hot. It's been in the nineties most of the day. It's fine in the shade but smoldering in the sun, where the games and the dugouts are. The game is delayed about thirty minutes by another game that is running over. The commissioner of the division comes up and begins chatting with one of the Marlins' assistant coaches. Aaron's mother wanders up and asks the commissioner if the game will be delayed long enough for her to run over to Fresh Fields, the new, highbrow, organic grocery store in the neighborhood, and get some salad and sushi before the game. "Take your time," he responds neutrally. As they watch her walk off, Tommy asks good-humouredly, "Now what she's got against our pork rolls? Ha. Ha."

After Kate announces the lineup, the boys standing or sitting out of order move toward their proper positions. Jackson is batting last today, instead of Jorge. Vic, who bats fourth, leans forward to examine the order of the boys on the lower bench and then calls out, "Hey! Jorge's not the last batter. Movin' up in the world!" Why does Vic care? Julio and Roland, both better players than Vic, ignore the entire exchange. Jorge talks to Jackson, happy in his new spot. Kate turns to Diego and says, "And you can sit wherever you want." I ask, "Is that because he's a hero?" "That's right. Heroes sit where they want." Diego has a bandage and cast on his left hand, having broken it at bat in the earlier game. Despite not being able to play, as usual he's in full uniform. During the game, he wanders the dugout, cheering, laughing and talking with the boys. He listens to a different drummer anyway, almost never paying proper homage to the rigidities of the hierarchy.

Jorge misses a lot of games. Today he's here, and Dan tells him he's going to play catcher. He looks up through his thick glasses at his father, thrilled. His father, a Puerto Rican truck driver, desperately wants Jorge to be a star player, something Jorge will never become. But Jorge understands the expectation and wants to please him. He stands by the bench, beaming with delight, looking very much like a model being dressed by her assistants, as Kate and Dan hook on his knee pads, thread his arms into the chest protector, and fit the helmet and mask over his head. Dan hands him a catcher's glove, and he waddles into the backstop. There is no stealing in seven-to-nine, and normally on plays to the plate, the first baseman comes in to get the throw. So, Jorge's job will be to catch the pitch if he can and throw it back to Dan on the mound. Still, with all the equipment, it must feel pretty special.

Finally, the earlier game ends. The Marlins are home team today, so they quickly take the field. Today will be tough, because the Angels are the top team in their division. However, in the top of the first, amazingly, the Angels fail to score. The coach is having all sorts of problems with the pitching machine, between pitches trying desperately to alternately adjust the armature, the tripod, and the speed dial, in order to get the pitches over the plate. He isn't very successful, and two of the three outs are on strikeouts, which almost never happens to the top of a lineup, even for the weakest team in the league.

Dan tries, but doesn't do much better with the machine. It seems to be one of those days. Aaron leads off with a ground out to second, trying to make contact with a pitch above his head and outside. Following him, Roland takes two bad pitches, swings through two others, and strikes out on a terrible fifth pitch. Like the rest of the boys, I am curious about how he will respond to this. He comes into the dugout with a sheepish expression on his face but doesn't seem to be totally devastated. At first, there is utter silence. Then commiserating, Aaron says, "Hey, that's not the real Roland. You get a hit every time." Inspired by the idea of an imposter in Roland's body, Ralph rises from the other end of the bench, walks over to Roland, looks at him, and says jokingly, "Hey, you're not the REAL Roland. You're not the real Roland. You're an alien from outer space." He repeats this several times, each time a little louder, until Roland finally jumps up and, somewhere between play and punishment, grabs his cheeks and squeezes them. Ralph sits down, still rubbing himself and not quite smiling any longer. Pecking order reestablished. In any game, there are dozens of incidents like this between the boys, incidents in which the hierarchy is negotiated, challenged, and enforced. The main ingredients of the interpersonal dynamics negotiated are age, skill level, confidence, and aggressiveness. The "winners" depend on traditional sources of male power: individual success, independence, domination, exclusion, and violence.

Julio saves the inning and puts the Marlins ahead with a home run. The throw beats him to the plate, but scoots into the backstop, so Julio slides in safely. He stands up at the same time as the catcher, now with the ball in his glove, thrusts out his chin at him, and then turns away slowly in a cool in-your-face, put-down move. An older boy I know from another team, standing next to me behind the dugout, mumbles, "AND aren't I a little show-off?" Several of the top players approach him as he comes into the dugout to give him five. He touches their hands passively, never smiling. When he arrives at his spot on the bench and sees his cherry drink sitting upside down on the ground, he stamps his feet and shouts "WHY do you guys always mess up my stuff?" Anger comes so easily to him. It's often the only connection he has with the other boys. He takes his drink and finds that some remains. After several sips, he gives a satisfied look. But the satisfaction comes from his solitary drinking pleasure and perhaps the memory of the play. He doesn't directly take in anyone's affirmation, and his pleasure doesn't coincide with the group's expression of it.

As we watch Vic come to the plate, Julio looks over his shoulder at me and notices that I am writing in my notebook. In contrast to his coolness toward the boys, Julio is always friendly and warm when he speaks to me. I wonder if it is because he sees me as an insider to the Spanish-speaking world of his parents. He moves over, close to me, and asks timidly, "Are you keeping score?"

"No, writing a story about the games."

"About me?"

"Well, about everybody, but you too. But don't worry, I won't say your name or anything."

Silence.

"But then you probably want me to use your name, right?"

"Yeah."

"I'm following the Marlins and some other teams."

"Which ones?"

"The Blue Jays, but also the D'backs and the Bisons in the ten-to-twelves."

"Why did you pick us?"

"Well, I knew Dan already; my son used to play for him."

Julio ponders this for a moment, and then inquires, "Which dugout you gonna stand behind when we play the Blue Jays?"

"Wow, that will be hard. I hate it when you guys play them. I guess I should stand right behind the batter's box, don't you think?"

[Smiling] "Yeah."

"But maybe I'll just walk back and forth between both dugouts."

"Okay. But who do you *want* to win?" Not waiting for an answer, he adds, "We beat them before."

"Yeah, that's right." I look away, to steer us away from this theme.

Vic gets on base, but Pete grounds out to first to end the inning. He swings so late, and has so little power, that he is often an easy out. "If he could only get it on the left side," Kate says to me, "he'd be okay. He's got good speed." In the top of the second inning, when the boys are in the field, Diego sits on the bench singing out to them his own peculiar versions of standard chants. His parents come into the dugout and keep him company on the bench. The batting machine is a bit more cooperative in the second, and the middle of the Angels' lineup is able to score two runs before hitting the dead wood at the bottom of the order.

In the bottom of the second, the Marlins begin with their number six batter, Jeff. As he comes to the plate, Alvaro starts a chant that is common in the division, "He may be small, but he can hit the ball." Julio looks down at him, and says "Hey, that's a bad luck cheer." Alvaro says nothing but quits chanting. Then he starts up a new chant, one hopefully more acceptable. "Hit a little single, just a little single. . . . " This is an interesting moment. Julio, a star Puerto Rican player from a very working-class family, shuts down the weaker Latino athlete with the professional Chilean parents. As a new immigrant, Alvaro is still unsure of his footing in American boys' culture, and he defers to Julio's authority and to his definition of the chant as bad luck, despite the fact that it is widely sung across the division. Skill and nativity trump class and immigrant status. Jeff does hit a single to start things off, but it comes to naught as the lineup after him is pretty weak: Alvaro, Con, Ralph, Jorge, and Jackson. Alvaro strikes out. Con is safe on an E–4. And Ralph and Jorge both strike out as well. So far, it's a low-scoring game: 2–1 Angels at the end of two.

In the top of the third, the Marlins get a quick out, but then the last batter in the Angels' lineup hits a swinging bunt (real bunts are not permitted) and is safe on first. Top of the lineup. This time there are no pitching machine problems, and the skilled Angels lineup begins to do what it does best: score runs in bunches. At short, Julio is frantic. Each time a ball goes to the outfield, he runs all the way to whoever has the ball, takes it as a handoff, and then runs in with it as quickly as possible. He has less confidence in his teammates' ability to throw to him at the cut-off than in his own ability to run fast. Kate laughs about how ridiculous this is. But she and Dan don't intervene nor give corrective advice to him about his play. He wouldn't listen anyway. However, when Julio does make a mistake, such as the two fielding plays in a row that he misses in this inning, Dan calls out "Don't worry, Julio. Bad hop!" He knows how disconsolate Julio can become with his own mistakes. He doesn't want him psychologically out of the game, especially this early. The Marlins finally get out of the inning, but not until six runs have crossed the plate.

The Marlins' third starts off with Jackson, who has improved his play a lot lately. He hits a foul pop outside first baseline, but in easy fielding range. Their first baseman snags it, and the umpire calls the out. Jackson comes into the dugout complaining loudly to Kate, "But that was a foul. It was PAST the line." Kate smiles and explains, "But if they catch it—no matter where it is—it's an out." "Oh." He smiles, instantly taking it in stride. Jeff calls to him from higher up on the bench, "Can't you hit it any harder?" Jackson's smile fades, and he shrugs.

Aaron, who hits well but usually without much power, hits a very hard

ground ball into right field. Since the outfield on that side is level, as opposed
to the up-sloping grade in left, the ball rolls forever. He comes in easily with a
homer, enters the dugout triumphantly, eyes wide open, and screams to his
Dad, "THREE HOME RUNS!!!!!" At first I think he means this game, but then I realize
that he means during the whole season. Several guys, of course, have about ten
home runs, so this indicates his openness about expressing his happiness at his
own success. He is not yet a top dog who feigns minimal satisfaction. He gets
high fives all around and congratulations from Kate. Diego is standing on the
bench next to his spot and begins to recount, to anyone who will listen, his
memories of life in the womb. "I remember when I was in my Mommy's stomach. I opened my eyes just a little bit, and I could see her, some part of her
body." His brother, Alvaro, counters, "You did not." Diego insists, "I did too! A
part of her body. I don't know which part it was, but I could see A LOT!" Meanwhile, Aaron, still basking in the glow of his home run, is looking up at Diego
during this entire speech in wonder, smiling with wide open eyes, considering
the miracle of Diego's pre-birth memories.

     Roland follows Aaron with a shot to left, successfully sliding into home base
for the second home run of the inning. Everyone is cheering. It's amazing how
a few hits can dispel the depression that ensued after the Angels' high-scoring
top of the inning. Roland sits down with the look of the returning hero on his
face. Jeff turns enthusiastically to him and says, "I *told* you to slide," taking
credit. Roland responds, "No you didn't." [Silence.] In a disgusted tone, Roland
adds, "I know when to slide."

     Julio, Vic, Pete, and Jeff all get hits, and it looks like the Marlins are back in
the game. Since Kate and Dan don't believe in telling the boys the score, even
though they ask constantly, the boys spend much energy and subversive time
figuring out what it could be. Some are more obsessed than others with monitoring it. They all lose track, just as the adults do, and constantly check their
memory with each other. They also make constant efforts to trick Kate into
revealing it. "I have never told you once. Why should I tell you now?" she sometimes says. She goes so far as to leave the dugout to whisper it to the umpire
when he forgets. But the boys are also aware that she will whisper it to parents.
Yet she refuses in a good-humored way to tell the kids. After he scores, Julio
tries to figure it out by confirming his tally with her. Looking up at her with his
big, brown eyes, he asks, "Kate, it's 5–4, right?" She says, "You have never been
right yet, Julio. Forget about it. It doesn't matter." But they know this is not true.
It matters to her. It matters to all the adults. I spend a good deal of the season
wondering about this practice. When everyone knows the score, as is the case
in the older boys' games, then everyone shares the intensity of certain moments
equally. But when only the kids, the actual players, are not allowed to have their
fuzzy memories corrected, then they are excluded from some of the meaning

of the game. They therefore organize to overcome their exclusion from this knowledge.

Later in the inning, one hilarious example of this happens. The Marlins have scored a number of runs, even though they are now in the bottom of their lineup. The boys are wild with excitement at the prospect of beating the Angels. At this point, even Julio is dancing around (but only with the higher-status boys, like Vic and Roland) and tolerating the other boys' antics graciously. There are two outs. Ralph is up, and he hits a slow ground ball up the middle, past the pitching machine. Carlos, coaching first, is thrilled. He calls out to Ralph, encouraging him "Run fast. Run fast." In the excitement of the play he ends up shouting "*Corriendo. Corriendo,*" and waving his arm in a wide circle. Ralph, despite being clueless about the Spanish, does indeed run faster and is safe at first, despite a decent play by the fifth infielder (who plays on the second base bag), and Julio's father, still caught up in the thrill of the close play, lingers emotionally in his native language for a few more seconds: "¡Lindo! ¡Qué lindo." Ralph nods knowingly. Two more runs are scored, making it now five for the inning. The score is now 8–6 Angels, something I verify with Kate on the sly. But the boys are jumping like grasshoppers with Ralph's two RBIs, squealing among themselves, "We're winning 8 to 5, we're winning!!!" Psyched by the idea that they may be winning, Jackson leaps to the ground and begins doing pushups. He gets to about twenty when Alvaro falls off the bench and joins in. The others jump around screaming, pounding each other. Calls ring out of, "Hey! We're ahead by three" and "Hey, we're winning by two. Pass it down the line." Jorge makes the last out of the inning, stranding the heroic Ralph on first.

The top of the inning is pretty uneventful. The Angels score one run on two hits, making the score 9–6 in their favor (despite what the Marlins' players may believe). The Marlins batted around in the third, so Jackson leads off again this inning. The heat adds a whole different dimension to the dugout. The big jugs filled with ice water mean that the boys have a new source of amusement that must be regularly monitored and censored by the coaches. They are allowed to fill a cup to cover their heads with water. Kate spends a great deal of time telling them to sit down, to stop wasting water, and to not spit the water in lines on the dirt. As soon as they stop the line-spitting, several put tiny holes in the tip end of their cone cups so that the water can drip out. They use the drips to draw patterns in the dirt. Ralph, the most creatively subversive of the group, and perhaps the least interested in the game, waits patiently until the coaches and his grey-haired, distinguished-looking father are focused on the field. Then he picks a new victim to dump a cup of water on. He restricts most of his dumping to the lower end of the bench. All except Jorge take it well. The antics keep escalating. Kate grows agitated as she attempts to settle them down. Dan leaves this task to her. Ten seconds after Kate has shouted, "SEATS ON BENCHES!" Ralph stands on the bench and jumps up and down like a monkey, giving out loud ape cries. Inspired by Ralph, Jorge stands up as well, looks at me as the only audience who might not have heard, and calls out, "I'M HAPPY! We're winning!" I think, Oh boy. Such delusional joy.

Jackson hits the first pitch straight into the pitching machine. Foul ball. This is another of the oddities of seven-to-nine ball. The blow seems to throw the pitching machine off just a bit, and he ends up striking out on some off-center pitches. Next, Aaron grounds out to second for an easy second out. The ball is in the first baseman's glove well before he is there, in fact when he is about halfway. Nonetheless, he keeps running full speed to first base, and then curves dramatically out to the right side of the foul line just as he has been taught to do. I can see by the run, and the drama of his full circle, that he is deeply engaged in the pleasure of running the right way. His circle finally closes, and he trots back to the dugout with an open, happy face. After all, he's already hit a home run today. His dad laughs. He is doing just what he was taught in the last practice, and he is pleased by his following it through. In this moment, at least, the out is irrelevant compared to the fun of sprinting. With two outs, Roland, Julio, Vic, Pete, and Con combine for three runs, before Alvaro makes the last out of the inning.

I go over to sit on the bleachers for the fifth inning, and all the parents are wondering what the score really is. "Ask her," someone says, pointing to me. "She always knows." "Tied at nine," I tell them. This may be the last inning too, because of time. Each game in seven-to-nine is allotted two hours, so the last inning isn't supposed to be played unless there is at least fifteen minutes left of the allotted time. We started late, but it's already almost 3:00. It'd have to be an awfully quick inning for us to get in the sixth. Everybody knows that if the Angels hit like usual, the game is lost. I realize how very caught up I am in wanting the Marlins to win. I find myself praying for the Angels' batter to strike out. I turn to one of the parents, and mention my thoughts. "Isn't it terrible when you find yourself praying for a small child's defeat?" She says, "I know. I say to myself, 'Oh, I hope he gets a good hit the next game, but now, let him strike out. Yes, let him get a home run the next game, but not this one.' That way, I don't feel so bad about myself." Aaron's father, who is listening, adds, "I tell myself it is okay to think it. You just can't say it out loud. You can't just say, 'Strike out, little guy!'" But the Angels don't all strike out. In fact, they score three runs on solid hitting, despite a pretty good defensive effort in the Marlins' infield.

I decide to go back to the dugout for what will probably be the last half inning. This isn't likely to be pretty, since the bottom three in our lineup are up. Ralph strikes out for the first out of the inning and returns to the bench without comment, unfazed. He probably has no idea whether or not this is a close game, or whether his at-bat was significant. Alvaro, who made the last out of the fourth inning, sits next to him. He wears several multicolored cloth bracelets, with fringe, on his wrists. Along with his long ponytail, they give him a hippie flair. Ralph asks Alvaro, "Why do you wear bracelets, if you are a boy?" "They are not bracelets." Several minutes later, Alvaro gives him a very hard, side punch in the stomach. Ralph seems to be genuinely hurt and doubles over for a long time. He then glances sidelong at Alvaro to see if Alvaro is witnessing the human agony he has caused. Alvaro ignores him and blithely watches the game. Ralph complains, "Hey, you almost knocked the air out of my stomach! Why did you do that?" It doesn't seem to occur to Ralph to tell an adult about the punch, despite feeling indignant. He often positions himself beyond the adult order. He is in the complicated position of being a very confident, assertive kid who is objectively doing very badly at this game. He turns away from Alvaro and asks his brother, "Hey, Diego, did you get to miss any school when you hurt your finger?" Diego answers, "No, I'm a home schooler."

Jorge and Jackson both have weak at bats, and the Marlins go down with a whimper at the end, having played a great game against one of the strongest teams in the league. I watch the lineup for their expressions—smiles and rage. Most faces register just "good game" with neutral glances. Alvaro has a slight, but polite, smile as he hits the other boys' hands. Aaron positively beams as he comes out. Once back in the dugout, as usual, Dan sets the tone, taking it in stride with his understated summary of the game. "Okay, you guys had a very good chance of winning that game. I thought we had it. But that's okay. That happens. Now tomorrow, be here at 12:30. Okay? Now go get your hot dogs." By the time I walk home at 4:00, I am stumbling because of the heat.

THE OVERALL POSITIVE feel of the Marlins is related to various dynamics of the boys' culture of the bench. The relative benevolence of the two most talented players, aloof Julio and cheerful Roland, made life tolerable, even pleasant, for the less talented boys. Even without the benign posture of the team leaders, however, the resilience of two of the weakest players, Ralph and Alvaro, matters as well. They discovered alternative sources of play and pleasure, which made their shortcomings tolerable to themselves and which enhanced the experiences of the lower end of the bench. But the upbeat feel of the team, its celebratory tone, owes much to the positive emotional work of the two immigrant brothers, Diego and Alvaro, who have only recently entered this new culture of baseball, but who rapidly embraced its spirit and chanted, cheered, and consoled the collective egos of their teammates. Their voices were a constant reminder to the "top dogs" and to the "slugs" that among their peers someone would come to the rescue if the ever-present threat of failure were realized.

Blue Jays

The Blue Jays combine a more even mix of middle-class and working-class boys than do the Marlins. Eight of the boys live nearby, in either Fairmount or Spring

Garden. Three come from old-timer Fairmount families, the other five from newcomer parents. All of the five newcomer boys attend expensive private schools. Unusually, three of the boys from other neighborhoods have parents who are not professionals but who grew up in the neighborhood and chose to bring their sons back to the neighborhood to play. Of the twelve players, nine are white, one is black, one is Asian, and one has a mixed Puerto Rican–Jewish ancestry. The newcomer head coach, Sal, is assisted by two newcomer fathers, one of whom is black, and two Fairmounter fathers. In contrast to the Marlins, the Blue Jays have a larger gap in skills and a cluster of exceptionally weak players. As a team, they are competing for the bottom of the league. At the beginning of the season, they have one A player, one B player, six C players, and four coming up from T-ball. Most of the C players are the youngest boys, so their rankings are not good predictors of how well they will do, since some will improve dramatically. In fact, two of the C players will end up being selected for the All-Stars at the end of the season. But the newness of their ascendance makes them insecure about their status, leaving a negative imprint on the Blue Jays' bench. A glimpse at the dynamics of two Blue Jay games should reveal the negative collective culture that haunted the team.

Early June. Blue Jays versus Angels: Sunday 1:00 P.M.

Before I even get to the field, I know that the Core States Bike Race is happening about thirty feet behind the baseball field. Helicopters circle above the area. Enormous buses line the Parkway. Loudspeakers scream announcements. According to the *Philadelphia Inquirer*, the Core States is "the richest race in the world!" I see Aaron's father and ask him, "So what do we call the bike race now that First Union Bank has bought Core States?" He says, "The F.U. race, what else?" A much larger crowd than usual surrounds the field. French tourists pass through the park in search of the race behind our game. The race is a constant, loud, and imposing backdrop to the Blue Jays' game. About every twenty minutes, crouched bikers zip past, occasionally visible through the narrow gaps between the buses, as they make their loop from the baseball field area up to the northwestern Philadelphia neighborhood of Manayunk. While some parents wander the few yards to see the bikers pass, it is striking how few want to leave the game, and its intrigue, to watch the international competition behind us. A vote for local over global. Occasionally, strangers from the race wander slowly across the outfield grass between the two ball fields, a big "no no." Voices from our crowd complain about how inconsiderate they are for not hurrying as they disrupt our games.

It is still a little grayish today. It has rained so much this season that it's been hard for the teams to get into a rhythm. Rain means many cancelled games. It takes most teams about five games, along with the related practices, to come together and develop a team identity. During May, the Blue Jays were especially unlucky with rainouts. Now, in early June, they find themselves facing teams who have played together more and who have more cohesiveness. In addition, the talent pool on the Blue Jays is very weak. On any given day, winning is something of a miracle for these guys. This is a challenge for Sal, the head coach. He needs to find a way to keep these guys from getting dejected and to keep them interested in the game.

Today, the Blue Jays are the visiting team. Before the game begins, the dugout seems crowded with adults and a little chaotic. Besides Sal, there is his assistant coach, Roy; three other fathers "helping out"; and a teenager, Lennie's brother, who keeps score and watches out for Lennie, the Handful. Most of the Blue Jays' parents are standing or sitting behind the dugout. Sal calls the boys together before the game, and gives them their positions. He is about five feet, ten inches, with a solid build and just a hint of a belly emerging. His face is partially concealed by a big mustache and, usually, sunglasses. He moves with a quiet athleticism, clearly coordinated, but he also downplays it. He speaks in a calm, measured voice and goes right to the point. "Guys, the other night we played four innings and struck out eleven times. They made exactly four plays. They didn't have to beat us. We beat ourselves. Let's see if we can't put the ball in play today and make them get us out, okay? Guys, we're in the field first, so let's go. Everybody to their positions. Good luck, fellas!" Since the Blue Jays lose most of their games, Sal knows not to put too much emphasis on winning. He pays a lot of attention to small victories, and he tries to keep the team from becoming depressed.

In contrast to the Marlins, who have only one player—Ralph—who almost never hits, the Blue Jays have many strikeout artists, including two players who seem completely out of it: Lennie, the emotionally disturbed boy described earlier in the book, and Marcos, a tiny Greek boy who never speaks to anyone and avoids all eye contact. Besides these two, there are three others—Gary, Sam, and Pete—who strike out a lot owing to their lack of experience and nervousness. These weaker players are often targets of ridicule by three of the four most talented boys on the team. This bottom-heaviness of the Blue Jays, combined with the insecurity of three of the talented players, gives a somewhat negative overall feel to the boys' bench culture.

Sal goes out to the mound and takes two practice pitches with the machine, just to make sure everything is working before the first batter steps up to the plate. Samuel, a thin tall boy, is the one exception to the pattern of "negative top dogs" on the Blue Jays. The only A-ranked player Sal succeeded in drafting, Samuel is remarkably mature for his age. He usually looks pitifully at the boys who offer rude comments. With delicate features and deer-like movements, he is coordinated and always graceful. His considerable talent and athleticism are somewhat disguised by his slight build and unassuming character. Also, despite his tremendous skill, his shyness disqualifies him from leadership among the boys. On defense, he plays first base, which, along with shortstop, is one of the key positions in the seven-to-nine. On the first pitch, Samuel hits a grounder between short and third, but easily runs it out for a standing double, because the left fielder can't get the ball back in with any efficiency. Immediately, he assumes the ready position on second, left foot firmly on the bag, right foot stretched towards third, both legs slightly bent, arms dangling between his legs. He's a ball player who knows how to play the game.

Craig bats second. He is one of the group of three at the top of the boy's hierarchy on the Blue Jays bench. Like Lee, who follows him in the batting order, Craig is new to the top-dog position on a team. Craig comes from a blue-collar Fairmount family, is eight years old, and has only this year moved from the outfield to the infield and to the top of the lineup. Thus, he is still somewhat insecure about his dominant status, and often engages in behaviors designed to denigrate the weaker players on the team in order to build up his own status. In fact, this male-dominance behavior often characterizes the group of three, and gives the team its killjoy personality. Craig hits a grounder to shortstop, which should be the first out, but he lucks out—the throw bounces in front of the first baseman and scoots under his glove. On the overthrow, Craig takes second base, and Samuel, having taken off for third on contact, goes home to score. "Way to run the bases, guys," Sal calls out, clapping his hands in encouragement.

Lee, an African American boy from West Philadelphia, comes up third. He hits with the most power on the team and is deeply invested in winning and in his own success. He punctuates his play with a fragile cockiness that can evoke everything from admiration and laughter to scorn or pity from the adults in the stands. He watches the first pitch, and then hits a shot to left field. It's a homer all the way and he knows it. He slows up as he rounds second, to scornfully take a long look at the left fielder struggling to get the ball back in to the cut-off man, and then speeds up again to make it home without a play. Unlike the stars of the Marlins, such as Julio or Roland, Lee is far from indifferent to the glory of a home run. He enters the dugout with a broad smile across his face and gives high fives to everyone in sight. It's the top of the first, the Blue Jays are winning, he has just hit a big home run, and the world looks and feels good. His glowing smile and the bounce in his step communicate this to everyone.

The rest of the inning goes downhill from here. Gene, who bats fourth, hits a single. But after Gene, the Blue Jays lineup is truly pitiful, and this is the biggest reason why they lose most of their games. Sometimes it can take two innings to get back to the top of the lineup, because most of the guys from five down strike out most of the time. Kevin strikes out for the first out of the inning. Then, Pete squeaks out an infield single on the fifth pitch (the last pitch). This puts runners on first and second with one out. On the next play, Sam hits a roller right to first base. Pete takes a short lead off of first but is confused by the play and seems paralyzed in space. The first baseman steps on the bag at first and then runs hard after Pete. The shortstop comes in to cover second base and easily tags out Pete on a nice throw from the first baseman. His out ends the inning. He stomps into the dugout with an anguished face to get his glove. As he passes Craig and Gene in the infield and heads for center field, both boys yell at him about why he didn't run, and what was he thinking, and so on. Pete holds out his arms dramatically, as if to say, "I tried," but the ridicule and criticism are devastating. He reaches center field and stands forlorn, arms at his sides, chin to his chest, shaking with sobs. Sal calls time, trots out, and puts his arm around him and says a few consoling words. They don't seem to have much effect; Pete continues to look distraught throughout the inning.

The Angels, with their hyperactive Fairmounter coach who yells constant instructions on both defense and offense, have a solid but not great team. The first batter hits a pop fly between the second baseman and the right fielder. This is bad news, because Lennie is the right fielder. But, to everyone's surprise, Lennie, who seems to be in rare form tonight, actually moves towards the ball as if it were a relevant event in his life. As the ball drops dead in the grass fifteen feet in front of him, he raises his glove above his head and pounds his left hand into the pocket as if he were preparing for something spectacular. Then, he continues forward toward the ball as if to pick it up. Meanwhile, Pete is racing in from right center field, because he is used to Lennie completely ignoring the ball. They collide at the ball, but Lennie somehow comes up with it and throws it slow motion toward the infield. The batter is in for an easy triple, and Pete looks disgusted. Lennie, overwhelmed with emotion, lies down on the grass, spreading his arms like a snow angel. He doesn't rise until two batters later. In the end, the Angels score three runs in the inning, tying the score.

In the top of the second, the Blue Jays score no runs, and leave one man stranded. This brings up Lennie, who bats last (today this is the eleventh spot), to lead off the top of the third. The bottom of the second is equally uneventful. The Angels score one, to take a 4–3 lead. At one point during the inning, a mother from another team walks by and tells a Blue Jays' mother, Jessie, who is standing next to me behind the dugout, that she "may not be able to make the surprise party" for the birthday of a mutual Fairmount friend, scheduled for this weekend. She has "out-of-town friends coming." Jessie answers, "Oh this is not the party to miss. Bob [her husband] has arranged for a stripper to make a surprise appearance at 9:30, right after dinner." Then she giggles, "But I have another plan. I looked in the paper and got my own stripper. She is a 300-pound woman. I thought I would make that contribution. She's coming at 10:30. They say she is very funny. [Laughing at the deviousness of it] They say she'll take off her whole top—not just leave those little things on." She goes on to try to convince the other mother to come. "Oh, just bring 'em. Nobody cares." I happen to know that this same birthday man has a daughter who attends Temple

University and is currently enrolled in a sociology course dealing with gender roles and sexual discrimination. I smile thinking about a household where your mother's girlfriend solicits strippers for your father, and you listen three days a week to lectures about sexual objectification.

In the top of the third, things start to get snippy on the bench. Sal asks Samuel's father to work the pitching machine so that he can stay in the dugout. He warns the guys to "stop playing around and to sit down on the bench." To lead off the inning, Lennie strikes out, returns to the dugout talking loudly and incomprehensibly to an imaginary audience, and assumes his customary spot at the end of the bench, where he begins to shake the fence behind him and continues speaking to his audience. From the top of the bench, Craig, annoyed, calls out in disgust, "Hey! Lennie can't play on the bench either." Lennie leans back and shouts at him, "Shut up." "You shut up." Lennie now stands up, turns toward Craig, and puffs out his chest like a cartoon character. "Hey watch it, butt head," he says, basking in the dramatic glory of the confrontation. Craig doesn't answer but turns back to Lee and Freddie, who are close beside him on the bench. Behind them, I am writing notes as fast as I can. "Hey," Freddie asks, turning to me "are you writing how many times we say 'shut up?'" (Smart kid.) "Not really," I answer.

In contrast to the Marlins, who tend to spread themselves more or less evenly across the two benches in the dugout, the Blue Jays cluster as much as possible on the first bench. There are about ten or eleven players present at any game, and all of them are in the lineup even if they aren't in the field. Sal and his coaches have trained them to sit in the order of the lineup. This insures that no one forgets and bats out of order, thus causing an unnecessary out. It also constitutes a public display of the skill hierarchy on the team, reinforcing it. Interestingly, the boys follow the seating arrangement but don't distribute themselves equally between the two benches. Instead of five or six to a bench, as many as possible crowd onto the first bench, physically grouping themselves with the top dogs. Today, eight boys have pressed themselves together onto the first bench like pigeons on a wire. Only the two extremely marginal players sit on the other bench. Of course, Lennie is one of those, and he sits on the far end of the bench in his own world. Pete, who bats toward the bottom of the lineup but passionately dreams of baseball greatness, uses his glove to fill the space between the two benches and sits on it as if to avoid the demasculinizing contamination of the lower bench. In the middle of the bench, by himself, sits Marcos, today's catcher, a small, painfully shy player who never speaks to anyone and always strikes out.

Samuel comes to the plate, and Craig puts on his helmet and batting gloves and steps outside the dugout to take a few practice swings in the on-deck circle. Taking the opportunity afforded him by the absence of the other two top players in the dugout, Lee turns to Gene and says, "Last game, I hit one all the way to the fence," pointing toward center field. "You never hit it to the fence," Gene responds. "Yes, I did," Lee says. Kevin and Sam watch curiously to see where this conversation is going. Posturing and conflict are always interesting. Today's scorekeeper, Lennie's teenage brother, Joe, who stands against the fence watching Samuel bat, turns around and interjects with authority, "In your dreams it went to the fence." "No, well, I hit to the sidewalk."(This is at the edge of left field.) By this time, Craig has reentered the dugout, intrigued by the debate. "NO WAY you hit it that far," he says. "But I hit one to the trashcan before." (This is just beyond the sidewalk.) Gene, who is always slightly outside the circle of the top dogs, is inspired by the competitive bragging and jumps in with, "Well, I hit almost there, but it fouled out." "It couldn't foul out if it got to the sidewalk, pal," Craig counters sarcastically. Joe, pretending to be disgusted, turns to the boys again, raises his hands dramatically, and announces loudly, "Nobody HIT IT TO THE SIDEWALK, all right?" Watching the field from the crease in the fence, Sal pretends not to notice the exchange. The bantering might easily have continued, if Samuel hadn't driven the next pitch to right center field. Most of the boys stand up and move toward the fence to watch as the ball rolls past the outfielder's reach, and Samuel runs hard around the bases, quick, rounding each bag smoothly. Home run. Craig is first to greet him with a high five, followed by Lee and several of the other boys. Samuel looks happy, though perhaps also slightly embarrassed by the acclaim, as he takes it all in.

Now Craig squares up in the batter's box, and Gene, enthusiastic because the Blue Jays are scoring again, yells, "Okay, Craig, hit another one!" Gene is a boy who has the potential to do important emotional work for the team, and occasionally he does. But usually his self-consciousness and insecurity get in the way. I think of him as a worrier, because he openly frets about his own performances and almost everything else. He is also quite adult-oriented, which dilutes his influence with the boys. He talks to me, for example, more than all the other boys, regularly trying to clarify if I am a psychologist, or a teacher, or what. After a couple of supporting cries to Craig, he looks around and realizes that he's the only one cheering, and says, mostly to himself, "Hey! Am I the only one cheering on this bench?" Worried, he stops chanting. But then Craig belts a double, so Gene instantly stands to cheer again, momentarily forgetting himself in the excitement.

Things look good. Lee, the best hitter, is up. Gene's on deck, so he dons his helmet and pulls a single batting glove onto his right hand. As he exits the dugout to take a few swings, his elderly grandfather approaches him. He's talked to Sal about the schedule. In a friendly, Eastern European accent, he says, "You have game Friday, Saturday, Sunday." Gene nods and returns his smile, then asks, "What time did he say pictures were?" concerned that his grandfather hasn't procured all of the vital information. Without waiting for an answer, he runs over to Sal to ask the same question. He returns to his grandfather with a calculation. "Oh God," he says, "this means three hours and forty-five minutes between pictures and the game. But what time did he say for Sunday?" The old man looks puzzled. Gene dashes back to Sal and confirms the time for Sunday's game. A repeat of the whole cycle. "Did he say what time the Monday game was?" He heads back to Sal with the seriousness of a businessman clarifying times of crucial board meetings. With all of these pressing concerns, Gene has no time to take practice cuts, much less watch Lee's at-bat. Amazingly, Lee hits his second homer of the game, bringing in two runs and putting the Blue Jays up 6 to 4. Gene follows with a single, and Kevin, who has been steadily improving, hits a slow grounder to short and is safe on the wide throw, allowing Gene to advance to third. When Pete hits an easy out to the second baseman, at least it allows Gene to score. This part of the lineup barely makes contact, much less produce RBIs. Sam hits a nubber toward third, and the Clipper coach yells for the third baseman to hold onto the ball and call time, because he knows that a wild throw will score a run and that the bottom of the Blue Jays lineup will strike out. So, it's two down with Kevin on third, and Sam on first, and little Gary, a middle-class kid who attends private school, is up. He is baby-faced and has bulging blue eyes. The boys are feeling good. They're winning, and they know it. Unusually, Lee and Gene lead a few energetic cheers for Gary. All the attention makes Gary extra timid during his at-bat. He swings late on each pitch, striking out without even coming close to the ball, and returns to the dugout with an airy but stunned expression. He passes Sal at the dugout entrance and looks up at him. Sal holds his hands out to his sides, dramatically open, and offers an exaggerated shrug, as if to say, "So it goes," or "Such are the breaks." Gary passes him and looks up to meet the troubled eyes of his mother, who knows next to nothing about the game and announces this regularly. Dramatically, he repeats Sal's gesture and seems satisfied to file it away as a "whatever," until he sees the cold stares of disapproval coming to him from Lee and Gene, who lean across other players to scowl at him. The boys take the field, up 7–4 against a pretty good Angels' team. Also, they've managed to bring nine batters to the plate in one inning, which will give the top of their lineup at least one, and maybe two more at bats. Sal looks pleased, as do many of the parents. There is a lot of cheering for the boys in the field. "Okay, boys, let's get these outs," Sal calls, clapping his hands three times.

The bottom of the Angels lineup goes down in order in the third, so the Blue Jays hold onto their lead. When they come in to bat in the fourth, Gene asks various adults if they know the score. The Blue Jays boys haven't developed a system, unlike the Marlins boys, to get around the adult rule of not telling the score. They don't have a Julio, who has taken on the job and barters out the information. Samuel, given his intensity, might know the score, but no one ever asks him, and he is too much of a loner, and too little interested in status points with the other boys, to offer up the knowledge. When Gene asks his father for the score, his father answers, "Well if you're having fun, then it doesn't matter." Gene answers, "You can't have fun without knowing the score!!!" One of the assistant coaches, Craig's father, joins in. "Winning isn't important, OK?" At this point, a Fairmounter mother who grew up in the league turns to me and whispers sarcastically, "I love it when they say that." Then in a voice directed to the men, she adds, "But winning *is* something." Finally, more loudly, she says, "I'm here to win. I'm sorry."

Marcos strikes out to lead off the inning. His mother comes up and says quietly to him, "Marcos, you'll hit the ball next time." He manages to avoid all eye contact, insuring that no conversation will start. He looks so incredibly sad all the time, I can't imagine how he thinks of this experience. Lenny follows with another strikeout—he strikes out every time. In fact, the timing and location of his swing—when he swings—seem to have nothing to do with the ball itself. In any event, this brings up Samuel, the top of the lineup, with two outs on the board. Samuel gets his third hit of the game, and Craig follows with a home run to center, thus putting the Blue Jays up by five, 9–4. This brings Lee up. The first two pitches are way high, and Lee doesn't swing. Samuel's dad over-adjusts the machine and delivers a third pitch so low it almost hits the plate. Lee takes a huge swing anyway, misses, and shakes his head in frustration. More adjustments to the machine, but the fourth pitch also comes in too low to hit. Lee checks his swing, and walks out of the batters box in total disgust. "Alright, Lee, last pitch now. Gotta swing no matter where it is," Sal tells him. Samuel's dad tries again to adjust the machine. But, no practice pitches are allowed in the middle of an inning, so he can only guess. The last pitch comes in high, and Lee flails at it and strikes out for the last out of the inning. He comes in with a contorted face, and throws the helmet down on the ground, and the bat as well. It is dramatic, and qualifies as a violation, but nobody says anything. He sits on the bench and covers his face, shaking and sobbing. Then Sal puts his arm around him, and says, "Come on, pal. There was nothing you could do about it. Come on, now. I need you out there in the field." Wiping his eyes, Lee goes out to shortstop to suck up his pain and get himself prepared. For boys, the constant struggle to achieve success makes them surprisingly fragile— one failure, one mistake, and everything seems to come unglued. Later, as they grow older, this fragility becomes increasingly covert, pressed deeper into the psyche by the weight of masculinity.

In the bottom of the fourth inning, the Angels begin with the eleventh and twelfth batters in their lineup. The first batter is out on strikes, but the last batter is a pretty good player who is at the end of the lineup because he arrived late to the game. He hits a single, and you can feel the tension mount among the Blue Jays parents, as the top of the Angels lineup comes up. "All right, boys, let's get the outs," Sal calls out, encouraging them. The Angels' lead-off hitter pounds a ground ball right at Lee at short. He picks it up cleanly and makes a nice throw to first for the second out. As is almost always the case, a force out at second is not a choice, because the boy who plays on the second base bag (seven-to-nine works with five infielders) cannot be trusted to catch a short toss and step on the bag. On the throw, the runner takes off all the way to third and Samuel, instead of risking the run, runs the ball into the plate, raising the glove and ball above his head and calling time. The next batter slams a line drive that Lee is able to just barely snag, at head level and just to his right. It is, by seven-to-nine standards, an amazing play. Lee comes running in, yelling, "Yeah!" and gets a big slap on the back from Gene at third, and one from Sal as he comes through the dugout. He is buoyant and deliriously happy, redeemed from his strikeout, which is already forgotten. "Way to stop 'em, fellas," Sal says to the guys as they stream into the dugout. It's the top of the fifth, and somehow, the Blue Jays have a five-run lead. But it's been a slow game, and it looks like there might not be enough light for a sixth inning. This is probably it.

Of course, the Blue Jays won't get the top of their lineup back to the plate, so they'll have to win on defense. Gene leads off the top of the fifth. The boys are quite animated on the bench, feeling the victory in their hands. Pete and Sam, for example, both middle-ranked players who have slowly developed a bond since the beginning of the season, are standing in front of the bench, facing each other and talking excitedly. They are the same height, both tiny, and the tips of their hats interlock. Both were so shy at the beginning that they rarely talked to anyone. Now they chirp away at each other. Sam even playfully takes Lennie on at one point, and stands in a joking way with raised fists posed to fight. Lennie takes it wrong and yells back belligerently. The inning is quickly over, however, as Gene, Kevin, and Pete go down in order, one-two-three.

The bottom of the fifth begins predictably, with a home run from the Angels number three batter, their best hitter. "All right, guys. Let's get these last three outs," Sal calls. The next batter hits a lazy fly ball to center field right at Pete. He doesn't even have to move his feet to catch it. As the ball reaches him, he shoves his glove up towards it, as if protecting himself, and it drops into the pocket of the glove and bounces out onto the ground in front of him. Lots of groans all around, from Blue Jays parents. As the runner reaches first, Pete steps back from the ball as if he has just been shocked by it and fears it may still contain some charge. Other fielders wave and scream for him to do something, and he finally moves toward the ball, almost in slow motion, and throws it in to Lee, who has come out for the cut-off. This happens just in time to make the runner decide to go back to first, and not to risk a foot race with Lee to the second base bag. After Lee makes the play, he turns back toward Pete in the outfield, gesturing with his hands in exasperation. Pete answers back, something. But after Lee turns away again, he throws down his glove in the outfield and kicks the ground.

The next batter hits a roller between second and third into left field for a single. On the play, the runner from first charges around second and heads for third base, but Lee quickly gets the cut-off throw from Sam in left and makes a nice throw to Gene at third. The throw beats the runner, who slides into the bag as Gene drops to his knees and applies the tag to his helmet. He's out. The Blue Jay parents cheer. Usually, in seven-to-nine, when the throw beats the runner and a tag is made, the runner is called out without too much scrutiny about the when/where of the tag itself. But the umpire, who has come running half way up the third base line, calls the runner safe. As I stand behind the dugout, in shock, the head of the organization passes close behind us and whispers to me conspiratorially, with an ironic chuckle, "He was out." The call, and the chuckle, are possibly informed by two extraneous considerations. In the first place, the ump is the father of one of the Angels players, which makes a call like this always the subject of much grumbling and controversy. In addition, he normally umpires in the older boys' league where a tag to the head usually means that the runner's feet have reached the bag first. Whatever. The Angels now have runners at the corners with no outs. They follow with two weak infield singles to the right side, both of which could have been outs if not for a bumbling play at second base. Now, two more runs have scored, and there are men at first and second with still no outs. The lead is down to 9–7. Tension is mounting, and parents behind the dugout begin pacing around and confirming the score among themselves, to verify that the winning run is at the plate. Gene eases away from the line at third base, and his father, who is looking increasingly tense, yells out sarcastically, "Hey, Gene, are you playing third or short stop? You want to hold hands with 'em or what?" Without expression, Gene takes several steps back toward the base. The eight-twelve batters are coming to plate now, so there is still hope. The eighth batter strikes out, which produces an audible sigh of relief from Sal and several of the parents. One down. The next batter swings over a pitch and nubs it down into the dirt in front of home plate. Gene comes charging in and calls time. Now, it's bases loaded. The next batter strikes out, and Sal becomes animated, yelling to the guys, "Okay, guys, two outs now. Get the easy out. Force at any base. Gene, if you get the ball, tag third. Come on, guys, let's go." Many of the Blue Jays parents are clapping and smiling. The number eleven batter is a tiny boy who looks like he's drowning inside of his helmet. But, he takes a healthy cut at the first pitch, which is quite high, and misses. The helmet tips over his eyes on the follow through. The Angels coach taps down on the front of the machine housing, to lower the next pitch for his midget hitter. The boy looks at the next pitch, which comes in at his waist. On the third pitch, he hits a hard ground ball on the right side which squirts into the outfield. The Angels third base coach is screaming and waving his arm in a circle for the runner coming from second to round the bag and head home. Lee charges to the plate from shortstop to get the throw, which never arrives. A booming roar rises from the Angels' side of the field, the boys, the coaches, and the parents all clapping and yelling kudos to the little boy on first base. They have tied the game. The last batter strikes out to end the inning, but it's too late to save the Blue Jays top dogs from complete emotional collapse, this time over their own mistakes.

Lee stumbles in from shortstop, face contorted by tears. Gene is openly furious, stomping his feet in disgust. They both collapse on the bench, joining Craig, who is crying and shaking, and Lee, also already seated and heaving as he sobs. Craig' mother, leaning over the dugout and rubbing her son's head, says, "There's another inning, honey. Don't worry. You can take it back. It's just a game, honey." He wails, "But we're never gonna win now. They get an extra at bat too!!" then cries even harder. Gene, starting to recover, stands up and announces, "Hey it's a tie. We're still gonna win!" Slow to return from first, Samuel enters. As he puts his bat down, he scans the emotional wreckage on the bench. He stays quiet and looks at them respectfully, but at the same time with an air of disbelief. Very mature kid. The coaches huddle with the umpire, and a few minutes later, Sal comes in and announces, "Okay, guys. The game is over. Line up." They cry out, "But why? I thought we got a chance. Why? Why?" Sal, in a dejected tone, says, "Just because. They say it's too late. They called it. Just line up." As they slowly move toward the field for this ritual, Gene pushes Sam, who has separated him from Lee and Craig by moving in front of him, backward, and moves in front of him. The boys move through the line, touching hands with the Angels, all looking shell-shocked. No one offers any consolation to anyone else.

After the game, Sal gathers his players around. "Listen up. Tough game. [Pause] You played well. You deserved to win that one. [This is as close as he comes to implying an umpire fraud.] Things happen." Lee calls out, "It's not fair!" Gene leaps up, "Coach, if you put a glove in someone's face, touch his face, don't you think that it's some indication of an out?" Sal answers, "If the ump calls it, that's it. You played your positions fairly well. And you've got an opportunity to play them again. Hopefully we'll get better results. Good job. See you tomorrow."

Late June, the Playoffs. Blue Jays versus Grays: Monday 6:00 P.M.

Today could be the last game of the season. The Blue Jays face their first playoff game against the Grays, and it's a single-game elimination. Before heading over to the dugout, Sal sits the guys on the grass and gives them a pep talk. "Listen up. Maybe I didn't say this last time, but you had a really great game the last time. We are a great team. We may not have a great record, but we are a great team. Our record doesn't show what we can do. Remember, we beat the Senators once. The Marlins beat us only by one. We played well against the Mets. We may not have the greatest record, but we are a great team." Seated in a meandering circle, they all stare up at him, giving him their rapt attention. I walk around to see their faces. They drink in the sincerity of his voice, liking the elevated and serious tone of the whole thing. "Okay. Now I want you all to follow through on your swings. And on defense, keep your gloves down. And I want you to stick with each other. Be positive. Got that, Gene and Craig? Let's support each other out there and don't give up. Okay, boys? Now, here's the lineup: Samuel, Kevin, Craig, Lee, Gene, Ira, Pete, Gary, Sam, Marcos, Lennie. All right, let's go, guys."

Despite Sal's plea for community, bickering starts even before the game gets started. Craig, who is standing with Lee, turns toward Pete and says, "Hey, Pete, you strike out, and Lee and I are gonna get you. We're gonna give you a jackhammer." Pete looks at them, somewhat confused, straining to see if the words are meant in jest. "Yeah, we're gonna come lookin' for ya, Pete," Lee adds. They don't even wait for his response, but turn away and keep joking among themselves. Of course, they don't say this kind of thing to Marcos or Sam—the real sure bets for strikeouts—but to one of the middle-range guys, one who sometimes does deliver. Pete looks devastated but sits on the bench and looks down at his shoes for a few moments until he can recover his equilibrium. It's one of those painful, often secret moments that serve to discipline the middle-range boys, to remind them who's on top. It's also emblematic of how the ritual cruelty of the hierarchy can work at cross purposes with the goal of winning. The game begins with a potential contributor nursing bruised feelings and wounded self-esteem. Sal may never know how, or why, his effort at encouraging solidarity has been undermined.

The Grays have a better record than the Blue Jays, so they are the home team. Samuel leads off the inning with a ground ball that should be an out, but the throw bounces under the first baseman's glove and into foul territory. Samuel goes to second. Kevin now comes up to bat. He has recently improved his position in the batting order from much lower down to second. He puts the ball into play on almost every at bat, although he gets thrown out at first a lot, because of his unusual running form, which seems to be copied from his skating motion in ice hockey. This means, along with the fact that he looks like he's about two feet tall, that he needs considerably more steps than the others to get there. Kevin hits a grounder to second and is out easily at first, although Samuel advances to third on the play. This brings up Craig, who scorches a line drive right at the shortstop, who doesn't even have to move to catch the ball. Samuel, who has taken a couple of steps towards home, gets back to the bag quickly. Lee comes to the plate looking very aggressive, pounds his bat on the plate several times, and swivels his cleats into the dirt to get set—the clean-up hitter supremely aware of his role. After an over-anxious first swing on which he pulls the ball way foul, on the second pitch he hits a long ball into left. Samuel scores easily, but the left fielder is able to get the ball in quickly, and the third base coach holds Lee up at third. Since Gene does sometimes make contact, I suppose this isn't a terrible call, although with weak hitters coming up many seven-to-nine coaches might have taken more of a risk to score the run, even with two outs.

Fighting about space on the bench breaks out again in this game. The boys sometimes leave their gloves on a spot on the bench when they go to bat and expect others to honor their glove reservation, which happens rarely. Craig returns to the bench and finds Kevin, who has been moved ahead of him in the lineup for this game, wedged in where he thinks he belongs. He sits down forcefully and gives Kevin a hard side shove, adding, "Why don't you just go home?" Kevin continues to face forward, ignoring the question and the shove. He must weigh about twenty pounds less than Craig. Samuel, standing by the fence but near them, turns around and scans the scene. He decides to rescue. He leans down toward Craig and asks blithely, "Why don't *you*?" (Just what I wanted to say.) Silence for a few minutes. Kevin eventually glances over to Samuel, considering him, and then asks, "Samuel, how old are you?" "Eight and a half." Kevin nods. He seems to be wondering, with that little question and several more stolen glances, if their age gap is too big for friendship. Gene hits one off the pitching machine for a foul ball, and then swings way late on the next pitch, sending it straight up the first base line into the glove of the first baseman, who steps on the bag for the easy out.

In the bottom of the first, the Grays and their adult entourage start their maniacal cheering. It's what they're famous for. Timmie, the Grays coach, inspires most of it. He goes out to the pitching machine, takes a few practice pitches, adjusts things, and then starts up with his first batter. "Okay, Mitch, stand tall and hit the ball. All right, pal. You're the man. Say cheese and bend those knees. Level swing, level swing. Stand tall and hit the ball." Kate looks at me and rolls her eyes.

I spot Jessie standing alone on the other end of the dugout and walk over to her. I figure I can use a diversion from Timmie's frenetic chanting. "Hey, Jessie, how'd that birthday party go?" I ask, remembering the surprise birthday party for her friend's husband that she had told me about. She winces with pain at the topic. "Oh Sherri, you can't imagine such a bunch of sticks in the mud, ridiculous people in your life. All the fun of the whole thing was ruined for me. First the fat stripper arrives at 8:30 instead of 10:30. I tell her, 'Hey, you are way too early.' She says, 'I'm sorry, but I have 8:30.' I say, 'But I confirmed 10:30 twice. I'm sorry, but we are just having our dinner, we can't have you just walk in now.' [Like there was ever a good moment.] And, she is supposed to be *after* the thin one—for effect, you know. So I say, 'Okay, you can start at 9:30, and we'll just have to hold the other one off until 10:30 then.' Well, she comes in, Sherri, and these women start running to the bathroom to hide. You know, I think, What is wrong with these people? Have they never seen a naked breast before? Have they never looked at themselves in the mirror? What is this? Can't look at a naked breast? I was so upset. People all giving me evil eyes like I was . . . " her voice trails off. "Oh, I was so disgusted. It just ruined it for me. I paid $145 dollars for that! I say to my husband, 'There are a lot worse ways to make a living.'"

The first batter grounds the ball to Lee at short, who bobbles it and hurries the throw, but Samuel makes a great scoop at first for the out. This doesn't diminish Timmie's enthusiasm at all. You have to admire his pep, and the way he gives the boys such encouragement and positive energy. "Way to run it out, Mitch. Nothing you can do, pal. Sometimes they make the plays. You'll get 'em next time."

Jessie's husband, who's heard her telling me the story, comes over from the bleachers. Looking at me and smiling devilishly, he points to her, saying, "Sher, they got a bounty out on her head." Jessie laughs. "Even my mother, she comes up to me and says [speaking weakly in a pleading voice], 'Oh, Jessie. I think maybe you better just tell her to go home. People are kind of upset.' I say, 'What? Ma, you should be standing up for me. Backin' me up. Tell 'em to put towels over their heads. This woman is going on.'"

The second batter hits a lazy fly to right center field. Kevin stands, waiting for the ball with his glove close to his face and, incredibly, he squeezes his glove on the ball as it drops into the pocket. "All right, Kevin," I hear a parent yell. Cheers all around. Lee runs out to get the ball from him and to slap his glove. In seven-to-nine, a catch by an outfielder is universally regarded as miraculous. After trying to adjust it for his big number three hitter, Timmie has quite a bit of trouble with the machine, and the kid strikes out on five pitches, none really close to the strike zone. The Blue Jays have survived the first and are up 1–0.

Ira starts out the second with a ground out. Pete follows with a grounder to second, but the first baseman bobbles it as Pete arrives at the bag, and the ump calls him safe. Several of the Grays' parents are not pleased with the call. Pete looks happy and bouncy on first, ready for more glory. Now, Jessie remembers our conversation and goes back to her story. "Even his wife, my friend Mary! Well, her daughter [the one who is taking the sociology course] was having a fit and giving me the evil eye. Mary even defends her, and says, 'Oh Jessie you know how she is, she's just. . . . ' Well, yeah, but that is your responsibility as a mother to say to her, 'Now listen, you know your father and I have been together a long time, we have a good solid relationship—it is not going to affect anything if this happens.' That's what she should tell her daughter—not just whimper to me because I gave the present." Gary hits a nubber in front of the pitching machine for an easy single, putting runners on first and second. But Sam and Marcos both strike out to end the inning. As the boys come in to get their gloves, Pete, one of the favorite victims of the group of three, turns to Sam and complains, "Couldn't you strike out when the bases were empty? Geez, just wasted my hit." Sam pretends not to hear him as he heads for the field.

I ask, "Did he like it? The birthday boy?"

"Of course, he liked it. He was laughing. Now why can't they just see that he was having fun. It was for him, not them, and just shut up and give in to what he would like? I tell you."

"Did they like the second stripper, the thinner one?"

"Oh, yeah, that's it. That was the funny thing. Oh, that was fine. Nobody had a problem with her at all. Come right on in. . . . "

"Well, it is ironic that the perfect body one was acceptable, because presumably, their critique is that this was sexist or something, right?"

"Right."

I add, "Well, it's just as sexist, isn't it, to say that a woman should expose herself only if she has a good body, but a fat woman exposed is disgusting."

"You know, that's right. That's exactly right! The fat one is disgusting, but the other one is fine. Oh, people, sometimes. . . . You know—I'm telling ya. I said to my husband, not a bad way to make some fast money. Sherri, I'm thinking of eating myself out of house and home and then goin' out and making some quick cash." She laughs at herself with me.

My attention drifts from the game, as the Grays bat in the bottom of the second and Jessie and I continue talking. They get some base runners and, as I find out later, score three runs in the inning. But Jessie and I are talking. It's one of those things that sometimes happen out on the field: you find yourself in an interesting or intimate conversation with a neighbor, or even an acquaintance, someone you might know only for a season. Jessie and I talk about people's ungratefulness for the labor of others. I share a story with her about how rude people sometimes are at our Christmas party: coming late, eating like crazy, and then leaving to rush home to get to bed, so they can grocery shop the next morning. "What about pleasure?" I ask. She agrees, "Yeah, pleasure, and recognizing other's efforts." It is funny how we manage to translate soliciting strippers and hosting parties into unrecognized female work. Such a nineties moment. But as we linger for a few minutes longer, I can see how very pained she is at the memory, even as she laughs at herself.

The Blue Jays come up to bat in the top of the third inning, behind 3–1. Lennie leads off with his second hit of the season. When his bat hits the ball, he lets go instantly so that the bat and ball fly together into the infield. The ball rolls toward third and the bat ends up in front of the pitching machine. Meanwhile, Lennie is running like a big bear with his arms flailing in the wrong directions, in opposition to the trajectory of his body. The umpire, Billy, mumbles to somebody, "No way I'd ever call *him* out on a thrown bat!" All rules are suspended for Lennie, and I am deeply moved by the humanity of the group accommodation. After that, the top of the lineup produces some good hits behind Lennie, and the team ends up scoring three runs, thus pulling ahead 4–3. Lennie is delirious with his hit. The Grays go down almost in order in the bottom of the inning, so the game is turning out to be a good one. I'm glad it's not a blowout because they're so deflating, especially in the playoffs.

The fourth inning goes by in a flash. The Blue Jays go down easily, scoring none, and the Grays score one run on two hits to tie the game. In the fifth, with Kevin on first and one out, Craig comes up to bat. Jessie leans on the fence, expectant that her son will do something good here. Craig hits an infield fly, and Kevin is off at the crack of the bat. Roy and Sal are both yelling to Kevin to get back to first, but he doesn't hear them. The shortstop catches the ball and throws to first, for the double play. This hurts, especially with the meat of the lineup coming up. Both looking very solemn and pained, Craig comes back to the dugout with Kevin behind him. Pete walks over to them and stands with arms extended out to the sides, palms upwards, asking in what seems almost a conciliatory way, "What were you *doing?*" He has learned this demand for accountability from the top players, but he is demanding it with more good humor than they do when they do it to him. Craig blasts back, "Be quiet, Pete. You get outs all the time." Pete backs away from the hostility, saying, "So. I know." Craig continues, "Besides, you're at the bottom of the order. So shut up." Pete defends himself with, "I don't always strike out!" Sal enters, obviously frustrated, kneels down in front of Kevin, and says, "Kevin, lesson number one: always wait to see where the ball is hit before you run. You can't just charge off and hope it isn't caught. Wait long enough to see what it is. Okay?" Kevin nods but says nothing.

The Grays come back in the bottom of the fifth to score three runs on some good hitting. In fact, without a spectacular play by Lee at short, and good solid fielding plays from Gene at third and Pete at second, the inning might have been much worse. So, despite now falling behind 7–4, the Blue Jays are still very much in the game emotionally. It's the final inning, of what is potentially the final game. One of those classic, tension-filled moments where the parents seem to stop breathing, waiting to see how it's all going to unfold.

When Lee comes up to bat in the top of the sixth, his face is like a bulldog's. He psyches himself into ferocity, his way of coping with the building tension. Jessie, the serious baseball mom, now stands over by the exit from the dugout, right behind the cluster of coaches, which includes her husband. She is talking to Lee's father when I come up. She explains, "I have to stand here. I need to be this close. Oh, I have such a headache over this." Lee hits a double. "That helps," she mumbles. Gene follows with a single that drives in Lee. Then Ira too hits a single, putting men on first and second. On the fifth pitch, Pete manages a dribbler to second that is so slow that Gene, who is off on the swing, is able to score. On the throw home, Ira takes third, and Pete makes it to second. He stands with both feet on top of the bag, as if to increase his stature, and smiles broadly at the second baseman. His pleasure is evident. No effort at coolness. This never happens in the ten-to-twelve division. Ira, who has made it to third, moans out loud when he sees his teammate, Gary, a weak hitter, come up to bat. It's 7–6, with runners on second and third, no outs, and the bottom of the lineup coming up.

Gary, who often uses a kind of baby talk (his mother does too) that is inappropriate for his age, has large bulging eyes that give him a constantly startled or confused look. He now turns these confused eyes toward Ira, waiting on third, considering his meanness. Ira looks away. On the second pitch, he drives one into left field, shocking everybody, and takes off running. Ira and Pete score, and Gary gets to second and never stops running despite the fact that the shortstop is running in with the ball from shallow left. Eric, as third base coach, holds up his hand to stop him at third, as the shortstop is running behind him, ball in hand, trailing him by only about six feet now. Incredibly, Gary, who must be completely drunk on the glory of the hit, never slows up and charges around third, seemingly unaware of the shortstop behind him. But the shortstop has also stopped running, I suppose because he just assumed that Gary's only possible action at this point would be to stop at third. When Gary rounds the bag and keeps going, the shortstop resumes his chase but then realizes that he'll have to throw it home to get him. By this point, Sal and Roy and all the coaches are yelling "SLIDE" at the top of their lungs while everyone else holds their breath, watching the play unfold in an intense, almost painful, slow motion. The throw is easy, and right to the catcher, but he is unused to even trying to catch the ball, and so he misses it, and Gary slides into the plate as the ball bounces off the backstop like a pinball. The crowd goes berserk. First, Gary never hits. Second, he has pulled off a home run on the most reckless, daredevil running of the entire season. Total chutzpa from the bottom of the lineup. Third, he's driven in three RBIs, putting the team up by two runs, 9–7. The boys are also jumping around like crazy. He comes in with his already bulging eyes now almost half way out of their sockets. He walks around in circles, unsure what to do. He openly shares his amazement with all, as we indulge in our own amazement. He has none of the swagger of the top dogs, none of their repressed boyishness. Gary just falls down on the bench and keeps turning his head around to everyone and rolling his eyes like, "Where have I been? What has happened to me? Am I back yet?" His astonishment keeps feeding the crowd's pleasure. We call out more. He is further amazed. "How can I possibly be this kind of star?" his face asks. Most of the support here comes from the parents, although Pete feeds him a stream of high fives. The group of three quickly move back to their spots on the bench, happy, but unwilling to indulge him beyond what seems appropriate.

Unusually, Gary's father is at today's game. After things have settled down, his father says to him, "Good hit, Gary," and starts to hold out his hand. Gary slaps it. His father moves his hand away and adds, "Hey, give me a hug. I want more than a high five." [I have the distinct impression that he is saying this for my benefit. His wife is very aware of my study and has mentioned it to several people.] Gary stands on the bench to face him, looking almost like a toddler as he reaches up. "You're still huggable, right?" They embrace. While I find it tender, I can't help thinking that he is screwing up this kid's chances of entering the big boys' circle. Gary doesn't have enough status to tolerate this kind of display from his dad.

Sam hits a pop-up that lands behind the third baseman and makes it to first. Delirium seems to be contagious, as he does a little jig on the bag, swinging his arms back and forth in a brief dance of self-pleasure. Marcos however, comes to the plate looking Zen-calm, as if the game were in the way of his deeper thoughts. He strikes out on three pitches and comes in with no expression, and no one says anything to him at all. His silence is like a bubble that protects him from the insults or humiliations that might erupt in the dugout. Lennie, who is about to come up to bat, suddenly points to Lee and Craig and cries out, "They made me cry. I'm gonna strike out." He stomps up to the plate and makes nothing close to contact on any of his swings. With two down, there is much expectation for the top of the line up now.

Samuel takes his time but only squeezes out a single. Kevin hits a grounder toward short, but slow enough to allow his tiny legs to beat out the throw to first. Craig drives a ball into the gap of left center field and takes off around the bases. After Kevin rounds second, he slows up for no observable reason. Meanwhile, Craig is running hard into second and catching up fast. At this point, Sal and the third base coach are shrieking, "Kevin, run, run." He continues to hesitate, even after he rounds third. By now, Craig is directly on his heels and looking nervously over his shoulder at the shortstop who has the ball and who is winding up for his throw to home. Sal screams again, "RUN! KEVIN, MOVE, GO FORWARD!" Finally, Kevin seems to wake up, and begins running full speed toward home. The throw is strong to the plate, but over the first baseman's glove and high into the backstop. Kevin slides, and Craig, right behind him, slides as well, crashing into him. They stand up together in a bundle of dust, and make their way back to the dugout.

With the score now 12–7, the Blue Jay supporters are coming off the stands to stand behind the dugout. As Kevin enters, Sal grabs him by the shoulders and says intensely, "Now, Kevin, lesson number two. Always listen to what the coach tells you. *Run* if I say run." Kevin, holding up his hands in exasperation, answers, "But I MISSED THE BAG!!" The umpire is standing only about four feet away. Sal shifts Kevin toward the bench quickly, puts his hand over Kevin's mouth, and whispers as he kneels down in front of the boy. "I know. I know, *but*" Kevin looks deeply into Sal's face, waiting to hear the final moral. "It's just that when [stammering], when you have Craig moving in on top of you, you just have to go." [Silence.] Kevin shrugs, but then smiles, suddenly enjoying their joint deviousness. After another head nod, he sits down quickly, hoping the moment and the attention are over. Seconds after he sits down, Gene, who has been whispering with Lee, says to him, "Next time you do that, he's gonna flatten you on the plate like a, like a taco."

Pete and Sam have figured out that the Blue Jays are leading by five runs. They now sit on the bench, excitedly guessing which team they will play in the next playoff game. "If we play the Mets, that's good, 'cause they have almost no players left. Gone to camp. And the Padres are in last place!" (As if the Blue Jay's next-to-last-place position means nothing.) They turn to discussing body injuries. Kevin, now looking to their end of the bench for his only hope of inclusion, joins in: "I have stitches right here," he says, and lifts up his shirt to show his side. Several others start mobilizing immediately to show their injury points. This is the last inning in a playoff game, and they seem equally interested in body wounds. Someone tells of getting poked with a stick in the groin area and whispers to two others exactly where it happened. The other boys double over. One holds his crotch in mock drama at the thought of such an injury.

Lee hits a triple, but Gene grounds out to second to end the top of the sixth. Things look good, because the Grays are bringing the middle of their lineup up to bat. The Blue Jays should be able to avoid the top of the lineup and pull out the win.

The Grays score two runs with the middle of their lineup, and then things really start to fall apart. The last five kids in their lineup somehow all manage to get on base, except for their youngest player, who strikes out. On one play, Samuel fumbles a throw at first and then stands there looking knotted, his body turned inward, head down, with finger in mouth—his personal way of expressing distress. His father notices and calls out, "Samuel" and then demonstrates a loosening up gesture—bending knees and opening extended arms and swaying them—and adds, "It's okay," but saying something more with his body, like, "Get back this feeling. Let it go." It is a very perceptive intervention, one of the things that work between people who know one another very well. Within minutes, his body is loose and relaxed again. However, three runs have scored and the Grays are bringing up their leadoff hitter with only one out. After the batter hits four foul balls, probably out of nervousness at the drama of the moment, the Grays' coach calls time and goes into the box, puts his arm around his player's shoulders, and whispers for a few minutes into his ear. The boy gains enough composure to hit a hard line drive that looks like it is headed for foul territory again but stays just inside the third base line. As the Grays runners round the bases, their teammates, coaches, and parents are all screaming and clapping and jumping up and down. In a flash, the game is over. I'm standing next to Jessie, who instantly drops her head to her folded arms on the top of the dugout fence and moans to me, "I hate losing!" I feel the same way. It will be hard to make the transition to an end-of-the-season celebration. Sal calls out, "Everybody line up." As the boys come back into the dugout, Sal signals for them to sit back down on the bench. "All right, guys, listen up. Okay. First of all, I want to thank all of you for all this new gray hair I have. Blue Jays, you were a lot of fun." One boy asks, "What was the score?" Sal answers, "I have no idea." (WHAT? I think. He *still* won't tell?) "Don't worry about it, all right? You guys played hard. You did your best. That's all we could ask for. It wasn't our year, all right? That's all now. We're done. Okay. We'll get 'em next year. I want to thank you all." A parent calls out, "Thank you, Sal." Sal continues, "All of you were a great, great team." A general applause follows. Another parent calls out, "Thanks for coaching." More clapping. "Good job. Good job."

Sal continues, "Now we have the All Stars." At the last practice of the Blue Jays, Sal had told the boys about the upcoming All Stars game and explained that he could only send three players. He followed the method that several other coaches use, namely, letting each boy vote for four players (since they almost always vote for themselves anyway) along with the coach and assistant coaches. Without benefit of a master list of names, he had asked them to write their choices on a small piece of paper. Since that practice had run late, Sal had told them he would announce the winners at this playoff game. He now prepares to announce those results. "Okay, Guys. The top vote-getters were Lee and Craig, and I had a tie between Gene and Samuel." Sal adds rapidly, "I wish I could send all four of you, but I can't." I am surprised that Samuel, clearly the most all-around talented boy on the team, is not among the top vote-getters. But his shyness and maturity set him apart, and the weight of the boys' votes over the coaches probably made the difference. His abilities were resented by the three insecure top players. Sal continues, "Okay. So I have your names on these pieces of paper, and I'm gonna put them in this hat, and we're gonna pick 'em, all right? He hands the hat to Ira's dad to pick. Lee begins laughing, in part because he thinks the hat is a funny idea, but clearly also expressing his joy at being selected. He and Craig happily punch each other, while Samuel and Gene look serious. After looking at the paper, Sal announces in a somber tone, "It's Gene. All right then. Samuel, sorry, bud. Okay, then." He seems not to know what more to do. But because Sal has highlighted Samuel's loss, the entire crowd of parents and other stragglers now turn and look at a stunned Samuel, mortified by the wave of emotion flooding over him. His father moves in quickly and tries to pull his head toward him saying, "I'm sorry." Samuel, trying to stuff the surging emotion, is frozen. I force myself to turn away to try to break the collective gaze on him. Being a shy kid, Samuel finds the attention itself hard to handle. But this humiliating attention is unbearable. Some of the boys start to leave for hot dogs, none of them saying anything to him. Samuel now bolts and runs out of the dugout with an anguished face. His father looks miserable, as does Sal. The rest of the parents trickle away with their goodbyes and "See you next years." I feel sick. I can't believe we are ending the season on this note, with Samuel's inappropriate exclusion from the stupid All Star game as the end point, with the one magnanimous top dog of the team whimpering under a tree. For the rest of the evening, I feel badly about how the Blue Jay season has ended, but sad also just because the season has ended. All of the cozy conversations behind the dugout with parents, the fragile community of boys on the bench, and the feel of the fading summer heat after sunset are now over. The annual neighborhood drama has ended and, for this team at least, ended on an upsetting, exclusionary note.

THE CHOICE OF A narrative of games, what might look like "mere storytelling" in traditional sociology, offers a perspective that differs from a purely analytic account. It attempts to disaggregate the ways multiple moments of human agency and social structure combine endlessly, and unpredictably, in the flow of social life. It might have been possible analytically to describe these dynamics as general patterns, as a series of themes, with brief examples of each dynamic. But the effect of traditional sociological representations is often not sufficient in terms of how they account for, or understand, the process of social life. In particular, they fall short in how they account for the emotional texture of interaction. While these limitations probably hold true for any analytical representation of social space, in this context, among boys in the ebb and flow of a baseball game, a strictly analytic discourse would be noticeably inadequate.

What does a narrative of games give us that an analytic typology, for example, does not? Perhaps pleasure, for one thing. But even if we reject this as a goal of serious sociology, as many no doubt will, we can recognize that narrative is descriptive and time-conscious in ways that analytical discourse is not. It allows us to represent the flow of interactions, emotions, and meanings *in time*. While I have occasionally relied on narrative accounts in other parts of this book to deepen the sense of process, the descriptive and time-conscious elements of narrative are especially well suited to expressing the amazing slow-motion time of baseball games. With these four games, or typifications of games across the season, I try to portray how the social dynamics among the boys contribute to the overall feel of different teams. We see the importance of hierarchy to both groups of boys. Among the Marlins, highly skilled boys tend to interact mostly with the other most talented players. Those who rapidly improve their skills and performance over the course of the season can often renegotiate their social position, as happened to Jackson, who became one of the few boys with whom Julio would socialize. This wasn't possible for Kevin on the Blue Jays, who also evolved dramatically from a C-ranked player to a surprisingly good hitter, despite his size. The Blue Jays, being a more status-conscious team, had access to the upper ranks controlled by a tight group of insecure leaders. We also see the growing pressure to play serious ball, rather than "play around" on the bench and on the field, despite a sustained resistance to the weight of this adult world by playful boys, such as Ralph on the Marlins, who are less burdened by high adult expectations.

The "posture of talent" on the two teams contrasted sharply, with a more benign or disinterested cluster of leaders on the Marlins, and a harsher group of gatekeepers on the Blue Jays. In fairness to the Blue Jays boys, the range of talent on their team was much greater than that on the Marlins. Their lower-skilled players, Marcos and Lennie, almost never contributed a play, requiring levels of patience the Marlins top dogs never had to attain. Nonetheless, the gang of three on the Blue Jays introduced two decidedly negative dynamics. First, they harshly judged the failures of weaker players, especially the middle players, by whom they felt most threatened. Second, they harshly judged themselves, tending to emotional collapse over their own periodic failures. This collapse was often contagious; the weaker Blue Jays players, who lacked the resilience of some of the weaker Marlins players, often felt the game was lost and gave up. That is, the Blue Jay bottom players offered the team little other than mishaps, while the Marlins bottom players saw themselves less tragically, and sometimes provided diversions, spitting contests, and humorous story-telling.

But especially critical to the glue of the teams was the presence or absence of "emotional workers," boys who, through a softer style of masculinity, offered emotional comfort to the downtrodden on the team—to both the talented and the not so talented—and poured positive energy into the team through chants, cries of support, and public rationalizations of failure (like the cry of "good cut" when a teammate swings and misses). Their pats and high fives, and their creative diversions from the game, offered their teams a constant reminder that community could trump victory. The Marlins had Alvaro and Diego, whose efforts congealed the upbeat team personality. The Blue Jays had no one doing sustained emotional work, and so the other dynamics, such as the harsher masculinity styles of Craig and Lee, took on even more weight. Here we see alternative forms of masculinity emerge and begin to take hold. We see, for example, boys developing different degrees of comfort with emotional expressiveness. We also see the surprising extent to which traditional forms of masculine hierarchy are made tolerable, even effective, by nontraditional forms, by expressive, softer versions that nurture the group and thereby further group goals.

The dynamics described above operated as undercurrents in the boys' world, a world also structured by the class, race, and neighborhood tensions discussed in other chapters. These dynamics help explain the feel of teams, the elements of group personality that interacted with the broader social divisions in the adult worlds of these boys. The obvious talent of Julio, for example, was not enough to keep him in the league. His benign "posture of talent" could not save him from the forces of gentrification that pushed his parents, two years later, like countless other Puerto Rican families before them, to leave their life-time neighborhood, priced out of the housing market. His acute awareness of the divergence of his probable social fate within the neighborhood from that of his teammates, played a role in his "indifference" to the group. As his father described it to me after their move, his new, less affluent neighborhood eventually offered him an inferior, underfinanced, and chaotic league. This reality underscores the heavy weight that social inequality would play in his and his eventual teammates' futures. But despite the specter of social divisions, based on class and race, that would grow in importance as these boys matured, the world they constructed on the bench before they reached the age of nine, slightly autonomous from the adult circles within the neighborhood league, was ordered more by the posture of talent, the balance of generosity and insecurity of individual personalities, and the positive emotional expressiveness of players of heart. They saw each other very closely, came to know each other well, before the weight of real social division was meaningful to them.

6

===

Conclusion

The Fairmount baseball field is one example of what multiculturalism in urban public space felt like at the beginning of the twenty-first century, forty years after the civil rights movement. Although far from a social utopia, its achievements would have been hard to imagine in the not so distant past. In a changing neighborhood space, residents and outsiders who have lived most of their lives in racially segregated neighborhoods come together voluntarily to watch their children play together. It is also a space in which divergent class backgrounds meet, with competing class cultures. The social world of Fairmount sports also taps fluctuating sensibilities about acceptable masculinity styles and emotional expression, reflective of broader gender transformations in the society and intergenerational connections between strangers from the diverse communities. The space generates enough cross-boundary understanding to qualify as a fragile success.

My early questions about neighborhood baseball centered on the how and why of racial integration, and the range of parental expectations for their children, given their diverse social backgrounds. But over time, these early questions extended to issues of masculinity, class cultures, and public space. I think of the various chapters of this book as probes into the different dimensions of social life at this site. The multiple competing realities within this space correspond to a wide range of subfields within sociology. Because we have journeyed through so many distinct layers of social life—from community change and gentrification, to class and race tensions in multicultural encounters, to organizational politics and the social boundaries within local culture, to the range of masculinity styles among coaches and preadolescent boys—a brief story of the story is in order.

We began with neighborhood space and the changing racial and economic transformations of two adjacent neighborhoods in Philadelphia, Fairmount and

Spring Garden. In the early 1950s, the two predominantly white working-class areas, bordered by poorer black neighborhoods, consisted of descendants of southern and eastern European immigrants. As Spring Garden, with a larger stock of rental property, underwent a racial transformation with the arrival of Puerto Rican residents, Fairmount developed a city-wide reputation for defending its turf racially. Subsequently, the low-cost housing market of Spring Garden attracted developers and young professionals looking to buy inexpensive residential property close to Center City. Thus, the rapid gentrification that began in Spring Garden in the early 1970s over time pushed the poorer Puerto Rican residents out, and soon spread into Fairmount, where it set the stage for new social tensions and suspicions between old-timer Fairmount residents and the college-educated professional new arrivals.

Well before the arrival of the new professionals, the working-class Fairmount residents had fought public officials for the right to use public park land for a central neighborhood passion, baseball. The claiming of this space for community use produced a collective memory that established baseball as central to the character of the community and as one of its central "beauty assets," a public ball field in proximity to major cultural and art establishments. We saw how, when faced with a scarcity of local children, the passion of the neighborhood men for preserving the integrity of the game made room for the sponsored entry of new children onto the teams, including children of color. This was facilitated through the networks the children of the new professionals had with children of color, often in school; through new interracial friendships resulting from the integration of the local Catholic school; the lure of the new, visible clubhouse; and, in the post–civil rights era accountability to newly elected local black politicians. All of these elements played a role in the surprisingly smooth racial integration of the neighborhood baseball league. In short, by the 1990s, Fairmount neighborhood baseball had changed from a mostly white league to one where a third of the boys were children of color.

I argue that the character of baseball was central to this transition. Framed in terms of broader debates about sports and social inequality, whether sports merely reflect broader social divisions or contribute to undermining them, this book is a qualified vote for the constructive potential of sport. The vote is qualified on several grounds. First, it mattered that it was baseball and not just any sport. Second, it mattered that it was local, voluntary youth baseball. Third, the racial and class understandings achieved within this baseball space were uneven.

Why did it matter that it was baseball? For one thing, the highly structured, slow pace of baseball, its imposed grace of waiting, offered structural possibilities for social connection. Baseball, with its suspension of time, allowed parents of different social backgrounds to sit together on the bleachers without much more to do than cheer for each other's children and talk to each other in the long moments between plays. The patience required of baseball locks folks together for sustained intervals, with a common focus and a common set of experiential elements that they can play with conversationally. Not just any sport can deliver this kind of holding environment for spectators. The fast pace of other sports such as soccer or basketball, played against the clock, offers fewer opportunities for connections on the bleachers. For another thing, baseball draws attention to individual players, to their struggles, defeats, and triumphs, and contributes to an evolving collective identification among groups of boys and parents who are reshuffled every season. The reshuffling inherent in this type of local league broadens the range of families who gossip together about the meaning of the game in the lives of their children. In the process, people come to know each other in textured ways, as individuals and not as social types. This goes deeper than the acquired street wisdom about fleeting encounters on the street, as described by Eli Anderson in another gentrifying neighborhood of Philadelphia.[1] Finally, the collective memory about baseball extends into white ethnic, black, and Latino heritages, providing the diverse spectators with strong emotional connections to the game linked to their own social identities.

The fact that the FSA was local and voluntary also contributes to my qualified vote for the positive cultural impact of the league. This is noncommercial boys' baseball, not corporate professional sports. The audience is local, organizational control is local, and accountability is local. The decision making of staff and FSA coaches is under more immediate scrutiny than at higher levels of sport. Unhappy parents have an easy exit; there are no long-term contracts. The local leadership *needs* the parents of color to sustain the organization. There are not hordes of rookies waiting to replace disgruntled boys or parents who might sniff unfairness. So their judgments matter more.

Third, baseball may have stimulated racial understandings at FSA, but it did so unevenly. Recall that I used the notion of "segmented understandings" to describe *both* the shifting race relations and the class encounters at this site. Despite the smoothness of the entrance of new children of color into the organization and the opening up of the organization to the new professionals, there were still teams on which children of color were concentrated, and "clubhouse teams" dominated by Fairmounter kids and favored by the organizational leadership. Most significantly, there was little integration in the leadership of the organization, even fifteen years after the newcomers arrived. This might have become more of an issue than it was if the newcomers had cared more about organizational control than they did. But the stakes were not high enough for them, so they deferred and peace prevailed.

The unevenness of the racial understandings discussed above had a parallel in the class sympathies generated in the space. Before the newcomer professionals even arrived at the ball field, the old-timer Fairmounters already harbored a stockpile of resentments toward them based on class tensions and earlier encounters in the neighborhood. Many Fairmounters blamed the loss of their neighborhood's village-like feel on the newcomers, who invested little in neighborhood space and pursued other, instrumental social networks, generally in non-local settings. Yet many of these newcomers saw themselves as distinct from their professional counterparts in the suburbs and had moved to the city in search of its diversity and cultural opportunities. Many professionals gentrifying Fairmount and Spring Garden fit the description of the "cultural new class," or the liberal sector of the middle class that concentrated in the social and cultural fields of the economy typically unconnected to the corporate sector (i.e., doctors, lawyers, professors). While Fairmounters often saw newcomers as uninterested in local friendships or issues, newcomers often felt shunned, their participation unwelcome. On the baseball field, these misunderstandings met and crystallized.

Among the many issues that divided the two groups in this baseball space were the unequal amount of time devoted to sustaining the organization; volunteering only when one's child was a direct beneficiary (the newcomer "father coaches"); unfair scheduling of games and changes in schedules at the convenience of insiders (old-timers) and their children; the extent and nature of adult socializing on the field; and the degree of competition encouraged or expected in a baseball league for youth. These differences reflected competing sets of cultural values related to individual responsibility, group solidarity, and the promotion of children's interests. While there was a range of opinions within each of the groups about most of these concerns, when differences did appear they often took the form of a conflict between what I have called Fairmounters' hierarchal communalism and the more child-centered individualism of the new professionals. But more than misunderstanding happened on the field.

Outside the inner circles of the organization, the sympathies forged among the diverse participants of FSA were equal to the discord, especially in the ordinary encounters between Fairmounter and newcomer parents and children during games. Many newcomers grew to feel a strong loyalty toward FSA and came to prefer its cultural feel over the other, more homogenous alternatives available locally. The sympathies that developed across the lines of class and race were especially apparent in encounters between FSA and the outside world, such as the traveling team encounters in the suburbs, in which the "othering" of opponents that is built into competitive sports solidified our sense of "we-ness," permitting our sense of community to trump our class and race divisions.

The complex negotiations of this space went beyond race and class. Because it was baseball that brought neighbors together, and not quilt-making, encounters often centered around issues of masculinity. Since baseball, and baseball expertise, was central to neighborhood identity, part of what was at stake for Fairmounters as they turned to newcomer coaches for help was the preservation of their style of baseball, a style based on expertise, sophisticated strategy, and discipline. The grown-ups in this league displayed a fascinating range of behavior and attitudes about such masculinity issues as competition, winning, failing, crying, emotional cruelty, and emotional leadership. While there were dominant narratives in both groups that tended to reduce the coaching style of each to a contrast with the other (i.e., between "the yellers and the fuzzies"), these narrative constructions, or group stereotypes, did not match my empirical observations over a period of years of a number of coaches. Mapping a selection of Fairmounter and newcomer coaches on four key dimensions of coaching—degree of expertise, emphasis on skill-building or winning, use of positive or negative reinforcement, and reliance on tough or tender styles of masculinity—provided insights into the origins of group stereotyping and the group process of "othering." Group perceptions of "others" relate to the fact that each group's outliers differ from one another in easily identifiable ways: the Fairmounter coach as the expert disciplinarian with a competitive emphasis, a negative style of discipline, and a tough style of masculinity versus the newcomer coach as a noncompetitive rookie relying on a positive pedagogy with a tender, emotional masculinity style. These outliers provided handy oversimplifications of how the two groups of coaches differed, despite the fact that they failed to account for the behavior of *most* coaches in either group. Most coaches, in the mix of their own personal styles, are social hybrids who select elements from all of the available styles around them, both within and across social boundaries. This is undoubtedly true in countless other areas of social life where group boundaries emerge and narratives of difference take hold.

By exploring a series of portraits of different coaches involved in concrete coaching practice, we see the way the contemporary landscape is stocked with a range of masculinity styles that are not only diverse, but often unstable within the same individual over time, and even internally contradictory within the same person in the same period of time. We saw how even a coach like Billy, who in many ways fit the stereotype of the Fairmounter coach, could change over time with age and marital status. His masculine "inconsistencies" occurred not only over time but within time as well. But it took close observation, or being an insider, to see this, because his harshness tended to be salient, and therefore apparent, while his softer, more tender gestures were generally understated. Only those who saw him regularly, up close, over many years, like his assistants, the parents of his traveling players, my son, and other boys, came to view him as a mostly kind, fair man prone to angry explosions. His public reputation remained that of a punitive tyrant.

The masculinity styles at FSA at the turn of the twenty-first century, both tough and tender, occurred within the broader context of changing contemporary American gender norms. As more and more women with children take up

full-time roles outside the home, many of the assumptions behind the traditional, tough style of masculinity meet with challenges, and this has left many
men unsure about what is appropriate.[2] But, as we have seen, while there are a
variety of styles available to men, the traditional narrative of masculinity continues to maintain a hold on men that exceeds its correspondence to their lived
experience. So much so that even men who self-consciously have adopted tender emotional styles in their dealings with young boys often find it extremely
hard to challenge the periodic mercilessness of their male peers. There also
remains a generalized sense of discomfort with expressions of fear and vulnerability by boys, even as they learn to confront a speeding ball in the batter's box.

This entire community had as its target the socialization of children into
the culture of baseball and softball. Yet, despite the weight of adult messages,
the children had their own impulses, their own meanings and practices, to
throw into the pot. Along the way, the culture they created, especially as it per-
tained to masculinity, mattered to the outcomes and was important to the
overall feel of the adult-orchestrated games.

At first glance, it seems boys pay considerable attention to asserting dominance and jockeying for position, as scripted by traditional masculinity. They
aggressively seek individual success, practice exclusion of the weak, enforce
self-isolation, and strive for baseball knowledge (i.e., figuring out the score).
The most aggressive and dominant boys are generally considered the team leaders and are seen as central to its success. There is a haunting parallel here with
the "self-made man" ethos of capitalist masculinity in which the qualities of
individuality, dominance, and competition are intrinsic both to the system and
to individual success within it, but also produce the Willie Loman style of masculine tragedies, in which family and community are made impossible and men
and boys must suffer alone. Despite the centrality of the high-skilled "top dogs"
and the exclusionary ways of treating the less skilled in boys' culture, many boys
quietly embrace alternative relational styles not centered around competition
and one-upmanship.

The pliability of boys who have not reached ten years of age makes them an
ideal locus for studying masculinity negotiations just as they are being learned,
practiced, and tested by the boys themselves. These boys are still learning how
they are both expected, and not expected, to embody the masculine behaviors,
feelings, and attitudes that become more socially coded and rigid with older
boys. In Bourdieu's terms, the capital that is being played out among the boys
is, above all, masculinity capital in all its various forms. The wonderful thing
about younger boys is the extent of ambiguity remaining in the "dispositions"
that pertain to masculinity and those that pertain to childhood. This creates
masculinity exaggerations, such as those performed by Julio, and provides won-
derfully interesting contradictions, as when Victor, a top dog, was still able to

cry. The field, both the baseball field and the "field" in Bourdieu's sense, is where it all happens.

In addition to the uneven masculinity of the younger boys, one of the most significant and unrecognized dimensions of masculinity styles among boys is the vital role played by boys who nurture. It is widely acknowledged that many aspects of traditional male roles have depended on an often unrecognized, or little credited, female counterpart, either through the doing of childcare and housework, or through kin support and/or supplemental wage work. But the importance of alternative forms of masculine expression—of the tenderer, more emotionally expressive versions—for sustaining the success or viability of traditional male roles is less understood. Yet traditional males thrive not only through the emotional work of supportive females, but through the work of more emotionally expressive males in their circles as well. The unrecognized social contributions of boys like Diego and Alvaro, the emotional workers of boys' culture, parallel the often unrecognized emotional sustenance provided by females.[3] I observed many boys who knew how to nurture their fellow players in meaningful ways, who provided humor or a pat on the back in the face of defeat. Ironically, teams without these players more often tended to turn on each other; they were less stable in tense situations, and less resilient after setbacks. They certainly had less fun. The lack of these players may be the answer to the question often posed by perplexed adults when high-skilled teams lay down.

There was a parallel in the adult world of FSA men. The kitchen management of the organization, for example, was assigned not to women but to men.[4] The main ones responsible took great pride and care in the space. In the winter, when volunteer men would spend hours on cold Saturdays rebuilding the pitching mounds and setting fences, a man named Buddy would work in the kitchen, preparing hot sandwiches of Italian sausages and peppers, and steaming pots of boiled ham and cabbage, and serve them to the other men with comforting words of encouragement about their labor. In the world of professional sports, Jerome Williams of the Toronto Raptors is this type of emotional worker.[5] Because he was a scrappy, hustling player, many Toronto fans loved him even more than they loved Vince Carter, whose athletic talent far outmatched his. When he was hurt and barely playing, he was a cheerleader for others, selfless. After he was traded to the Chicago Bulls, his old team went downhill despite the fact that the trade improved the team on paper. But the old chemistry, along with Williams, was gone. Not coincidently, while in Toronto Williams was a supporter of the Canadian "White Ribbon Campaign" opposing male violence against women.[6] We usually imagine women doing this kind of supportive, empathic work. But inside masculine space, these male emotional workers often make the hierarchical relations tolerable to those not at the top. Still, their contributions are rarely recognized or valued. We'll know something has changed when we hear coaches, especially the most competitive ones, recruit a player because of his emotional skills in nurturing the team or offer a "MVN" trophy for the team's most valuable nurturer.

The connections forged between boys of different backgrounds through their FSA baseball experiences over the years endured, in many cases, beyond these games. After the late 1990s, most of the visible interracial friendship circles of older adolescent boys in Fairmount, hanging on corners, working out together at the local gym, or bagging groceries together in local grocery stores, were carryovers from their younger years at the baseball field. In many cases, these neighborhood connections took precedence over friendships from their schools, even among the middle-class boys whose external opportunities to socialize were often great. There were still all-white cliques of adolescents in Fairmount that resembled those of the old days. Many of these boys had also played baseball. But there was a comfort zone in the relationships between the homogeneous white groups and the mixed-race groups that their parents had never known.

From the beginning of this project I struggled with how best to narrate this story. While I find much about social life hilarious, I don't often laugh when I read sociology. Ruth Behar set out to transform anthropology into a discipline that "could break your heart." To do so, she violated disciplinary norms and shared her emotional vulnerabilities. Making the researcher more human, more exposed, she believed, would better level the playing field between the observed and the observer.[7] In that vein, one of my goals for this project was not so much a sociology that would break your heart as one that would make you smile. I wanted this book to celebrate the amusing inventiveness and intelligence of social process. This is how storytelling found its way, more and more, into the foreground of my project.

In the first four chapters, I used a consistent narrative approach, but one that departs in some ways from the analytic mode of much of sociology. The theoretical insights and implications that are more traditionally framed analytically I often placed into the weave of narrative. It is up to the reader to judge whether this was asking too much of the story.[8] In chapter 5, I deepened the strategy and relied almost exclusively on narrative "typifications" to capture the immediacy of boys' interaction in the context of the games. I used these composites, truncated into game vignettes, to illustrate the way four specific features of boys' teams mattered to the character of those teams. In a sense, these features were the parts that made up the whole, the elements that lent distinctive character to the teams: the range of athletic ability, the posture of talent, the emotional resilience of underdogs, and the presence of positive emotional workers. But since the social whole is always greater than the sum of its parts, they combined in unpredictable and constantly changing ways. For this reason, it was in chapter 5 that the many thorny issues of how to tell the story of Fairmount baseball appeared to me most salient. Like life, games unfold in starts and stops, contain multiple events that are simultaneous, parallel, or contradictory, and simply don't hold still for the analytical eye. But without a feel for the games themselves, what context would my reader have from which to understand this world? The focus on social practice led me to opt for a narrative mode for these games, because it allowed me to plot the various and disparate events of a game—from parents' comments, to boys' interactions on the bench, to plays on the field—in a temporal sequence, rather than in the less dynamic, structural mode of analytic discourse.

One of the blind spots of sociology is that it often fails to capture the flow of life, the process and feel of social practice as actors spontaneously respond to, resist, and transform their inherited social order. Yet the need to understand and capture practice is central to several theoretical traditions of sociology. It is, of course, a regular feature in the work of Bourdieu and central to much of the field of symbolic interaction and conversational analysis. Concentrating on practice takes us closer to, in Deustcher's terms, "what they do" as much as to what they say.[9] That's what drew me to sociology in the first place, but somehow, like many of us, I got derailed by the humorless reductionism dominant in social science. Don't misunderstand me. The sharp, analytical gaze of sociology has many perceptual advantages. It offers grand insights, synthesized generalizations, and sometimes, accurate predictions. But it also tends to disaggregate process, thereby losing too much flesh and too many bones. Sadly, it often bores its readers. Once my lens shifted to the social order of the boys on the benches as it unfolded, showing their practice became my focus. I don't mean to present this effort as some boldly original step, paving the way for mainstream sociology. It is a humble move to take up the challenge that has rung out, in many voices, since the publication of a wave of writing that expressed deep concerns about the exclusionary politics and deadening style of much of our cultural writing.[10] It wasn't until I had almost finished the book that I fully understood how it might be possible to use narrative—not the extracted and reconstituted narratives of subjects described by the godlike voice of the sociologist or anthropologist, but narrative as a conscious prioritizing of a story that builds in the flow of time to give a feel for the immediacy, color, and unpredictability of social life. The stories give us partial truths, glimpsed in the fragments of fieldwork, but they are at least in form as honest and valuable as the "realistic narratives"[11] that sociology prefers.

A PUERTO RICAN mother, down at the field one evening, told me that she dreaded the day when her son would reach fifteen and she would no longer have an excuse to come down to the field. "I don't really do much besides go to work and come home. My husband doesn't really talk to me. This gives me something to look forward to. I get to talk to people." There are many homes that a place like "the field" could enrich. This applies to my extended family members, who live far from the realities of Fairmount. I have a disabled, home-bound sister, who lives with my eighty-year-old mother, who requires oxygen therapy for congenital heart failure. Since neither one drives, it is a rare treat for them to go anywhere other than to the doctor's or to visit my father in his nursing home. My scheduled visits, every two months for a few days at a time, are the center of their reduced social spheres. Although they live in a small Texas town, they receive few visits, know few neighbors, and have trouble finding someone to take my sister, with her cumbersome walker, to church on Sunday, even from within her own congregation. I often think of how much richer their lives might be now if they had lived near us for some time in Fairmount and had invested years in this community instead. They could go to the ball field five nights a week for at least three months a year and sit in a lovely, vibrant place, filled with juicy gossip, and not feel so alone.

My experience with "the field" has left a deep impression on my psyche. It was not just that my family, my husband, myself, and our children spent so many hours and emotions there during the formative years of our children's lives. It went deeper. It was the only place, in my entire life, where I experienced a geographically grounded sense of community. And that's a strong statement from an outsider. Of course, these bonded feelings weren't present at every moment, not even in most moments, as there were countless alienations and solitary feelings along the way. But I did find a wonder of place there, as did many others. It was the opposite of the "dead public space" as described by Sennett.[12] I once told one of the Fairmounter coaches, after our interview, that when I died I wanted to be cremated and have my ashes left on the base path between third and home on the seven-to-nine field. Without pausing for a second, he answered, "Yeah, I understand that. But save the circle around home plate for me."

The coaches at FSA lived at a time described by many as father-absent or father-oblivious.[13] But in this space, boys without fathers, as well as those with fathers, got to see men up close, for long periods of time—not just as teachers, not as paid professionals who interact as part of their job requirements, but as men who *choose* to spend time with children. Regardless of the adult socializing that occurs in the clubhouse and on the sidelines, any man who agrees to coach a season at FSA has the outcome of spending more time with children than with adults. Children watch the coaches, and the coaches watch each other, make heavy sacrifices of time for the community, and they all learn something about masculine involvement and about the diversity of social styles that exist among men outside their homes and public and private schools.

In standing back and looking at the implications of a space like Fairmount baseball, it is worth considering the argument put forth by Robert Putnam in his much discussed and densely documented book, *Bowling Alone*. According to Putnam, what is drastically wrong with American society at the turn of the twenty-first century is a lack of civic involvement at almost every imagined level.[14] He contrasts the first two-thirds of the twentieth century, a time of deep engagement in community life, with what he calls a "treacherous rip current" pulling us apart from one another and from our communities. Americans, it seems, have withdrawn their investments from civic life and from their neighborhoods. The loss of civic-mindedness is evidenced by a decline in active involvement in face-to-face organizations like clubs and voluntary organizations, by declining church attendance and involvement, by a decline in numerous measures of social connectedness (like having friends over and card playing), by diminished participation by adolescents in most major sports (with the exception of bowling—hence the title), by reductions in altruism including charitable giving and philanthropy (except among the oldest generation of Americans), and by a decrease in "thin trust" between strangers as documented in survey data.[15] The loss of the community connections and civic-mindedness, as extensively documented by Putnam, has had dire social consequences for communities and is seen in a wide range of quality-of-life measures—from health and personal happiness, to crime and security levels in neighborhoods, to democracy itself and governmental accountability. Putnam and his colleagues[16] have prescribed a collective therapy to cure the damaged social fabric of American communities, a pathway to return to an era of civic investedness: "I challenge America's urban and regional planners, developers, community organizers, and home buyers: Let us act to ensure that by 2010 Americans will spend less time traveling and more time connecting with our neighbors than we do today, that we will live in more integrated and pedestrian-friendly areas, and that the design of our communities and the availability of public space will encourage more casual socializing with friends and neighbors. One deceptively simple objective might be this: that more of us know more of our neighbors by first name than we do today."[17]

Was the golden age of early—and mid-twentieth-century associations, described by Putnam, all that golden? This is the doubt raised by Jason Kaufman, who studied voluntary organizations in fifty-three American cities in 1880 and concluded that the motivations behind the drive to associate, celebrated by Putnam as civic virtue, were really about the desire for exclusive social spaces that would keep out individuals of different genders, races, and ethnicities.[18] They built ties of solidarity for members, and in the process exacerbated existing differences by reinforcing them through exclusive associations.

I often thought of Putnam's and Kaufman's arguments as I completed my fieldwork at the baseball field. Much about the place seemed like an exception to Putnam's dismal argument. I thought I understood well the vastness and the density of the social networks that emanated from this baseball field, until an experience I had toward the end of my project. After finishing most of the manuscript, I set about getting the releases from the parents of minors who would be featured in Janet Goldwater's photographs for this book. Since Janet had taken the pictures on her own schedule, often when I was not present, I was not sure who half of the hundred or so minors in the photographs were. One Saturday morning during the season, I went down to the field and started talking to folks. By moving around on the bleachers and talking to parents seated outside the field house, within about two hours I learned the names, and means of locating, about one-third of the unknown children. In any cluster of parents I approached, there were usually two or three who could give a location or a way of finding four or five of the kids in question. The next morning, I returned for about four more hours. I found out who on my list was related to whom, who hung out with whom, who had always lived in New Jersey but worked as a mailman in the area or who had now moved to New Jersey but still worked with Peggy's husband in facilities management at the University of Pennsylvania, who had become a drug addict since leaving baseball and would be hard to locate. I gave my number, written on torn pieces of paper, to anyone who might know how to reach one of the unidentified kids. One Fairmounter coach identified one of the boys as one of his former players, who he used to pick up in North Philadelphia and bring to the games. Then he took it upon himself to drive the release form to the home of the boy. He ended up waiting for several hours outside the house before an adult returned, and then dropped it off at my house the next day. Two days later, the mailman I was trying to track down rang my doorbell, wanting to sign his release. In short, over a three-day period, through these dense networks, I secured more than fifty release signatures. Although I had known that Fairmount ties were tight, the rapidity of the flow of accurate information about these randomly photographed residents over several seasons made me realize how I had underestimated them. I thought about the double-edged sword of such ties: the security they bring and the social control they represent. As sometimes lamented by Fairmounters, everybody, I mean everybody, can find out what you are up to. Most amazing, this was not small-town America, but a neighborhood within one mile of the central business district of a major U.S. city, Philadelphia.

What Fairmounters brought to the table was a cultural tradition founded on dense social capital, norms of reciprocity, and solidarity. But their early social capital was the inward kind that often relies on exclusive identities among homogeneous groups, precisely what Kaufman laments about voluntary organizations. We saw this in their historic treatment of blacks and Puerto Ricans in nearby areas. It would be wrong to romanticize the process of neighborhood transformation that brought about changes. The tragedy behind the gentrification of Fairmount and Spring Garden remains in the displacement of most of the poorer Puerto Rican residents from the area. But once gentrification was under way, it presented Fairmounters with a new challenge in the central physical site of their local culture—a chance to move beyond their local identities and connect with people different from themselves, to bridge their capital in terms of both class and race. They did this, although in a tentative way.

The new professional residents, most open to the baseball culture of Fairmounters, also learned to esteem the security and possibilities for connection that such a place can sometimes provide. We can't forget that essential to the organizational transformation was the claiming of public space for neighborhood use, a shift that required obedience to new community dictates for inclusion linked to the new external accountability to politicians prepared to enforce community-minded thinking. The inequality of effort toward maintaining the space by different groups of social actors has resulted in a sense of entitlement to organizational control by those making the biggest time sacrifices. How they confront demands for greater inclusion by those who don't fully appreciate these inequalities of sacrifice will remain a challenge to the stability and well-being of the organization in the future.[19] Drawing limits on the brutalization of young boys with the end of "making players of them" by weeding out abusive coaches, even among insiders who contribute heavily, also remains an important agenda for the organization's future. But this can't happen without a cadre of parents equally willing to do what Brett Williams calls the work of local culture by "building deeper, denser, more textured, and rooted political action."[20] Reforming local space requires local investment. Beyond these remaining challenges, the segmented understandings achieved across the diverse social groups who came together in this neighborhood lot are an important accomplishment in a place so racially divided thirty years earlier. Many elements of Putnam's recommendations for urban planners, looking toward the year 2050, are already at work in this Philadelphia neighborhood at the century's turn.

Appendix

Methodological Considerations

The problem of the male audience is taken up by Adrienne Rich as she discusses women writers: "Male writers do not write for women, or with a sense of women's criticism, when choosing their materials, themes, and languages. But women writers, even when they are supposed to be addressing women, write for men; or at least they write with the haunting sense of being overheard by men, and certainly with the inescapable knowledge of having already been defined in men's words."[1] There are probably only a few themes where this haunting sense of being overheard by men could assail women writers more than on the subject of baseball, and worse, on men's masculinity styles within baseball. This discussion elaborates on the overall description of the research process addressed in chapter 1 and explores some of the research dilemmas of involvement, vulnerability, and objectivity I confronted as a woman studying men and boys playing baseball.

The Setting

At the time of the fieldwork, the Fairmount Sports Association was relatively large for a neighborhood league. It sponsored an in-house, co-ed T-ball division for children aged five to seven. After that, for boys, there were the seven-to-nine, ten-to-twelve, and thirteen-to-fifteen divisions, with approximately six to seven teams in each division. There were also traveling teams that competed in city-wide leagues, like the Devlin League, or the one referred to as the "Rec League," which is sponsored by Philadelphia's Department of Recreation. There were traveling teams for those aged eleven and under, for those who were twelve, for those who were thirteen to fifteen, and for sixteen-year-old boys. Girls could join the co-ed T-ball teams, but starting at age seven, they played softball, which continued until about age sixteen, depending on how many signed up each year. Because fewer parents signed up their daughters, the girls' divisions typically extended over a broader age range, like twelve to sixteen, in order to insure enough teams for the divisions. Given my interest in masculinity issues, as well as my long participation (prior to the fieldwork) as a parent of a boy, my research focused on the boys' side of the organization. Periodically, I regretted the decision to study only the boys' league, especially when some of the serious baseball women from the neighborhood wanted to tell me about the historical struggles to claim a space for the girls, the glory of their memories of playing there as girls, and their ongoing complaints about the treatment of girls—the scheduled times of their games or how "their field" was being taken over by the little boys. I winced when they implied that all anybody cared about was the boys. I admit to having found myself watching the girls' space sometimes, with a sense of longing for the greater comfort zone their world might have offered me.

FSA does not belong to the Little League, the best known youth, sports program in the United States. Given the small-town origins of Little League[2] and its extension to predominantly suburban areas, its membership requires access to considerable space. The urban nature of FSA—less than one mile from the central business district of Philadelphia—means that space is at a premium. Consequently, its outfield fails to meet Little League requirements. This means that FSA is not a branch of a large national corporation, as many youth baseball leagues are, and this serves to fortify its local character. The organization is financed by the per-child registration fees paid by parents ($80 per child in 1998), by sponsorship of teams by local businesses, and, more recently, by occasional small grants.

By external standards, the baseball organization could be considered relatively competitive in the sense that there is a clear distinction between practice, play, and games. Known boys are ranked according to skill level and drafted onto teams before the season. Teams practice for as many as six weeks before the season begins. There is a great deal of talk about "being ready" for the season, for "games that count," more so than there is about learning baseball only in the context of the games. Every division has playoffs, championships, and All Star games to which each team sends its top three players. Games are often played despite extreme heat. In an effort to shorten the time it takes to complete games in the younger division, where in the past they might have lasted three or four hours, the seven-to-nine division years ago turned to pitching machines, fed by coaches. Most seasons, most teams have eleven or twelve players. Therefore, the range of skills on any team is not extremely wide when compared to leagues that draft much larger teams. The entire team fields in the seven-to-nine division. In the ten-to-twelve division, four boys play outfield. This means that no one is on the bench in the younger division, while one or two players are on the bench in the ten-to-twelve. For in-house games during the regular season, but not for playoffs or championships, rules require that coaches play each of their players in the field for at least half of the game. The full team bats sequentially in both the seven-to-nine and the ten-to-twelve divisions.

Entry, Presentation, and Consent

Because I began as a participant in FSA, as the mother of a player, and then shifted to the position of a researcher, I was already an insider before I started fieldwork. Since my son had played on a traveling team for years, I knew quite a number of the organizational leaders. In the FSA office, one Saturday in the winter of 1997, I approached the president of the organization and explained that I wanted to both write a history of the organization and do a sociological study of the role of sports and coaches in the lives of boys. I wondered aloud if he might also, at some point, agree to an interview about the history of the organization. Being a "can do" kind of person, his initial agreement to the project took the form of his beginning on the spot to recount for me the organization's history. He, and another staff member who happened to be present, proceeded to give me my first deep sense of how long this tradition of baseball had already existed in the neighborhood and of how many folks, then present in the FSA, had grown up playing ball in the organization. It was a wonderful way to begin, receiving at once both a historical frame of the space and his agreement to the project. Later, I returned for a more formal approval, including his signature. This good beginning set the tone for his toleration of me in a mostly good-humored manner. Occasionally, however, it was clear that he sometimes considered me a pest. Once, I entered his office looking for an updated schedule for one of the divisions, and in a loud, booming voice, he announced in the presence of an office full of insiders, "Sher, you are really starting to get on my nerves." As curious faces eyed me, I was mortified but nonetheless answered, "I know what you mean. I'm starting to bug myself as well." There were other moments when we used humor to conceal zones of discomfort. For the most part, I ignored that discomfort as I went about my business on the two fields. This made me wonder sometimes if he, and others who had been informed early on about the research, had forgotten along the way about the ongoing nature of the project and had returned to seeing me as merely a mother watching her son's games (which, often, I was).

Once I selected the teams I wanted to follow, I approached the coaches of those teams and explained to them that my project dealt with the history of FSA in the neighborhood, the role of sports in boys' and parents' lives, and the ways in which they handle various kinds of experiences, like winning and losing and their interactions with coaches. I asked for their permission to follow their team over the course of the season, which would involve me attending games, practices, and conversations with parents. Of the eight coaches either I or my research assistant approached, six agreed immediately. Two newcomer coaches, who were approached by one of my research assistants, were reluctant. One newcomer coach said that he would present it to his group of parents himself and see how they felt and get back to us. Not surprisingly, he came back to say that the parents were not interested. Josh, my assistant, was convinced that the coach had presented the prospect to the parents negatively. By the time another newcomer expressed his doubt, we had already obtained enough agreements. Four coaches offered us the balance of backgrounds and a good representation of boys: from Fairmount, from outside the neighborhood, and from varying ethnic and racial backgrounds.

Typically, the manager or head coach recruits a few assistant coaches from among the fathers of his players. Because the leadership on one of the teams we selected was shared between a newcomer head coach and his more dominant Fairmounter assistant coach, we were really dealing with five coaches, two newcomers and three Fairmounters. These coaches differed in ways that seemed typical of the coaches I had observed over the years, in terms of residence, religion, education, and years of coaching experience. Of the three Fairmounters, one had lived in Fairmount his entire life, one had grown up in Fairmount but now lives elsewhere, and one had lived in Fairmount for twenty-three years. In contrast, both of the newcomers lived outside the neighborhood. All three Fairmounters were Catholic, had attended Catholic schools either in the neighborhood or in a nearby parish, and had sent their children to Catholic schools. One newcomer was Jewish and the other was Catholic, but both had attended public schools in other neighborhoods. The children of one of the newcomers attended an expensive private school, while the children of the other newcomer attended public schools. None of the three Fairmounters had attended college, whereas both of the newcomers had completed college and one had a Master's degree. Of the three Fairmounters, one had coached in FSA for twenty-two years, one for eighteen, and one for thirteen. One of the newcomers had coached for seven years and the other for only three.

The coaches of the four teams Dylan and I followed during the 1998 season introduced us to their players during a preseason practice. At the end of one of the first practices of the seven-to-nine Marlins, their coach, Sal, gave me my first introduction, simply saying, "This is Sherri, and she wants to talk to you." They all looked up at me from their circle on the ground as I explained that I was writing a book on Fairmount and its baseball league and on the kinds of experiences boys have playing baseball. I explained that I wanted to follow their team and another one, to tell the story of the teams. I then told them that I had explained it to most of their parents and would be getting to the rest during the next game. Immediately, one boy asked if I was a teacher, since the term "sociologist" was smoky. Lennie, discussed in chapter 4, immediately stood up by my side and began shouting to them that he too was an explorer and that they should listen up. They seemed relieved by his outburst, as if it gave them a break from the seriousness of the moment. I asked for their questions. One boy asked which of the other teams I was following and sneered when he heard the names, but no one else asked any more questions. With the other team I followed, my introduction was similar, with the exception that the coach did not turn it over to me, but instead explained it to them very generally and added that I would be around during all of the games and practices. Most of their questions about what I was up to came out intermittently, throughout the season. Like other researchers, I found in working with children that they were always disappointed to learn that I would not be using their real names.

Field Observations

I adjusted my approach to this project several times along the journey. I started out imagining it as something close to what it ended up being, an integration of my family's personal experience in the baseball organization with more systematic ethnographic data. However, during the exploratory phase of the data collection in 1997, I began to think of the research in more traditional terms, as a project that would put my personal involvements at bay and draw primarily on comparative observations of coaches and teams with which I was not directly involved. This led me to solicit the collaboration on the project of my colleague, Kevin Delaney, during the 1997 season as Josh Freeley, a sociology graduate student, and I informally observed two coaches in the seven-to-nine division. We even went so far as to write a conference paper based on these preliminary field observations. However, sometime in the process of writing up those observations I began to have doubts that collaboration with colleagues who were not personally involved in the space would permit me to adopt the narrative approach I had originally imagined. I struggled with imagining how we would integrate our formal collection of data with my deeply engaged personal experience. I could feel myself shifting more and more to third person and losing contact with my personal emotional stance in the space. I am very grateful to Kevin Delaney for his graceful acceptance of my under-articulated sense that I needed to go it alone.

While chapter 1 gives a general overview to the process of data collection, I include here methodological details and issues that might bore the general reader. The phases of research and the sources of data are summarized in Table A.1. In the summer of 1997, Josh Freeley and I began by observing the informally selected practices and games of two teams of boys, aged seven to nine. We did so through most of the 1997 season. Two men, each judged to be tied predominantly to either the Fairmounters or the newcomers, coached the two selected teams, the Angels and the Senators.[3] The Angels were coached by Jerry, a man from the neighborhood who worked various manual jobs and had a high school education. This was Jerry's seventh year coaching the Angels, although he had also coached other teams prior to that, when his older children played. The second team, the Senators, was coached by a newcomer professional, Kyle, who had coached baseball at Fairmount for only three years. Kyle held two Master's degrees and resided outside of Fairmount, in a nearby neighborhood. Beyond the two teams Josh followed, I observed the playoffs and finals that season of another four teams of seven-to-nine boys, for a total of about fifteen games. I also attended another twenty-five games of my son's team, the more competitive "ten-and-under traveling team," which represented the neighborhood that year in the city-wide league competition and, as it turned out, went on to win the city-wide championship and competed in a regional championship in a neighboring state

Dylan Galaty, also a Temple graduate student, worked with me during the second season. Before the season began, Dylan and I sat down and reviewed the themes and the comparable game moments that we would monitor, observing the coaches, the parents, and the boys of our four teams. I was especially interested in monitoring tensions between coaches, parents, and boys, and tensions between neighborhood folk and newcomers and parents of color who had more recently entered the organization. Since I was focusing exclusively on boys' baseball, I wanted to pay close attention to how and when themes of manhood emerged, to expressions about expectations of male behavior, and to implicit models of masculinity that might be behind the comments and reactions of parents, coaches, and boys. Did these expressions vary in systematic ways as people watched, coached, or played baseball?

First, in order to capture the range of coaching styles, we agreed to concentrate on certain dimensions of coaching: the coaches' speeches to the boys before and after the games; the frequency, intensity, and timing of their interventions; the types of chatter (at batting moments, at fielding moments, at moments when physical and mental errors were made); their game strategies and the stress they put on winning, having fun, and instructing individual players; their reactions to the range of emotional styles of their players; their tolerance for displays of vulnerability and anger; and their encounters with parents. Second, we would monitor the boys' responses to their team's winning or losing, their own and teammates' errors and successes, and coaches' and umpires' interventions and comments. We also would pay attention to team group dynamics—how more talented players treated less successful players; whether or not, and how, teams had fun; how teams handled clutch situations, disciplined themselves, and treated their competitors. Third, we would record the comments and reactions of parents about the coaches, the FSA organization, and the players, as well as the types of justification they gave for their approval or disapproval.

During the 1997 and 1998 seasons, there were thirty-one slots open for head

TABLE A.1.

Overview of Data Sources and Samples

Field Observations

1993–2000

Observed all of the seasonal events of the organization, such as the annual fund-raiser: "Booster Day," Opening Day, Picture Day, All-Stars Day, and "Trophy Day," as well as numerous team barbeques.

Summer 1997

Observations of two seven-to-nine teams, coached by one Fairmount resident and one newcomer professional, by Freeley.

Observations of the playoffs and championship games of four other seven-to-nine teams, by Grasmuck.

Informal observations of 25 games of the ten-and-under traveling team, leading to city-wide championship, by Grasmuck.

A total of approximately 35 games for the season

Summer 1998

Observations of games and practices of two seven-to-nine teams, the Marlins (18 games) and the Blue Jays (13 games), by Grasmuck.

Observations of games of two ten-to-twelve teams, the Bisons (8 games) and the Diamond Backs (11 games), by Galaty; a third team intermittently by Grasmuck (8 games), and occasional games of other teams in league by Grasmuck (5 games).

Observations of games of one FSA traveling team, home and away, by Grasmuck (14 games).

Observations of 12 practices, by Grasmuck and Galaty.

A total of 81 games and 12 practices for the season

Interviews

May–January 2001–2002

Conducted in-depth, semistructured interviews with 18 current FSA coaches from the seven-to-nine and ten-to-twelve divisions, and 4 former FSA coaches or staff members: 9 longtime residents of Fairmount (all white); 8 high school graduates and 1 with a college degree; 9 newcomers (6 white, 3 black)—1 to Fairmount, 1 to Spring Garden, 7 of other neighborhoods; 7 with college degrees, 2 with graduate degrees; 4 coach/organizational leaders; 2 of 22 coaches were female, by Grasmuck.

Conducted in-depth, semistructured interviews with 21 parents: 9 males and 12 females; 10 grew up in Fairmont/Spring Garden, high school education; 10 newcomers with college degrees (7 in Fairmount/Spring Garden, 3 from outside); 6 parents "of color"(3 black women, 1 black male, 2 Puerto Rican males, 1 Puerto Rican female), by Grasmuck.

coaches of boys' teams at FSA, either in the seven-to-nine division or in the ten-to-twelve division, and a few more for several of the traveling teams. During both of these seasons, all of the head coaches, or managers as they are called, were white. It was not uncommon during these years, to see black or Hispanic parents working as assistant coaches, but at that point none were managers. The following year, three black managers were given teams, two in the seven-to-nine division and one in the ten-to-twelve division. But at the time of our study there were no black managers, and therefore all of the managers we selected that season were white.

During the games, Dylan and I would usually stand immediately behind the dugout of our respective teams, as that vantage point maximized the possibility of watching the boys interact with each other when their team was at bat, hearing the public and "private" comments of coaches to the boys, and monitoring the comments and interpretations of the "insider parents" (who stood there as well) about what was happening in the game, with the umpire, with the coach, or with the boys. Other parents rarely approached the dugouts. They stationed themselves instead, either alone or in clusters, on the bleachers. A few gravitated toward the grass. Therefore, we also spent time during every game in the bleachers. It was there that parents most openly discussed the boys' performances and reactions, their evaluations of the coaches and of parents standing behind the dugouts, and their experiences with the organization of the FSA. On an individual basis, we explained our research in general terms to the parents of the teams we followed. Beyond them, many of the parents of the opposing teams never noticed our existence.

The younger boys' field is separate, but adjacent to, the older boys' field. This meant that Dylan and I were often present at the ball field at the same time, even though observing different games. In fact, often, as I stood behind my dugout taking notes, I could see Dylan's large frame and shiny, shaved head, across the two adjacent fields, bent over, writing on his clipboard behind his team's dugout. In addition to taking notes at the games, I preferred sometimes to retreat from hearing range and dictate my observations and reactions into a tiny tape recorder I kept with me. I found this to be much more efficient than note-taking, as I could then capture a conversation or a comment I had just heard more precisely. After games, I would return quickly to my house, located just a five-minute walk from the field, and spend about two hours typing up my notes and transcribing my taped comments. Throughout my field notes, I included in bracketed form my emotional reactions to notable game moments or poignant events. Also, for each set of field notes, I made a set of separate analytic observations about that day's events as they related to the broader themes of the study and I instructed Dylan to do the same. From just the four teams we followed, we ended up with more than 400 pages of typed, single-spaced field notes. We also ended up with notes from other organizational events and from occasional strategic games with other teams. I read and reread the field notes multiple times, thematically labeling each section or paragraph.

We structured our observations of the four teams around themes that had emerged from my first year of observations. I found that there were gender-relevant differences in our field notes. Dylan's notes were much more game-centered than mine. He dutifully reported plays, errors, and the formal benchmarks of the game, with the score at the end of every inning. I sometimes wondered about other things happening around these plays or on the bleachers. Dylan's field notes showed a verbal mastery of the genre of sportscasting and of the sports pages. In contrast, in my notes it was not always clear what was happening in the game, but I included elaborate commentary about the comments of the boys on the benches, the mumblings of parents, and the facial expressions and body language of coaches. We both set out to pay attention to the social dynamics and the specifics of each game. But he ended up focusing more on the way the game framed other social events, while I focused more on the way social dynamics altered the games.

Interviews

I had intended to stop my research with the ethnographic observations of the games and practices, and I had even completed several draft chapters in 1999. However, it became apparent as I struggled with these chapters that my field observations had yielded a set of observations about the game behavior of coaches, parents, and players, and a good deal of my interpretations of these behaviors, but little about the intentions, philosophies, or interpretations of coaches or parents, regardless of their behavior at games. So I stopped writing for a year and developed interview guides for coaches and parents, conducted the interviews, transcribed a few myself, and had the rest transcribed by others. Subsequently, I listened to all of the interviews on tape and corrected the transcriptions for accuracy.

Half of the coaches I interviewed were longtime residents of Fairmount who had been involved with the organization for more than two decades and, with two exceptions, continued to live in the neighborhood of Fairmount. In fact, eight of the nine Fairmounter coaches had grown up in the neighborhood. Only one of the Fairmounter coaches had attended college, and all of them were white. These Fairmounter coaches held jobs that ranged from manual, working-class to clerical, lower-middle-class positions. Several were comfortably self-employed, and one worked as a professional city employee.

The other nine coaches interviewed were newcomers whose length of participation with the organization ranged from one to nine years, and who, with one exception, lived outside of Fairmount, either in nearby Spring Garden or in other, more affluent nearby neighborhoods. All of the newcomer coaches were college educated. All but two also held advanced degrees or training. With two exceptions, the newcomer coaches held professional jobs involving high levels of autonomy and little direct supervision of their work. Three of the newcomers interviewed were black. In addition to the coaches, I interviewed four other former coaches or individuals with a long history of participation in the organizational leadership of FSA in past decades. Only two of the twenty-two coaches interviewed were female. The range of issues covered in these interviews included the coaches' personal historical experience with baseball and the league, their reactions to various game scenarios, their assessments of their own strengths and weaknesses and those of other coaches, their experiences with parents, and their reactions to a range of emotional styles in the boys they coached.

For the parent interviews, I selected most cases from the 1998 registration sheets, the forms that parents fill out when they register their child and pay their registration fee. These forms provided a complete listing of all parents who registered children between the ages of seven and twelve that year. On most of these sheets, the boy had been given a ranking by FSA officials for purposes of the draft. The ten parents I define as Fairmounters had either grown up in Fairmount or had married someone who did. Only two no longer lived in Fairmount, having recently moved away. In contrast, only two of the newcomer parents lived within the Fairmount neighborhood, although half lived in the adjacent, more gentrified area of Spring Garden; the remaining four traveled from neighborhoods outside either Fairmount or Spring Garden, areas typical of the neighborhoods of a growing number of FSA children.

The themes covered in the coach interviews included the history of each coach's own childhood experience with baseball; their educational, occupational, and residential information; the history of their coaching experience; their subjective assessments of their goals, strengths, and weaknesses as a coach; their selections of the best and worst of the FSA coaching staff over time; questions about various game scenarios designed to tap their emphasis on instruction versus competition; questions about their reactions to a range of emotional expressions of players; their experiences with, and the challenges posed by, parents; their descriptions of the qualities of an ideal baseball player; and their assessments of the changes in the organization of FSA over time—the internal divisions or tensions of the organization and their assessments of the ways the neighborhood and FSA had changed over time.

Parent interviews covered themes similar but not identical to those in the coach interviews: the parents' childhood history with sports; their educational, occupational, and residential information; the history of their participation with FSA; their personal rankings of all the coaches their son/s had had in FSA and the justifications for their rankings; descriptions of the qualities of an ideal coach; their degree of intervention in coaching decisions related to their child;

game scenarios with questions about appropriate coaching strategy and justifications; their evaluations of the organization of FSA and its leadership, and
their assessments of the major divisions and cleavages between the neighborhood and FSA; their assessments of the impact of changes in the racial and ethnic composition of the league; their assessments of the emotional challenges of
baseball for their sons and the extent to which they felt these needs were
addressed in their coached experiences; and salient memories that helped
define their overall experience with FSA.

The interviews with coaches and parents averaged one and a half hours. I
interviewed most of the coaches and parents in their homes, but some interviews took place at a picnic table adjacent to the baseball field, a few occurred
in my kitchen or at a local deli, and a few coaches were interviewed in their
place of business. I taped all of the interviews and followed each session with
approximately one hour of note-writing about the "between the lines" moments:
the setting, the tone, the emotional dynamics, and the analytical themes of the
interview. Oftentimes, I would record these observations on tape after the interview and transcribe them later.

Once the interviews were transcribed, I created a data matrix with a
spreadsheet program, placing all of the questions of the interview guides across
the y-axis and all the interviewees across the x-axis with their summarized
responses filling the text cells of the table. I could manipulate the data matrix,
of more than 500 printed pages, to give me a quick overview of how the entire
sample had responded to any given question. I could also arrange the cases
according to categories, such as Fairmounter coach versus newcomer coach,
parent of high-skilled child versus parent of low-skilled child, or parents of
color versus white parents, in order to observe patterns, or absence of patterns,
around themes. The data matrix helped me while I was writing to distinguish
more honestly between quotations from parents or coaches that were typical of
a group, and quotations from parents or coaches that were salient, dramatic, or
juicy, but not necessarily representative.

Conducting ethnographic fieldwork in a small public space combined with
the formal interviews in private spheres provides interesting challenges to confidentiality. All of the people I formally interviewed completed consent forms in
which I guaranteed them confidentiality in the sense that nothing they said in
the interview would be associated with them as individuals. Although I name
the community, to protect their privacy I changed the names and many partic-
ulars about all of my interviewees, including identifying details in their stories
when I quote them directly. Although I wanted to actually name a few of the
original founders of the organization, as a way of honoring their efforts, at least
one of them preferred that I not do so. Therefore, I have changed the names of
the founders of FSA to pseudonyms as well. Although a journalist might not
have done so, given that it was a public space, I also assigned pseudonyms to

and changed some of the characteristics of individuals I quoted or portrayed in the context of the games and the ball field, even when they had not been promised anonymity. One coach, disappointed that his identity would not be revealed, urged me to use a code name he selected, so that he could track himself in the text. However, in a relatively small organization, in such a small space, with continuing dense interactions and a long history, the issue of recognizability remains tricky. If I perceived that too much of the social or aesthetic meaning was being lost by the distortion of identity, there were limits to how far I was willing to go in distorting the descriptions of individuals, like giving them a false ethnicity or radically altering their physique or tone. While no one is definitively recognizable, some readers with deep experiences in the organization will have strong hunches and others may well recognize themselves. In confronting this dilemma, I sought to balance confidentiality with descriptive integrity as much as I could.

Nature of Involvement and Vulnerabilities

When Gary Fine wrote *With the Boys: Little League Baseball and Preadolescent Culture* in the late 1980s, he confessed that his not being as athletically skilled as most of the coaches in his field sites limited his role, and he was sometimes teased by players for his lack of skills. As a male researcher, he needed to deal with the cultural expectation that, as a male, he ought to possess an acceptable level of skill and know-how. He ultimately saw his "not adding up" as an advantage since it excused him from the expectation that he help adult coaches or be an "expert" to the boys he wanted to befriend. My situation, of course, was different. Very few of the coaches or boys expected much of anything from me in relation to the game or practice. There were exceptions. It was more likely to be Fairmounters who might, on a rare occasion, wonder if I might be useful in baseball terms. They came from a community where girls and women played ball. There was a whole softball side of FSA controlled by neighborhood women who were passionately devoted to the game. The Fairmount men were more likely than the professional coaches to ask in a pinch if I might be able to help out, with scoring for example. I did occasionally volunteer to run to the concession stand for ice when a boy was injured, and I remember agreeing, during a practice at adjacent parkland, to lead a desperate boy across a four-lane street to the bathroom behind the concession stand. But I can't remember one instance of anyone ever approaching me to help with anything technical.

My two male research assistants did confront some participation pressures. I remember arriving once at the field and finding, to my astonishment, one of them umping a seven-to-nine game. He whispered to me, "They were desperate!" We subsequently established that they would do no umpiring and no keeping score, although they might occasionally help out with drills in practice, both to pay back the coaches for their intrusions and also as a way to get to know the boys better. Fine and Glassner have argued that adult researchers working with children might adopt one of four roles: leader, observer, supervisor, or friend.[4] In the context of the games and practices, our research role was mostly as "observers." We engaged in no supervision of the boys, had no formal authority over them, and with few exceptions, had little personal involvement outside of the baseball space. Our contact with the boys, even the many sidebar conversations, occurred in the near proximity of many other adults who assumed primary responsibility for the boys' behavior. We were therefore almost never solely responsible for them and faced no dilemmas about potentially harmful situations or about disciplining or restraining them. Since we were following only a few teams, we permitted ourselves to cheer for their successes, both because we all found ourselves very swept up in the group enthusiasm, and because joining in made us less conspicuous.

The exception to personal involvements came in terms of my own role as a mother of a player in the older division. Quite a number of boys did know me as my son's mother, had been to our house, or, more likely, had played basketball behind our house in the evenings over several summers (until our neighbors discreetly protested). I regularly negotiated with some of these boys to keep it down, or to tone down their language because the neighbors were getting antsy. And I listened to their mumblings when they pointed out that no one would complain about the noise if they were all white. Part of the reason I chose to concentrate this research on the seven-to-nine teams, and to have Dylan concentrate on the ten-to-twelve division, came from my personally knowing so many of the ten-to-twelve boys, and from having a son and a husband active in the older division.

My involvement with adults was different. Since my participation conformed in many ways to what many mothers did during games—namely, sitting on the bleachers or standing behind the dugout—I engaged in many more informal conversations with them about topics beyond the games than I did with the boys. My interactions with them paralleled many of the adult encounters in the space. The happenings of the game framed the pace and the attention span of our conversations. This made it easy to approach almost anyone. I could position myself next to anyone without causing suspicion, as long as I also watched the game. Since a great deal of baseball is about talking about baseball, folks watching the game typically make comments, informed or uninformed, about what is happening. While it is true that the nature of one's comments rapidly establishes one's degree of knowledge, and that there are some who will avoid chatting with anyone who shouts out something like "Slide!" as a runner advances to first base, most welcome the opportunity to share insights and knowledge. The cultural expectation that we talk about the game and our children as we watch it helped make developing connections fairly easy.

As the season wore on, Dylan and I discussed how hard it was not to get wrapped up in the game, how easily, after standing with them and their children for several months, we were drawn into solidarity with the team's parents. Somewhere along the way, we decided that we would not restrain ourselves from cheering for our teams, unless they were playing against the other team we were both observing. For one thing, it helped the boys, especially the younger ones, to accept us more easily if they didn't think we were just scouting them for someone else or studying them without the usual range of emotions. For example, once, some of the younger boys on one team I followed, the Marlins, understood that I also went to all the games of their competitors, the Blue Jays. They asked me where I would stand when we played the Blue Jays. They seemed mildly relieved to learn that I would go back and forth between the two teams' dugouts and bleachers. Also, paying attention to how easily I became swept up with the game, and with the specific victories of particular boys, was important in understanding the rapidly fluctuating emotions of the parents of the team. By permitting ourselves occasionally to cheer for our teams, we defined ourselves as casual team insiders. In any case, I found myself incapable of not cheering.

Although I entered the research site as a professional, a college professor, I had lived in various class circumstances growing up. During my childhood, my family of origin made a rather rapid ascent to the upper middle class in terms of income, but not in terms of cultural style. Neither of my parents went to college. One of my sisters and a few cousins were the first in our extended family to attend college. My father lived with much unspoken shame about his status inconsistency that translated into a constant series of warnings to his children about the pretenses and cruelties of the educated class. This left me, as it left many with similar backgrounds, with a powerful legacy of ambivalence about academia but also with a sense of familiarity and loyalty toward those aspects of working-class, or lower-middle-class, culture that express defense in the face of cultural humiliation. This fortified my empathy with many Fairmounters as they dealt with the professional newcomers.

While in the Introduction I presented many of the aspects of my identity, and of my husband's and son's identities, that have mingled with this research project, I do not wish to give the impression that I have "told it all." Given the complex role my family played in this space, I had to consider more than just how exposed I wanted to be. In spirit, I accept the notion that sharing our positioning and the complex range of identities we each hold gives the reader insight into potential biases or blind spots that might condition our research observations. Yet I agree with Pablo Vila, who argues that some identities are more acceptable than others and that some are "not yet authorized subject positions" and cannot be shared without peril.[5] Over the course of the project, our family suffered tragedy that ravaged us, but required a social silence. This silence crept into the manuscript at various junctures and rang out to me like a trumpet. But whatever limitation it imposed on the book was worth the price.

Objectivity as Fairness

I note in chapter 1 that my compass for objectivity in the project was fairness to the multiple viewpoints and perspectives of the diverse groups of the FSA. This notion of objectivity as fairness draws on the methodological sensibilities of Gideon Sjoberg. This perspective on a plausible objectivity for social science is linked to the representation of different perspectives, or standpoints, embedded in diverse social locations and combined with the researcher's obligation to analyze his or her own moral or value position relative to the topic under investigation.[6]

Throughout the project, I fretted about how to balance fairly my representation of the sometimes competing perspectives of Fairmounters and of newcomer professionals. At one point, my editor, after reading an early draft of one chapter, proclaimed that I had an "anti-yuppie" bias, as expressed by the fact that I used fewer quotes from their interviews. Yet, after reading the same draft, a colleague worried that the Fairmounter perspective was not fleshed out enough. In each instance, I made revisions, trying to address their mutually contradictory concerns.

After I completed a more final draft of the manuscript, I selected two people from the community and asked them to read it and to give me feedback. Both of these individuals were "crossovers," in that they moved freely in both newcomer and Fairmounter circles. But they also crossed from different origins. One reader was a longtime resident of the neighborhood who had coached, umped games, and held various staff positions for more than a decade; the other community reader was a newcomer professional, but one who had been involved with FSA for more than a decade. Both had provided some of the most insightful comments of my earlier interviews, reflecting keen sociological imaginations. Specifically, I asked them to point out any factual inaccuracies they noticed, but more importantly, to signal any places in the text where they sensed any unfairness in my representation. I left it at that.

From the newcomer reader, I received an overall evaluation of fairness, with one qualification about the chapter on coaches. If several coaches were who she suspected they might be, then she disagreed with my implicit evaluation of one's style as preferable to the other's. She provided several detailed examples about the tricky ways in which competitive coaches hide their competitiveness, and stressed the inconsistent ways parents viewed coaches, depending on how close to them they had become. As someone who had spent much time inside dugouts, close to coach mumblings, she, like the boys, saw many instances of subtle tenderness, even from the harshest coaches. She also noted that standing back and seeing the place through my eyes made her see its social achievements as fragile and made her worry more about its future.

The evaluation from the Fairmounter reader was more complex. We first spoke briefly after he had read about half of the manuscript. His first reaction was, "Well, I now know all there is to know about Fairmount Sports Association. I've been down there for years and had no idea all that was going on." But then he expressed his discomfort with the use of the term "old-timer" to refer to longtime Fairmount residents, which, to my surprise, he found pejorative. Yet with probing, he revealed that his problem with the word choice really reflected a discomfort with the representation of the neighborhood in terms of its racial past, its posturing toward bordering black areas. He said, "If you had explained more how the Fairmounters developed their value system, how that 'we-they' came from their parents and grandparents trying to survive the '50s and the Depression, then using 'old-timer' would have been all right. . . . I mean, I didn't find anything unfair, or hurtful toward anyone. But it is the outsider's perspective." After he had read the manuscript through twice, we then had a conversation that lasted almost four hours, where we explored this theme and others further. "It is not that you say anything untrue about Fairmount's history. That is how it was. But you don't explain how those Fairmounter values came from the struggles of their parents to survive. We learn a lot about Fairmounter racial pasts but we don't get to see what all those newcomers were doing back then. Maybe they were worse. I mean, you probably can't do it cause they came from all over the place, no particular place like Fairmount. . . . It just seems that Fairmounters are there as a backdrop for the newcomers." We discussed how hard it was to hear one's complex historical experience, filled with memories of community sacrifice and struggle, reduced to a particular relationship with outside groups. His point was valid. Historic Fairmount was clearly much more than just a white, racially defended territory in Philadelphia. By focusing on its racial past, a past shared by many other white neighborhoods in the city in the pre–civil rights era, and by not describing the possibly equally racist neighborhoods of the childhoods of the white newcomers, I had left them more negatively exposed than the newcomers whose pasts were less clear. As we discussed this further, however, he allowed for the fact that the representation of the pasts of newcomers was an almost impossible task given the heterogeneity of backgrounds. I asked him if he had seen ways, other than racially, that the newcomers did not come off as well, perhaps, as the Fairmounters. We then explored together the extent to which the manuscript was also a celebration of Fairmounters' contributions to the community, a recognition that their labor had both sustained the organization and held it together for the benefit of newcomers and new families of color. He had appreciated the extent to which their labor was counted and documented, which showed the unfairness of many newcomer demands given their minimal contributions. About a month later when I ran into him with a group of boys, he came up to me. "Look at me down here. I quit coaching for four years, my kids are all gone, but after I read your book and thought more about all my years here, I just couldn't give it up. I signed up to coach again. You reminded me of too many good memories." In the end I had to content myself with his judgment that while the racially divisive history of Fairmount was hard to own up to in the post–civil rights era (a discomfort shared in many parts of contemporary America about the legacy of race discrimination), my representation of neighborhood encounters had, nonetheless, not been unfair in his eyes. Since fairness to the multiple viewpoints in this multicultural space had been my compass, I had to leave it at that.

NOTES

CHAPTER 1: SEEING THE WORLD IN NEIGHBORHOOD BASEBALL

1. See Ruth Behar, *The Vulnerable Observer: Anthropology that Breaks Your Heart* (Boston: Beacon Press, 1996).

2. Victor Lidz, in "The Sense of Identity in Jewish-Christian Families" (*Qualitative Sociology* 14, no. 1 [1991]: 84), distinguishes an "observing participant" from a "participant observer." An observing participant "enters the group or situation to be studied as a natural member meeting all the usual qualities or requirements of participation...one is a member who then asks the group for permission to carry out social scientific observation in conjunction with one's other activities of membership." Having spent years in the organization as a "bench mom," I then requested permission to study the organization.

3. See David Snow, Louis A. Zurcher, and Gideon Sjoberg, "Interview by Comment: An Adjunct to the Formal Interview," *Qualitative Sociology* 5 (1982): 285–311.

4. In three of the parent cases, once I began the interview, I discovered that the parent also had a history of coaching in the league. These three "double dipping" cases were drawn on for my discussions of coaches as well as parents.

5. There couldn't be a sharper contrast in tone between the way that Doris Kearns Goodwin in *Wait Till Next Year: A Memoir* (New York: Touchstone, 1997) and Adrienne Harris in "Women, Baseball, and Words" (in Gary F. Waller, Kathleen McCornick, and Lois Josephs Fowler, eds., *Lexington Introduction to Literature: Reading and Responding to Texts* [Lexington, Mass.: D. C. Heath, 1987], 1139–1157) position themselves as female fans of and writers on baseball. Harris possesses a double awareness of both the ideological features of baseball and the suspect nature of the female voice talking on the topic: "Woman as speaking subject is excluded, both specifically from the practice of baseball and generally from authority in discourse" (1156).

6. See Joe Feagin, Anthony M. Orum, and Gideon Sjoberg, eds., "A Case for the Case Study," in *The Nature of the Case Study: Introduction* (Chapel Hill: University of North Carolina Press, 1991), 7.

7. See Laurel Richardson, "Writing: A Method of Inquiry," in Norman K. Denzin and Yvonna S. Lincoln, eds., *Handbook of Qualitative Research*, 2d edition (Thousand Oaks, Calif.: Sage Publications, 2000), 923–948, for a comprehensive discussion of the rhetorical advantages of what she calls "creative analytic practices" such as autoethnography, fiction-stories, poetry, drama, and, among others things, performance texts. See also Carolyn Ellis and Arthur P. Bochner, "Autoethnography, Personal Narrative, Reflexivity: Researcher as Subject," in Norman K. Denzin and Yvonna S. Lincoln, eds., *Handbook of Qualitative Research*, 2d edition (Thousand Oaks, Calif.: Sage

Publications, 2000), 733–768, and Yvonna S. Lincoln and Norman K. Denzin, "The Seventh Moment: Out of the Past," in *Handbook of Qualitative Research*, 2d edition (Thousand Oaks, Calif.: Sage Publications, 2000), 1047–1065.

8. This section is in deference to Mitch Duneier's point in *Sidewalk* (New York: Farrar, Straus, and Giroux, 1999) that a scandalously small amount of scholarly attention is paid to the use of quotes and quotation marks.

9. See Andrew C. Sparkes, "Fictional Representations: On Difference, Choice, and Risk," *Sociology of Sport Journal* 19 (2002): 1–24.

10. I made this decision to name the communities early in the project, before Wolfe published his article accusing sociologists of using pseudonyms with little justification, a practice that prevents others from second-guessing their arguments about places. See Alan Wolfe, "Invented Names, Hidden Distortions in Social Science," *Chronicle of Higher Education* 49, no. 38 (2003): B13–14.

11. See Clifford Geertz, *Local Knowledge: Further Essays in Interpretative Anthropology* (New York: Basic Books, 1983), 36.

12. See the appendix for a more detailed discussion of this notion of fairness as a criterion of objectivity.

CHAPTER 2:   THE NEIGHBORHOOD AND RACE SPONSORSHIP

Chapter 2 is a revised version of an article previously published as "Something about Baseball: Gentrification, Racial Sponsorship, and Neighborhood Boys' Baseball," *Sociology of Sport Journal* 20, no. 4 (2003): 307–330.

1. R. Cybriwsky, "Social Aspects of Neighborhood Change," *Annals of the Association of American Geographers* 68 (1978): 17–33.

2. Eugene Ericksen, David Bartellt, Patrick Feeney, Gerald Foeman, Sherri Grasmuck, Maureen Martella, William Rickle, Robert Spencer, and David Webb, *The State of Puerto Rican Philadelphia* (Philadelphia: Temple University, Institute for Public Policy Studies, 1985).

3. Carmen Teresa Whalen, *From Puerto Rico to Philadelphia: Puerto Rican Workers and Postwar Economics* (Philadelphia: Temple University Press, 2001, 186). Whalen's data extend the area defined as Spring Garden to include an additional census tract, 133, just to the east of tract 134.

4. Of the thirty-five men arrested, most were in their twenties, and only five were Puerto Rican. See Whalen, *From Puerto Rico*, 189.

5. See Whalen, *From Puerto Rico*, 187.

6. Cybriwski, "Social Aspects," 22, calculates the rates of homeownership in Fairmount as even higher—almost three-quarters of Fairmount residents in the 1960s, based on real estate directories.

7. See Ralph Taylor, *Human Territorial Functioning: An Empirical, Evolutionary Perspective on Individual and Small Group Territorial Cognitions, Behaviors, and Consequences* (Cambridge: Cambridge University Press, 1988), 79–131, for a conceptual discussion of socially defended territories.

8. In the early 1970s, in high stress areas on the borders of Fairmount, David Ley and Roman Cybriwski, in "Urban Graffiti as Territorial Markers" (*Annals of the Association of American Geographers* 64 [1974]: 491–505), linked neighborhood feelings of encroachment to the content and placement of wall graffiti (502). Messages such as

"Fairmount Rules," "Fairmount is Boss," and "White Power" sent unfriendly messages to outsiders and signaled the neighborhood's insecurity.

9. See R. Cybriwsky, "Social Aspects of Neighborhood Change," *Annals of the Association of American Geographers* 68 (1978): 17–33; and Whalen, *From Puerto Rico*.

10. Whalen, *From Puerto Rico*, 197.

11. Lina Kadaba, "Relentlessly Striving for More," *The Philadelphia Inquirer*, Sunday, March 3, 1998, H3.

12. Ley and Cybriwsky, in "Urban Graffiti," 503, report two cases of large anti-black actions against black families settling in the area in the early 1970s.

13. Cary Goodman, *Choosing Sides: Playground and Street Life on the Lower East Side* (New York: Schocken Books, 1979).

14. John Logan and Harvey Molotch, *Urban Fortunes: The Political Economy of Place* (Berkeley: University of California, 1987).

15. Judith Goode and Jo Anne Schneider, *Reshaping Ethnic and Racial Relations in Philadelphia: Immigrants in a Divided City* (Philadelphia: Temple University Press, 1994).

16. Harvey Molotch, William Freudenburg, and Krista Paulsen, "History Repeats Itself, but How? City Character, Urban Tradition, and the Accomplishment of Place," *American Sociological Review* 65 (2000): 791–823.

17. Roger Kahn considers this the greatest moment in the history of American sports. In MacNeil/Lehrer Productions, *Memories of Summer: The Golden Days of Baseball*, transcript of interview between Roger Kahn and David Gergen, Online News Hour, *http://www.pbs.org/newshour/gergen/april97/kahn_4–11.html*, 2003. This is not to portray Reese as more heroic than Robinson. Rather, it underscores the need all heroes and heroines have for help from friends.

18. Jay Coakley, "Sport in Society: An Inspiration or an Opiate?" in D. Stanley Eitzen, ed., *Sport in Contemporary Society: An Anthology* (New York: Worth Publishers, 2001), 20–36; and Margaret Gatz, Michael A. Messner, and Sandra J. Ball-Rokeach, eds., *Paradoxes of Youth and Sport* (Albany: State University of New York Press, 2002).

19. Harry Edwards, *The Revolt of the Black Athlete* (New York: Free Press, 1970); Harry Edwards, *Sociology of Sport* (Homewood, Ill.: Dorsey Press, 1973); Richard Lapchick, *Racial and Gender Report Card* (Boston: Northeastern University Center for the Study of Sport in Society, 1998); D. Stanley Eitzen, *Fair and Foul: Beyond the Myths and Paradoxes of Sport* (Lanham, Md.: Rowman and Littlefield, 1999); George Sage, "Racial Inequality and Sport," in D. Stanley Eitzen, ed., *Sport in Contemporary Society: An Anthology* (New York: Worth Publishers, 2001), 275–284.

20. Eitzen, *Fair and Foul*, 18.

21. Coakley, "Sport in Society."

22. Eitzen, *Fair and Foul*, 18.

23. Michael Messner, *Taking the Field: Women, Men and Sports* (Minneapolis: University of Minnesota Press, 2002).

24. Goodman, *Choosing Sides*.

25. Paul Hoch, *Rip Off the Big Game: The Exploitation of Sports by the Power Elite* (Garden City, N.Y.: Anchor Books, 1972).

26. Coakley, "Sport in Society."

27. Margaret Gatz, Michael A. Messner, Michael A. Ball-Rokeach, and Sandra J. Ball-Rokeach,

eds., *Paradoxes of Youth and Sport 2002* (Albany: State University of New York Press, 2002), 5.

28. Coakley, "Sport in Society"; Harry Edwards, "An End of the Golden Age of Black Partic-
    ipation," in D. Stanley Eitzen, *Sport in Contemporary Society: An Anthology*, 6th ed.
    (New York: Worth Publishers, 2001), 285–291.

29. One of the most comprehensive reviews of this idea of "sport as secular sacrament"
    is found in Varda Burstyn, *The Rites of Men: Manhood, Politics and the Culture of
    Sport* (Toronto: University of Toronto Press, 1999). See also Donald Mrozek, Sport and
    American Mentality, 1880–1910 (Knoxville: University of Tennessee Press, 1983).

30. In the mid–1950s, the Phillies had the only all-white baseball club in the National
    League. Its first black member, John Kennedy, arrived in 1957. See Bruce Kuklick, *To
    Every Thing a Season: Shibe Park and Urban Philadelphia, 1909–1976* (Princeton, N.J.:
    Princeton University Press, 1991), 148. Two years later, the Red Sox signed Pumpsie
    Green, making it the last team in major league baseball to integrate, with the Phillies
    being the next to last. See Howard Bryant, *Shut Out: A History of Race and Baseball in
    Boston* (New York: Routledge, 2002).

CHAPTER 3:   THE CLUBHOUSE AND CLASS CULTURES

1. See Frank F. DeGiovanni, "Patterns of Change in Housing Market Activity in Revitaliz-
   ing Neighborhoods," *Journal of the American Planning Association* 49 (1983): 22–39;
   Jason Hackworth, "Post-recession Gentrification in New York City," *Urban Affairs
   Review* 37, no. 6 (2002): 815–843; Gary Bridge, "Gentrification, Class, and Residence:
   A Reappraisal," *Environment & Planning D: Society & Space* 12, no. 1 (1994): 31–51.

2. See P. Dreier, J. Mollenkopf, and T. Swanstrom, *Place Matters: Metropolitics for the
   Twenty-first Century* (Lawrence: University Press of Kansas, 2001), 100.

3. See John Logan and Harvey Molotch, *Urban Fortunes: The Political Economy of Place*
   (Berkeley: University of California Press, 1987), 287.

4. See Alvin Gouldner, *The Future of Intellectuals and the Rise of the New Class* (New
   York: Seabury Press, 1979); E.O. Wright and B. Martin, "The Transformation of the
   American Class Structure, 1960–1980," *American Journal of Sociology* 93 (1987): 1–29;
   S. Lash and J. Urry, *The End of Organized Capitalism* (Cambridge: Polity Press, 1987).

5. See M. Savage, P. Dickens, and T. Fielding, "Some Social and Political Implications of
   the Contemporary Fragmentation of the 'Service Class' in Britain," *International Journal of Urban and Regional Research* 12 (1988): 455–476; J. Ehrenreich and B. Ehrenreich, "The Professional-Managerial Class," in P. Walker, ed., *Between Labor and Capital*
   (Boston: South End Press, 1979), 5–45.

6. David Ley, "Gentrification and the Politics of the New Middle Class," *Environment and
   Planning D: Society and Space* 12 (1994): 53–74.

7. S. Brint, "New Class and Cumulative Trend Explanations of the Liberal Political Attitudes of Professionals," *American Journal of Sociology* 90 (1984): 30–71.

8. T. Butler and C. Hamnett, "Gentrification, Class, and Gender: Some Comments on
   Warde's 'Gentrification as Consumption,'" *Environment and Planning D: Society and
   Space* 12 (1994): 477–493. See L. Bondi, "Gender, Class and Gentrification: Enriching
   the Debate," *Environment and Planning D: Society and Space* 17 (1999): 261–282, for
   a review of literature on the role of gender as well as class factors involved in gentrification.

9. N. Smith's *The New Urban Frontier: Gentrification and the Revanchist City* (New York: Routledge & Kegan Paul, 1996) provides a comprehensive review of the literature on gentrification in the 1980s and 1990s, organized in terms of consumption and production side explanations. It is widely recognized that the arrival of "the gentry" in marginal housing markets produces a series of chain reactions, often leading to the displacement of lower-income native residents, as happened to Puerto Ricans in Spring Garden. More recently, scholars have turned their attention to the political and cultural impact of gentrification. See David Ley, *The New Middle Class and the Remaking of the Central City* (Oxford: Oxford University Press, 1996); and J. Betancur, "The Politics of Gentrification: The Case of West Town in Chicago," *Urban Affairs Review* 37, no. 6 (2002): 780–814. Also, J. Caulfield, in "'Gentrification' and Desire" (*Canadian Review of Sociology and Anthropology* 26, no. 4 [1989]: 617–632), has examined the way gentrification in Canadian cities involves a paradoxical outcome, initially a reflection of a cultural "emancipatory drive" by those critical of current city-building trying to establish new ways of urban social interaction only to be undermined by a "culture industry" led by modern property entrepreneurs, those who sell not just housing but commoditized lifestyles (626). See also S. R. Prince, "Changing Places: Race, Class, and Belonging in the 'New' Harlem," *Urban Anthropology & Studies of Cultural Systems & World Economic Development* 31, no. 1 (2002): 5–35); A. Ramos-Zayas, "Racializing the 'Invisible' Race: Latino Constructions of 'White Culture' and Whiteness in Chicago," *Urban Anthropology* 30, no. 4 (2001): 341–380; and see Joseph Barry and John Derevlany, eds., *Yuppies Invade My House at Dinnertime* (Hoboken, N.J.: Big River Publishing, 1987), for a hilarious account of the cultural conflict behind gentrification as reflected in letters to the local newspaper. Eli Anderson, in *Street Wise: Race, Class and Change in an Urban Community* (Chicago: University of Chicago Press, 1990), also documented phases in the process of gentrification, from old-timer Villagers, to ex-counter-culture types, both relatively positive toward racial diversity in their neighborhoods, to the latter arrival of "the yuppies," younger professionals, mostly childless, who appear to favor a more homogeneous community and are more uncomfortable with diversity.

10. See Judith Goode and Jo Anne Schneider, *Reshaping Ethnic and Racial Relations in Philadelphia: Immigrants in a Divided City* (Philadelphia: Temple University Press, 1994).

11. They explained how they lost this battle by pointing to a critical moment in the process of gentrification in the area. A meeting between neighborhood residents, dominated by several real estate developers, and city officials from the Redevelopment Authority and Philadelphia Housing Authority occurred in a church at the corner of Mt. Vernon and 22nd Street. At this meeting an explicit agreement was negotiated that there would be no scattered-site, public housing in Spring Garden beyond 21st Street. This resident claimed that this was a defining moment for the area. "Before then it was great; there were Hispanics playing dominos outside, bongo drums playing. But after that meeting, gentrification took off like crazy. The developers felt secure and poured money into their houses and then prices soared."

12. See Jay Coakley, "Organized Sport Programs for Children: Are They Worth the Effort?" in Jay Coakley, ed., *Sport in Society: Issues and Controversies* (St. Louis: Times Mirror/Mosby, 1990), 87–112.

13. In FSA head coaches are referred to as "managers." They both coach and manage the team. FSA leadership selects the head coaches, but the head coaches select their

assistant coaches, who may be a friend of theirs or may come from the ranks of parents. In the text, I sometimes use the phrase "manager-coach" and sometimes "head coach." Strategic FSA leaders estimated the intensity of the work contributions of the most active volunteers, and the twenty coach-managers provided estimates of the time they spent during the season on coaching and other support activities.

14. By 1997, the ratio of newcomer managers to Fairmounter managers in both the seven-to-nine and the ten-to-twelve divisions was even. From that point on, newcomers came to dominate in numbers, hovering around sixty percent for the next several years.

15. In addition to the registration fee, the hidden cost of joining the organization is really about $150, since on top of the registration players are expected to come with a glove and cleats. These expenses insure that relatively few poor families from the surrounding areas can afford entrance.

16. Based on the registration forms (contact sheets) for the 187 families who signed boys up to play in either the seven-to-nine or the ten-to-twelve division of FSA in 1998, 46 percent were from Fairmount/Spring Garden, and 54 percent came from nearby areas (26 percent from Center City, 16 percent from West Philadelphia, and 12 percent from other areas). Project data collected by author.

17. Between 1996 and 1999, 65 percent of Fairmounter head coaches agreed to take a team when they had no son playing in the division. By comparison, only 20 percent of the newcomer head coaches coached a team on which their son did not play over this same period. After 1998, newcomers came to dominate in numbers, hovering around 60 percent of head coaches over the next several years. This ushered in an increase in "father coaches," since newcomers typically coached only when they had a son on the team, unlike their Fairmounter counterparts.

18. See Annette Lareau, *Unequal Childhoods: Class, Race, and Family Life* (Berkeley: University of California Press, 2003).

19. See Andrew Greeley, *The Catholic Imagination* (Berkeley: The University of California Press, 2000), 137. Greeley's argument about the Catholic imagination is not merely a theoretical argument based on doctrine. He presents empirical evidence for a persistent, distinctively Catholic social orientation related to the sacredness of place or local, community ties and hierarchical structures in the community.

20. All of the Fairmounter parents I interviewed were Catholic, but none of the newcomer parents were. The eleven newcomer parents were equally divided between Protestants, Jews, and those who claimed no religious affiliation.

21. See A. Lareau, *Home Advantage: Social Class and Parental Intervention in Elementary Education* (Lanham, Md.: Rowman & Littlefield Publishers, 1989). Brett Williams, in *Upscaling Downtown: Stalled Gentrification in Washington, D.C.* (Ithaca, N.Y.: Cornell University Press, 1988), explored the implications for communities of this same tendency of middle-class parents to scout externally for social opportunities that maximize advantage for their children and in the process weaken the fiber of local communities.

22. See Robert Putnam, *Bowling Alone: The Collapse and Revival of American Community* (New York: Simon and Schuster, 2000).

23. Richard Sennett, *Respect in a World of Inequality* (New York: Norton, 2003), 207.

24. Seven of the ten newcomer parents described FSA as stressing competition (playing games to win) over instruction (teaching individual and team skills), whereas only

two of the ten Fairmounters described the ball club as relatively competitive. Most Fairmounters saw FSA as appropriately balancing competition with instruction.

25. Some of the differences at FSA between Fairmount parents and newcomer parents correspond to findings by Geoffrey Watson, in "Games, Socialization and Parental Values: Social Class Differences in Parental Evaluation of Little League Baseball" (*International Review of Sport Sociology* 9: 17–48), who compared parents in a middle-class Little League program with parents in a working-class league and evaluated their children's' experiences. Middle-class parents tended to view the games more as social events, whereas working-class parents saw them as primarily athletic events, as a "means," and therefore exhibited much more emotional involvement in game interactions and game decision making. Working-class parents also put more stress on the importance of children learning to respond to authority or to conform to highly structured social conditions. One can see why, once parents with such different expectations around the game come together in a shared space like the FSA, their different expectations might be translated into judgments by newcomers that Fairmounter are "too competitive," or judgments by Fairmounters that newcomers don't take the overall game seriously enough, or conform to the logic of the game, or for that matter, have the need to conform to a coach's authority or whims.

26. This was the wording of the original draft produced by the Philadelphia City Planning Commission, reduced and edited for the final version ("City Planning Commission Comments on the Central Philadelphia Development Corporation Parkway Plan," 2000, 6–7, unpublished memo).

CHAPTER 4:   THE DUGOUT AND THE MASCULINITY STYLES OF COACHES

1. See M. S. Kimmel, "Baseball and the Reconstitution of American Masculinity: 1880–1920," in M. A. Messner and D. F. Sabo, eds., *Sport, Men and the Gender Order: Critical Feminist Perspectives* (Champaign, Ill.: Human Kinetics Books, 1990), 55–66; A. E. Harris, "Women, Baseball, and Words," in G. F. Waller, K. McCornick, and L. Josephs Fowler, eds., *Lexington Introduction to Literature: Reading and Responding to Texts* (Lexington, Mass.: D. C. Heath, 1987), 1139–1157; V. Burstyn, *The Rites of Men: Manhood, Politics and the Culture of Sport* (Toronto: University of Toronto Press, 1983).

2. The seminal work that articulates the concept of "hegemonic masculinity" compared to its alternative versions is R. W. Connell, *Gender and Power: Society, the Person and Sexual Politics* (Stanford, Calif.: Stanford University Press, 1987), elaborated on in R. W. Connell, *Masculinities* (Berkeley: University of California Press, 1995), 183–188. Connell's concept of hegemonic masculinity set the stage for two decades of scholarship on variations in manliness. The concept refers to the "culturally idealized form of masculine character" that associates masculinity with "toughness and competitiveness," the "subordination of women," and "the marginalization of gay men."

3. The exact terms to apply to these two contrasting styles of masculinity are somewhat arbitrary. Many choices are fraught with problematic associations or implications. "Hard" versus "soft" masculinity has unintended erotic and/or homophobic associations. "Traditional" versus "modern" would be historically naïve. "Hegemonic" versus "subordinate" is too vague for this context, not to mention that it has a deadening ring. My choice of "tough" versus "tender" follows the description by A. M. Klein in "Dueling Machos: Masculinity and Sport in Mexican Baseball," in J. McKay, M.A.

Messner, and D. Sabo, eds., *Masculinities, Gender Relations, and Sport* (Thousand Oaks, Calif.: Sage Publishers, 2000), 74, of "tough machismo" versus "tender machismo" among a group of players on a Mexican professional baseball team. The Mexican players differed among themselves and from their Anglo counterparts on the same team in three areas: attitudes toward children, expressions of vulnerability, and physical touching of other men.

4. After making the placements of the coaches in terms of the four dimensions, I showed them to two coaches I knew well (who were included among the twenty), to see if they agreed with my judgments on both themselves and the others. These two conversations resulted in my changing the positioning of two coaches in terms of one dimension. In one case, I had attributed more baseball knowledge to one of the coaches than either of them did. In another case, I had judged one coach as less competitive than one of my consultants did. After he provided several concrete illustrations of the coach's strategies in various games I had not witnessed, I was persuaded that his assessment was correct.

5. See T. Carrigan, B. Connell, and J. Lee, "Toward a New Sociology of Masculinity" (in H. Brod, ed., *The Making of Masculinities: The New Men's Studies* [Boston: Allen & Unwin, 1985], 63–100), for an elaboration of the thesis that hegemonic forms of masculinity typically only correspond to a small proportion of men. Research in varying contexts has confirmed this insight. Also see C. Hasbrook and O. Harris, "Wrestling with Gender: Physicality and Masculinities Among Inner-city First and Second Graders," in J. McKay, M. A. Messner, and D. Sabo, eds., *Masculinities, Gender Relations, and Sport* (Thousand Oaks, Calif.: Sage Publications, 2000), 27; B. Thorne, *Gender Play: Girls and Boys in School* (New Brunswick, N.J.: Rutgers University Press, 1994); P. Hondagneu-Sotelo and M. A. Messner, "Gender Displays and Men's Power: The New Man and the Mexican Immigrant Man," in Harry Brod and Michael Kaufman, eds., *Theorizing Masculinities* (Thousand Oaks, Calif.: Sage Publications, 1994), 200–218.; S. Laberge and M. Albert, ("Concepts of Masculinity and Gender Transgression in Sport among Adolescent Boys," in Jim McKay, Michael Messner, and Don F. Sabo, eds., *Masculinities, Gender Relations, and Sport* [Thousand Oaks, Calif.: Sage Publications, 2000], 205) found that approximately half of a group of adolescent boys in Quebec, from different class backgrounds, expressed norms of dominant masculinity, while the other half criticized or challenged them in varying ways by social class.

6. The drawback to these portraits of coaches is that they freeze the behaviors of these coaches over the span of just a few years in their lives and at specific moments in their own life cycles. Yet, we know that what it means to be a man changes over the lifetime and life experience of most men (see M. S. Kimmel and M. A. Messner, *Men's Lives*, 5th ed. [Boston: Allyn and Bacon, 2001], xxvi). Numerous coaches reported to me that their approaches had softened over time, especially as they became parents and developed more realistic sensibilities about appropriate developmental expectations for children.

7. See B. Thorne, *Gender Play.*

8. See S. Ramos's discussion, in *Profile of Man and Culture in Mexico* (Austin: University of Texas Press, 1962), of "protest masculinity," as applied to Mexican men whose sense of economic and social powerlessness was often masked by a fierce demonstration of power and virility. For a comparative discussion of this work and other applications, see Klein, "Dueling Machos."

9. For a review of the literature on wives' power and authority, especially as it relates to income and employment, see A. Cherlin, *Public and Private Families* (New York: McGraw-Hill, 1996), 302–312; and P. Blumstein and P. Schwartz, "Money and Ideology: Their Impact on Power and the Division of Household Labor," in Rae Lesser Blumberg, ed., *Gender, Family, and Economy: The Triple Overlap* (Newbury Park, Calif.: Sage Publications, 1991), 261–288.

10. For a review discussion of the factors that keep men and boys at the margins of social groups, engaged in silent complicity about dominant and often abusive treatments of targets by more powerful leaders, see M. Messner, Taking the Field: *Women, Men, and Sports* (Minneapolis: University of Minnesota Press, 2002), 27–38.

CHAPTER 5:   THE BENCH AND BOYS' CULTURE

1. See G. A. Fine (*With the Boys: Little League Baseball and Preadolescent Culture* [Chicago: The University of Chicago Press, 1987]), who adopts a symbolic integrationist approach to his study of Little League baseball. Even though my book centers on baseball played by boys rather than adults, it has more in common with both B. Kuklick's *To Every Thing a Season: Shibe Park and Urban Philadelphia, 1909–1976* (Princeton, N.J.: Princeton University Press, 1991), which deals with the affective ties to place linked to baseball, and A. Klein's treatment of semiprofessional baseball on the Texas–Mexican border, *Baseball on the Border: A Tale of the Two Laredos* (Princeton, N.J.: Princeton University Press 1997) than with Fine's *With the Boys*. Like Klein, I am as interested in the diversity of the social space around the game—in his case, nationalist tensions; in mine, class, race, and masculinity—as I am in the game itself. The relative homogeneity of the boys Fine studied, and his greater concern with the way boys construct cultural meanings through their interactions with each other, lead him to mine the topic differently. This chapter is where we probably have the most thematic overlap, although I am adopting a very different narrative strategy for exploring these interactions. While I had seen the 2000 article in which Klein uses the terms "tender machismo" and "tough machismo" in reference to the Tecos transnational team, it wasn't until I had almost finished my book that I actually read his 1997 book, *Baseball on the Border*. I was surprised and very pleased to see his creative use of narrative storytelling in portraying the transnational, but internally divisive, team.

2. The valuable contribution of the emotional work of employers to adult organizations, as well as the cost of that sociability for workers, was explored by Arlie Hochschild in her examination of flight attendants and bill collectors in *The Managed Heart: Commercialization of Human Feeling* (Berkeley: University of California Press, 1983). Ronnie Steinberg has a long history of exploring the uncompensated emotional skill behind many female-typed occupations. See R. Steinberg and D. Figart, eds., *Emotional Labor in the Service Economy* (Thousand Oaks, Calif.: Sage Publications, 1999). Typically we see emotional work as women's work or girls' roles. I am exploring the importance of emotionally expressive boys for sustaining the high status of emotionally inexpressive boys.

3. This notion that there is often a hiatus between organizational structures and the "life world," in Habermas's terms, or between Bourdieu's "habitus and field" as a gap between the social grammar that we internalize and the way we convert it into real lives, real decisions, and living speech, is echoed in various theoretical accounts of social life.

4. This combination of integration and ethnic clustering is reminiscent of Troy Duster's description of the way multicultural social life at the University of California at Berkeley in the 1990s played itself out. See T. Duster, "Understanding Self-Segregation on Campus," *The Chronicle of Higher Education*, September 25, 1991, B1:179.

CHAPTER 6: CONCLUSION

1. In a study of another gentrifying neighborhood in Philadelphia, Eli Anderson (*Street Wise: Race, Class and Change in an Urban Community* [Chicago: University of Chicago Press, 1990]) applied the notion of "street wisdom" to describe individuals who have mastered the basic rules of etiquette for dealing with strangers in public space. The street-wise have learned to read the signs and symbols people different from themselves might exhibit, to distinguish between those who might mean them harm and those who might be potential allies. Street wisdom comes from accumulated social knowledge of a place, from walking streets, exchanging stories, and learning about the texture of a place. While the internal divisions of Fairmount are different from those of Anderson's Village-Northon area, sitting on the bleachers season after season with a changing set of parents of different backgrounds nevertheless provides something similar—a community wisdom about handling difference and recognizing commonality across social divisions in areas away from the street, a wisdom harder to achieve outside this space.

2. See Kathleen Gerson, *No Man's Land: Men's Changing Commitments to Family and Work* (New York: Basic Books, 1993).

3. Arlie Hochschild's *The Managed Heart: Commercialization of Human Feeling* (Berkeley: University of California Press, 1983) highlighted the importance of emotional work in several occupations and contexts, especially as performed by women, and showed how it greases the wheels of social encounters, allowing for the smooth functioning of many occupations, e.g. flight attendants and bill collectors.

4. FSA, at least at the organizational level, differed in this regard from the pattern observed in several other studies that stressed the central role of women's labor in sustaining the sports activities of male players, both of their sons and their husbands. Women were active participants in the organization, especially for organizational girls' activities, but were not as central as the men in holding up the organizational structure of the boys' leagues. See J. Chafetz and J. Kotarba, "Little League Mothers and the Reproduction of Gender," in J. Coakley and P. Donnelly, eds., *Inside Sports* (New York: Routledge, 1994), 46–54; and S. Thompson, *Mother's Taxi: Sport and Women's Labor* (Albany: State University of New York Press, 1999).

5. I am grateful to Michael Kaufman for this observation.

6. The White Ribbon Campaign is a mass-oriented campaign against violence by men against women. It was originally formed in response to the slaying of fourteen female engineering students at the University of Montreal in 1989 because they were perceived by their murderer to be feminists. Every year since then, on a selected day in December, men from the campaign lead workshops and public discussions about men's violence. The campaign has received widespread public attention in Canada, including at the level of Parliament, as well as internationally. See White Ribbon Campaign, "Education and Action Kit" (Toronto, 1996), or its home page (*www.whiteribbon.ca*). For a sense of how this organization links male violence to the emotional pressure required of traditional masculinity styles, see the work of Michael Kaufman,

International Director of the White Ribbon Campaign, *Cracking the Armor: Power, Pain and the Lives of Men* (Toronto: Viking Canada, 1993; New York: Penguin, 1994).

7. See R. Behar, *The Vulnerable Observer: Anthropology that Breaks Your Heart* (Boston: Beacon Press, 1996). Then see the introduction to Pablo Vila's *Ethnography at the Border* (Minneapolis: University of Minnesota Press, 2003), for his challenge to an assumption he finds in Behar's work, that all researchers can reveal their personal identities and still survive in academia.

8. There is more of a call in the anthropological literature for self-doubt about the researcher's ethnographic authority than there is in the sociological literature, although this may be changing. The anthology *Writing Culture: The Poetics and Politics of Ethnography*, by James Clifford and George Marcus (Berkeley: University of California Press, 1986), helped to usher in a "crisis of representation" in ethnographic work, in anthropology and beyond. For an excellent and brief review of the literature that has critiqued ethnographic authority, its meanings, practices, and possibilities, see Vila's, *Ethnography at the Border*, ix–xxxv.

9. See Irwin Deustcher's *What We Say/What We Do: Sentiments and Acts* (Boston: Addison-Wesley, 1973).

10. The highlights include: C. Moraga and G. Anzaldúa, eds., *This Bridge Called My Back: Writings by Radical Women of Color* (New York: Kitchen Table: Women of Color Press, 1983), a bold step in challenging the distancing and alienating forms of self-expression that cloud much of academia; the edited anthology by Clifford and Marcus, *Writing Culture*, a critique of "realism" in anthropology and a critique of the lack of attention given to literary foundations in much of the writing on culture; L. Abu-Lughod's "Can There Be a Feminist Ethnography? Women and Performance," *Journal of Feminist Theory* 5 (1990): 7–27; and R. Behar and D. Gordon's anthology, *Women Writing Culture* (Berkeley: University of California Press, 1995).

11. See C. K. Reissman's *Narrative Analysis* (Thousand Oaks, Calif.: Sage Publications, 1993) for a discussion of the dominance and distortions of "realistic representations."

12. R. Sennett, *The Fall of Public Man* (New York: Norton, 1974).

13. For a selection of diverse approaches to studying the issue of fathers' absence, their low participation in children's worlds, and the implications for families, see Kathleen Gerson, *No Man's Land* (New York: Basic Books, 1993); Sanford Dornbusch and Myra Strober, "Our Perspective," in S. M. Dornbush and M. Strober, eds., *Feminism, Children, and the New Families* (New York: Guilford Press, 1988), 3–24; David Popenoe, "American Family Decline, 1960–1990: A Review and Appraisal," *Journal of Marriage and the Family* 55 (1993): 527–555; Judith Stacey, *Brave New Worlds: Stories of Domestic Upheaval in Late 20th Century America* (Boston: Beacon Press, 1997); and Annette Lareau, "Invisible Inequality: Social Class and Childrearing in Black Families and White Families," *American Sociological Review* 67, no. 5 (2002): 747–776.

14. R. D. Putnam, *Bowling Alone: The Collapse and Revival of American Community* (New York: Simon & Schuster, 2000), 27.

15. Included in Putnam's analysis are weighted causes of the emptiness of contemporary social life, namely: pressures of time and money, especially among two-career families (weighted as 10 percent of the problem); suburbanization, commuting, and sprawl (10 percent); the privatizing effect of electronic entertainment, especially television (25 percent); and, most significantly, generational change or the replacement of a highly civic-minded generation by their more privatized children and grandchildren (50 percent).

16. Putnam's challenges emerged as one outcome of a concerted nationwide conversation on civic engagement sponsored by the Saguaro Seminar at the John F. Kennedy School of Government at Harvard University. See Putnam, *Bowling Alone*, 501.

17. Putnam, *Bowling Alone*, 408.

18. See Jason Kaufman, *For the Common Good? American Civic Life and the Golden Age of Fraternity* (New York: Oxford, 2002).

19. We shouldn't discount the possibility that social and racial conflicts could still blow up, especially if the class balance of people of color shifts from one that is predominantly middle-class to one that is more working-class. Part of the reason why this encounter worked was that very few of the new, middle-class members wanted to run the organization. It took too much time. But this possibility of control through running FSA might be more tempting to newcomers with fewer non-local confirmations of social worth. Also, the whole scene could crumble if real estate developers or urban planners convince city leaders that this real estate is too valuable for "mere community life."

20. Brett Williams, *Upscaling Downtown: Stalled Gentrification in Washington, D.C.* (Ithaca, N.Y.: Cornell University Press, 1988), 143.

APPENDIX

1. Quoted in R. Behar and D. Gordon, eds., *Women Writing Culture* (Berkeley: University of California Press, 1995), 6.

2. See H. Turkin, *Official Encyclopedia of Little League Baseball* (New York: A. S. Barnes, 1954); and G. A. Fine, *With the Boys: Little League Baseball and Preadolescent Culture* (Chicago: University of Chicago Press, 1987).

3. All of the FSA's boys' teams use the names of major league teams, like the Reds, the Orioles, or the Cubs. The girls' teams are named things like the "Cream Puffs," the "Shamrocks," and the "Wild Bunch." In order to protect the individual identities of coaches and boys associated with particular teams, I have substituted the FSA team names with team names from the major leagues not used by the FSA. Also, I often alter some of the descriptions of particular coaches or change some identifying details about them in order to make them less recognizable.

4. See G. A. Fine and B. Glassner, "Participant Observation with Children: Promises and Problems," *Urban Life* 8 (1979): 153–174.

5. See P. Vila, ed., *Ethnography at the Border* (Minneapolis: University of Minnesota Press, 2003), xxxii.

6. See G. Sjoberg, "Reflective Methodology: Foundations of Social Inquiry," in G. Sjoberg and R. Nett, *A Methodology for Social Research: With a New Introductory Essay* (Prospect Heights, Ill.: Waveland Press, 1997), I–xliv; B. Littrell, "Gideon Sjoberg: Methodology, and Symbolic Interaction," in Norman K. Denzin, ed., *Studies in Symbolic Interaction* 25 (2002): 129–152.

BIBLIOGRAPHY

Abu-Lughod, Lila. 1990. "Can There Be a Feminist Ethnography? Women and Performance." *Journal of Feminist Theory* 5: 7–27.

Adams, Carolyn Teich, David Bartelt, David Elesh, Ira Goldstein, Nancy Kleineiwski, and William Yancey. 1991. *Philadelphia: Neighborhoods, Division, and Conflict in a Post-industrial City.* Philadelphia: Temple University Press.

Alwin, Duane F. 1988. "From Obedience to Autonomy: Changes in Traits Desired in Children, 1924–1978." *Public Opinion Quarterly* 52: 33–52.

———. 1990. "Historical Changes in Parental Orientations to Children." In Nancy Mandell, ed., *Sociological Studies of Child Development* 3: 65–86.

Anderson, Dean F., and Gregory P. Stone. 1979. "A Fifteen-Year Analysis of Socio-Economic Strata Differences in the Meaning Given to Sport by Metropolitans." In March L. Krotee, ed, *The Dimensions of Sport Sociology.* West Point, N.Y: Leisure Press. 167–184.

Anderson, Elijah. 1990. *Streetwise: Race, Class, and Change in an Urban Community.* Chicago: University of Chicago Press.

Barry, Joseph, and John Derevlany, eds. 1987. *Yuppies Invade My House at Dinnertime.* Hoboken, N.J.: Big River Publishing.

Barth, Gunther Paul. 1980. *City People: The Rise of Modern City Culture in Nineteenth-Century America.* Oxford: Oxford University Press.

Behar, Ruth. 1995. "Introduction: Out of Exile." In Ruth Behar and Deborah Gordon, eds., *Women Writing Culture.* Berkeley: University of California Press. 1–29.

———. 1996. *The Vulnerable Observer: Anthropology that Breaks Your Heart.* Boston: Beacon Press.

Behar, Ruth, and Deborah Gordon, eds. 1995. *Women Writing Culture.* Berkeley: University of California Press.

Betancur, John J. 2002. "The Politics of Gentrification: The Case of West Town in Chicago." *Urban Affairs Review* 37, no. 6: 780–814.

Blumstein, Philip, and Pepper Schwartz. 1991 "Money and Ideology: Their Impact on Power and the Division of Household Labor." In Rae Lesser Blumberg, ed., *Gender, Family, and Economy: The Triple Overlap.* Newbury Park, Calif.: Sage Publications. 261–288.

Bondi, Liz. 1999. "Gender, Class and Gentrification: Enriching the Debate." *Environment and Planning D: Society and Space* 17: 261–282.

Bridge, Gary. 1994. "Gentrification, Class, and Residence: A Reappraisal." *Environment & Planning D: Society & Space* 12, no. 1: 31–51.

Brint, S. 1984. "New Class and Cumulative Trend Explanations of the Liberal Political Attitudes of Professionals." *American Journal of Sociology* 90: 30–71

Bryant, Howard. 2002. *Shut Out: A History of Race and Baseball in Boston.* New York: Routledge.

Burstyn, Varda. 1983. *The Rites of Men: Manhood, Politics and the Culture of Sport.* Toronto, University of Toronto Press.

Burstyn, Varda. 2001. "Sport as Secular Sacrament." In D. Stanley Eitzen, *Sport in Contemporary Society: An Anthology.* 6th edition. New York: Worth Publishers. 10–19.

Butler, Tim, and Chris Hamnett. 1994. "Gentrification, Class, and Gender: Some Comments on Warde's 'Gentrification as Consumption.'" *Environment and Planning D: Society and Space* 12: 477–493.

Carrigan, T., B. Connell, and J. Lee. 1985. "Toward a New Sociology of Masculinity." In H. Brod, ed., *The Making of Masculinities: The New Men's Studies.* Boston: Allen & Unwin. 63–100.

Caufield, Jon. 1989. "'Gentrification' and Desire." *Canadian Review of Sociology and Anthropology* 26, no. 4: 617–632.

Chafetz, Janet Saltzman, and Joseph A. Kotarba. 1999. "Little League Mothers and the Reproduction of Gender." In Jay Coakley and Peter Donnelly, eds., *Inside Sports.* New York: Routledge. 46–54.

City Planning Commission. 2000. "Comments on the Central Philadelphia Development Corporation Parkway Plan." Unpublished memo. 6–7.

Coakely, Jay J. 1990. *Sport in Society: Issues and Controversies.* 4th edition. St. Louis, Mo.: Mosby.

———. 2001. "Sport in Society: An Inspiration or an Opiate?" In D. Stanley Eitzen, ed., *Sport in Contemporary Society: An Anthology.* 6th edition. New York: Worth Publishers. 20–36.

———. 2001. "Play Group versus Organized Competitive Team: A Comparison." In D. Stanley Eitzen, ed., *Sport in Contemporary Society: An Anthology.* 6th edition. New York: Worth Publishers. 40–49.

Cherlin, Andrew. 1996. *Public and Private Families.* New York: McGraw-Hill.

Chodorow, Nancy. 1978. *The Reproduction of Mothering: Psychoanalysis and the Sociology of Gender.* Berkeley: University of California Press.

Clifford, James, and George Marcus, eds. 1986. *Writing Culture: The Poetics and Politics of Ethnography.* Berkeley: University of California Press.

Connell, R. W. 1987. *Gender and Power: Society, the Person and Sexual Politics.* Stanford, Calif.: Stanford University Press.

———. 1990. "An Iron Man: The Body and Some Contradictions of Hegemonic Masculinity." In Michael Messner and Don Sabo, eds., *Sport, Men and the Gender Order: Critical Feminist Perspectives.* Champaign, Ill.: Human Kinetics Books. 83–96.

———. 1995. *Masculinities.* Berkeley: University of California Press.

———. 2000. *The Men and the Boys.* Berkeley: University of California Press.

Cummings, Scott. 1998. *Left Behind in Rosedale: Race Relations and the Collapse of Community Institutions.* Boulder, Colo.: Westview Press.

Cybriwsky, R. 1978. "Social Aspects of Neighborhood Change." *Annals of the Association of American Geographers* 68: 17–33.

DeGiovanni, Frank F. 1983. "Patterns of Change in Housing Market Activity in Revitalizing Neighborhoods." *Journal of the American Planning Association* 49: 22–39.

Deutscher, Irwin. 1973. *What We Say/What We Do: Sentiments and Acts.* Boston: Addison-Wesley.

Dreir, Peter, John Mollenkopf, and Todd Swanstrom. 2001. *Place Matters: Metropolitics for the Twenty-first Century.* Lawrence: University Press of Kansas.

Duneier, Mitchell. 1999. *Sidewalk.* New York: Farrar, Straus and Giroux.

Duster, Troy. 1991. "Understanding Self-Segregation on Campus." *The Chronicle of Higher Education,* September 25, B1. 179.

Early, Gerald Lyn. 1994. *The Culture of Bruising: Essays on Prizefighting, Literature, and Modern American Culture.* Hopewell, N.J.: The Ecco Press.

Edwards, Harry. 1970. *The Revolt of the Black Athlete.* New York: Free Press.

————. 1973. *Sociology of Sport.* Homewood, Ill.: Dorsey Press.

————. 2001. "An End of the Golden Age of Black Participation." In D. Stanley Eitzen, ed., *Sport in Contemporary Society: An Anthology.* 6th edition. New York: Worth Publishers. 285–291.

Eitzen, D. Stanley. 1999. *Fair and Foul: Beyond the Myths and Paradoxes of Sport.* Lanham, Md.: Rowman and Littlefield.

————. 2001. "American Sport at Century's End." In D. Stanley Eitzen, ed., *Sport in Contemporary Society: An Anthology.* 6th edition. New York: Worth Publishers. 4–9

————. 2001. "The Democratic Ideal and School Sport." In D. Stanley Eitzen, ed., *Sport in Contemporary Society: An Anthology.* 6th edition. New York: Worth Publishers. 155–165.

Eitzen, D. Stanley, ed. 2001. *Sport in Contemporary Society: An Anthology.* 6th edition. New York: Worth Publishers. 285–291.

————. 2001. "Ethical Dilemmas in American Sport: The Dark Side of Competition." In D. Stanley Eitzen, ed., *Sport in Contemporary Society: An Anthology.* 6th edition. New York: Worth Publishers. 169–179.

Eitzen, D. Stanley, and George H. Sage. 1978. *Sociology of American Sport.* Dubuque, Iowa: Wm. C. Brown.

Eitzen, D. Stanley, and N. B. Yetman. 1977. "Immune from Racism?" *Civil Rights Digest* 9: 3–13.

Ehrenreich, J., and Barbara Ehrenreich. 1979. "The Professional-Managerial Class." In P. Walker, ed., *Between Labor and Capital.* Boston: South End Press. 5–45.

Ellis, Carolyn, and Arthur P. Bochner. 2000. "Autoethnography, Personal Narrative, Reflexivity: Researcher as Subject." In Norman K. Denzin and Yvonna S. Lincoln, eds. *Handbook of Qualitative Research.* 2nd edition. Thousand Oaks, Calif.: Sage Publications. 733–768.

Ericksen, Eugene P., David Bartellt, Patrick Feeney, Gerald Foeman, Sherri Grasmuck, Maureen Martella, William Rickle, Robert Spencer, and David Webb. 1985. *The State of Puerto Rican Philadelphia.* Philadelphia: Temple University, Institute for Public Policy Studies.

Ewing, Martha, Lori Gano-Overwazy, Crystal F. Branta, and Vern D. Seefeldt. 2002. "The Role of Sports in Youth Development." In Margaret Gatz, Michael A. Messner, and Sandra J. Ball-Rokeach, eds., *Paradoxes of Youth and Sport.* Albany: State University of New York Press. 31–47.

Feagin, Joe, Anthony M. Orum, and Gideon Sjoberg, eds. 1991. "A Case for the Case Study." In *The Nature of the Case Study.* Chapel Hill: University of North Carolina Press.

Fine, Gary Alan. 1987. *With the Boys: Little League Baseball and Preadolescent Culture.* Chicago: University of Chicago Press.

Gans, Herbert J. 1982. *The Urban Villagers: Group and Class in the Life of Italian Americans.* New York: The Free Press.

Gatz, Margaret, Michael A. Messner, and Sandra J. Ball-Rokeach, eds. 2002. *Paradoxes of Youth and Sport 2002.* Albany: State University of New York Press.

Geertz, Clifford. 1983. *Local Knowledge: Further Essays in Interpretative Anthropology.* New York: Basic Books.

Gerson, Kathleen. 1993. *No Man's Land: Men's Changing Commitments to Family and Work.* New York: Basic Books.

Goode, Judith, and Jo Anne Schneider. 1994. *Reshaping Ethnic and Racial Relations in Philadelphia: Immigrants in a Divided City.* Philadelphia: Temple University Press.

Goodman, Cary. 1979. *Choosing Sides: Playground and Street Life on the Lower East Side.* New York: Schocken Books.

Gouldner, Alvin. 1979. *The Future of Intellectuals and the Rise of the New Class.* New York: Seabury Press.

Grasmuck, Sherri. 2004. "Something about Baseball: Gentrification, 'Race Sponsorship,' and Neighborhood Boys' Baseball." *Sociology of Sport Journal* 20: 307–331.

Grasmuck, Sherri, Kevin Delaney, and Joshua Freeley. 1998. "'No Tears! I Hate That!' Masculinity, Ethnicity and Class in Boys' Baseball: Conflicting Class Cultures in a Local Setting." Paper presented at the Eastern Sociological Society Annual Meeting, Philadelphia, March.

Greeley, Andrew M. 2000. *The Catholic Imagination.* Berkeley: University of California Press.

Greenfield, Patricia, and Rodney R. Cocking, eds. 1994. *Cross-Cultural Roots of Minority Child Development.* Hillsdale, N.J.: Lawrence Erlbaum Associates.

Greenfield, Patricia M., Helen M. Davis, Lalita K. Suzuki, and Joakim Boutakidis. 2002. "Understanding Intercultural Relations on Multiethnic High School Sports Teams." In Margaret Gatz, Michael A. Messner, and Sandra J. Ball-Rokeach, eds., *Paradoxes of Youth and Sport 2002.* Albany: State University of New York Press. 141–157.

Greenhalgh, Susan. 2001. *Under the Medical Gaze: Facts and Fictions of Chronic Pain.* Berkeley: University of California Press.

Gruneau, Richard. 1983. *Class, Sports, and Social Development.* Amherst: University of Massachusetts Press.

Gupta, Akhil, and James Ferguson. 1997. "Discipline and Practice: 'The Field' as Site, Method, and Location in Anthropology." In *Anthropological Locations: Boundaries and Grounds of a Field Science.* Berkeley: University of California Press. 1–47.

Hackworth, Jason. 2002. "Post-recession Gentrification in New York City." *Urban Affairs Review* 37, no. 6: 815–843.

Handel, Gerald. 1984. "A Children's New York: Boys at Play in Yorkville." In Vernon Bogs, Gerald Handel, and Sylvia F. Fava, eds., *The Apple Sliced: Sociological Studies of New York City.* New York: Praeger Publishers. 33–49.

Harris, Adrienne. 1987. "Women, Baseball, and Words." In Gary F. Waller, Kathleen McCornick, and Lois Josephs Fowler, eds., *Lexington Introduction to Literature: Reading and Responding to Texts.* Lexington, Mass.: D. C. Heath. 1139–1157.

Hasbrook, Cynthia A., and Othello Harris. 2000. "Wrestling with Gender: Physicality and Masculinities among Inner-city First and Second Graders." In Jim McKay, Michael A. Messner, and Don Sabo, eds., *Masculinities, Gender Relations, and Sport.* Thousand Oaks, Calif.: Sage. 13–30.

Hoch. Paul. 1972. *Rip Off the Big Game: The Exploitation of Sports by the Power Elite.* Garden City, N.Y.: Anchor Books.

Hochschild, Arlie. 1983. *The Managed Heart: Commercialization of Human Feeling.* Berkeley: University of California Press.

Hondagneu-Sotelo, Pierrette, and Michael A. Messner. 1994. "Gender Displays and Men's Power: The 'New Man' and the Mexican Immigrant Man." In Harry Brod and Michael Kaufman, eds., *Theorizing Masculinities.* Thousand Oaks, Calif.: Sage. 200–218.

James, Cyril Lionel Robert. 1963. *Beyond a Boundary.* London: Hutchinson.

Kadaba, Lina. "Relentlessly Striving for More." *The Philadelphia Inquirer,* Sunday, March 3, 1998. H3.

Kaufman, Jason. 2002. *For the Common Good? American Civic Life and the Golden Age of Fraternity.* New York: Oxford University Press.

Kearns Goodwin, Doris. 1997. *Wait Till Next Year: A Memoir.* New York: Touchstone.

Kimmel, Michael S. 1990. "Baseball and the Reconstitution of American Masculinity: 1880–1920." In Michael A. Messner and Don F. Sabo, eds., *Sport, Men and the Gender Order: Critical Feminist Perspectives*. Champaign, Ill.: Human Kinetics Books. 55–66.

———. 1995. "'Changing Men' and Feminist Politics in the United States." In M. Kimmel, ed., *The Politics of Manhood: Profeminist Men Respond to the Mythopoetic Men's Movement (and the Mythopoetic Leaders Answer)*. Philadelphia: Temple University Press. 97–111.

Kimmel, Michael S., and Michael A. Messner. 2001. *Men's Lives*. 5th edition. Boston: Allyn and Bacon.

Klein, Alan. 1997. *Baseball on the Border: A Tale of the Two Laredos*. Princeton, N.J.: Princeton University Press.

———. 2000 "Dueling Machos: Masculinity and Sport in Mexican Baseball." In Jim McKay, Michael A. Messner, and Don Sabo, eds., *Masculinities, Gender Relations, and Sport*. Thousand Oaks, Calif.: Sage Publishers. 67–87.

Klein, Michael. 1990. "The Macho World of Sport: A Forgotten Realm?" *International Review for the Sociology of Sport* 25: 175–184

Kohn, Melvin. 1969. *Class and Conformity: A Study in Values*. Homewood, Ill.: Dorsey Press.

Kuklick, Bruce. 1991. *To Every Thing a Season: Shibe Park and Urban Philadelphia, 1909–1976*. Princeton, N.J.: Princeton University Press.

Laberg, Suzanne, and Albert Mathieu. 2000. "Conceptions of Masculinity and Gender Transgressions in Sport among Adolescent Boys: Hegemony, Contestation, and the Social Class Dynamic." In Jim McKay, Michael Messner, and Don F. Sabo, eds., *Masculinities, Gender Relations, and Sport*. Thousand Oaks, Calif.: Sage Publications. 195–221.

Lamont, Michèle. 1999. "Above 'People Above'? Status and Worth among White and Black Workers." In Michèle Lamont, ed., *The Cultural Territories of Race: Black and White Boundaries*. Chicago: University of Chicago Press. 127–150.

Lapchick, Richard Edward. 1998. *Racial and Gender Report Card*. Boston: Northeastern University Center for the Study of Sport in Society.

Lareau, Annette. 1989. *Home Advantage: Social Class and Parental Intervention in Elementary Education*. Lanham, Md.: Rowman & Littlefield Publishers.

———. 2002. "Invisible Inequality: Social Class and Childrearing in Black Families and White Families." *American Sociological Review* 67, no. 5 (March): 747–776.

———. 2003. *Unequal Childhoods: Class, Race, and Family Life*. Berkeley: University of California Press.

Lash, S., and J. Urry. 1987. *The End of Organized Capitalism*. Cambridge: Polity Press.

Ley, David. 1994. "Gentrification and the Politics of the New Middle Class." *Environment and Planning D: Society and Space* 12: 53–74.

———. 1996. *The New Middle Class and the Remaking of the Central City*. Cambridge: Oxford University Press.

Ley, David, and Roman Cybriwsky. 1974. "Urban Graffiti as Territorial Markers." *Annals of the Association of American Geographers* 64: 491–505

Lidz, Victor. 1991. "The Sense of Identity in Jewish-Christian Families." *Qualitative Sociology* 14, no. 1: 77–102.

Lincoln, Yvonna S., and Norman K. Denzin. 2000. "The Seventh Moment: Out of the Past." In Norman K. Denzin and Yvonna S. Lincoln, eds., *Handbook of Qualitative Research*. 2nd edition. Thousand Oaks, Calif.: Sage Publications. 1047–1065.

Littrell, Boyd. 2002. "Gideon Sjoberg, Methodology, and Symbolic Interaction." In Norman K. Denzin, ed., *Studies in Symbolic Interaction* 25: 129–150. New York: JAI Press.

Löfgren, Orvar. 1991. "Learning to Remember and Learning to Forget: Class and Memory in Modern Sweden." *Erinnern und Vergessen: Vortrage des 27. Proceedings from the 1989 Folklore Congress Conference.* Edited by Brigitte Bönischü-Brednich, Rolf W. Brednich, and Helge Gerndt. Göttingen: V. Schmerse.

Logan, John, and Harvey Molotch. 1987. *Urban Fortunes: The Political Economy of Place.* Berkeley: University of California Press.

Low, Setha. 1996. "Spatializing Culture: The Social Production and Social Construction of Public Space in Costa Rica." *American Ethnologist* 23, no. 4: 861–880.

MacNeil/Lehrer Productions. 2003. *Memories of Summer: The Golden Days of Baseball.* Transcript of interview between Roger Kahn and David Gergen, April 11, 1997. Mac-Neil/Lehrer Productions Online News Hour. http://www.pbs.org/newshour/gergen/april97/kahn_4–11.html.

McGuffey, C. Shawn, and B. Lindsay Rich. 2001. "Playing in the Gender Transgression Zone: Race, Class and Hegemonic Masculinity in Middle Childhood." In Michael S. Kimmel and Michael A. Messner, *Men's Lives.* 5th edition. Boston: Allyn and Bacon. 73–87.

McKay, Jim. 1992. "Sport and the Social Construction of Gender." In G. Lupton, T. Short, and R. Whip, eds., *Society and Gender: An Introduction to Sociology.* New York: Macmillan. 245–266.

McKay, Jim, Michael Messner, and Don F. Sabo. 2000. "Studying Sport, Men, and Masculinities from Feminist Standpoints," In J. McKay, M. Messner, and D. Sabo, eds., *Masculinities, Gender Relations, and Sport.* Thousand Oaks, Calif.: Sage Publications. 1–11.

Messner, Michael A. 1990. "Boyhood, Organized Sports, and the Construction of Masculinities." *Journal of Contemporary Ethnography* 18, no. 4: 4.

———. 1992. *Power at Play: Sports and the Problem of Masculinity.* Boston: Beacon Press.

———. 2002. *Taking the Field: Women, Men and Sports.* Minneapolis: University of Minnesota Press.

Messner, Michael A., and Don F. Sabo. 1994. *Sex, Violence, and Power in Sports: Rethinking Masculinity.* Freedom, Calif.: Crossing Press.

Messner, Michael A., and Don F. Sabo, eds. 1990. *Sport, Men and the Gender Order: Critical Feminist Perspectives.* Champaign, Ill.: Human Kinetics Books.

Molotch, Harvey, William Freudenburg, and Krista Paulsen. 2000. "History Repeats Itself, but How? City Character, Urban Tradition, and the Accomplishment of Place." *American Sociological Review* 65: 791–823.

Moraga, Cheríe, and Gloria Anzaldúa, eds. 1983. *This Bridge Called My Back: Writings by Radical Women of Color.* New York: Kitchen Table: Women of Color Press.

Mrozek, Donald. 1983. *Sport and American Mentality, 1880–1910.* Knoxville: University of Tennessee Press.

Ortner, Sherry B. 1993. "Ethnography among the Newark: The Class of '58 of Weequahic High School." *Michigan Quarterly Review* (summer): 411–429.

Passaro, Joanne. 1997. "'You Can't Take the Subway to the Field!' 'Village' Epistemologies in the Global Village." In Akhil Gupta and James Ferguson, eds., *Anthropological Locations: Boundaries and Grounds of a Field Science.* Berkeley: University of California Press. 147–162.

Prince, Sabiyha Robin. 2002. "Changing Places: Race, Class, and Belonging in the 'New' Harlem." *Urban Anthropology & Studies of Cultural Systems & World Economic Development* 31, no. 1: 5–35.

Putnam, Robert D. 2000. *Bowling Alone: The Collapse and Revival of American Community.* New York: Simon and Schuster.

Ramos, Samuel. 1962. *Profile of Man and Culture in Mexico.* Translated by P. Earle. Austin: University of Texas Press.

Ramos-Zayas, Ana. 2001. "Racializing the 'Invisible' Race: Latino Constructions of 'White Culture' and Whiteness in Chicago." *Urban Anthropology* 30, no. 4: 341–380.

Raudenbush, S. 1999. "Systematic Social Observation of Public Space." *American Journal of Sociology* 105, no. 3: 603.

Reissman, Catherine Kohler. 1993. *Narrative Analysis.* Thousand Oaks, Calif.: Sage Publications.

Richardson, Laurel. 2000. "Writing: A Method of Inquiry." In Norman K. Denzin and Yvonna S. Lincoln, eds., *Handbook of Qualitative Research.* 2d edition. Thousand Oaks, Calif.: Sage Publications. 923–948.

Rosaldo, Renato. 1993. *Culture and Truth: The Remaking of Social Analysis.* Boston: Beacon Press.

Sabo, Don. 1994 "Pigskin, Patriarchy, and Pain." In Michael A. Messner and Don F. Sabo, eds., *Sex, Violence, and Power in Sports: Rethinking Masculinity.* Freedom, Calif.: Crossing Press. 150–160.

Sage, George. 2001. "Racial Inequality and Sport." In D. Stanley Eitzen, ed., *Sport in Contemporary Society: An Anthology.* New York: Worth Publishers. 275–284.

Savage, M., P. Dickens, and T. Fielding. 1988. "Some Social and Political Implications of the Contemporary Fragmentation of the 'Service Class' in Britain." *International Journal of Urban and Regional Research* 12: 455–476.

Sennett, Richard. 1974. *The Fall of Public Man.* New York: Norton.

———. 2003. *Respect in a World of Inequality.* New York: Norton.

Sjoberg, Gideon. 1997. *A Methodology for Social Research.* Reissued edition. Prospect Heights, Ill.: Waveland Press.

Smith, N. 1996. *The New Urban Frontier: Gentrification and the Revanchist City.* New York: Routledge & Kegan Paul.

Snow, David, Louis A. Zurcher, and Gideon Sjoberg. 1982. "Interview by Comment: An Adjunct to the Formal Interview." *Qualitative Sociology* 5: 285–311.

Sparkes, Andrew C. 2002. "Fictional Representations: On Difference, Choice, and Risk." *Sociology of Sport Journal* 19: 1–24.

Spickard Prettyman, Sandra. 2002. "If You Beat Him, You Own Him, He's Your Bitch: An Analysis of What a Coach's Language Says to Student Athletes." Paper presented at the North American Society for the Sociology of Sport Conference, Indianapolis, November.

Stacey, Judith. 1988. "Can There Be a Feminist Ethnography?" *Women's Studies International Forum* 11, no. 1: 21–27.

Steinberg, Ronnie. 1999. "Emotional Demands at Work: A Job Content Analysis of Municipal Work." In Ronnie Steinberg and Deborah Figart, eds., *Annals of the American Academy of Political and Social Science.* Newbury Park, Calif.: Sage Publications.

Taylor, Ralph. 1988. *Human Territorial Functioning: An Empirical, Evolutionary Perspective on Individual and Small Group Territorial Cognitions, Behaviors, and Consequences.* Cambridge: Cambridge University Press.

Thompson, Shona. 1999. *Mother's Taxi: Sport and Women's Labor.* Albany: State University of New York Press.

Thorne, Barrie. 1994. *Gender Play: Girls and Boys in School.* New Brunswick, N.J.: Rutgers University Press.

Vila, Pablo. 2000. *Crossing Borders, Reinforcing Borders: Social Categories, Metaphors, and Narrative Identities on the U.S.–Mexico Frontier.* Austin: University of Texas Press.

Vila, Pablo, ed. 2003. *Ethnography at the Border.* Minneapolis: University of Minnesota Press.

Watson, Geoffrey. 1974. "Games, Socialization and Parental Values: Social Class Differences in Parental Evaluation of Little League Baseball." *International Review of Sport Sociology* 9: 17–48.

Weston, Kath. 1997. "The Virtual Anthropologist." In Akhil Guptal and James Ferguson, eds., *Anthropological Locations: Boundaries and Grounds of a Field Science.* Berkeley: University of California Press. 163–185.

Whalen, Carmen Teresa. 2001. *From Puerto Rico to Philadelphia: Puerto Rican Workers and Postwar Economics.* Philadelphia: Temple University Press.

Whiting, Robert. 1990. *You Gotta Have Wa.* New York: Vintage Books.

Williams, Brett. 1988. *Upscaling Downtown: Stalled Gentrification in Washington, D.C.* Ithaca, N.Y.: Cornell University Press.

Wolfe, Alan. 2003. "Invented Names, Hidden Distortions in Social Science." *Chronicle of Higher Education* 49, no. 38: B13–14.

Wright, E.O., and B. Martin. 1987. "The Transformation of the American Class Structure, 1960–1980." *American Journal of Sociology* 93: 1–29.

INDEX

ABOUT THE AUTHOR

SHERRI GRASMUCK is Professor of Sociology at Temple University. She is the coauthor of *Between Two Islands: Dominican International Migration*, with Patricia Pessar, and *Get Real Comics*, a series of female friendly, race-sensitive comics for preadolescents, with Debbie Rogow.

JANET GOLDWATER is a photographer and a documentary filmmaker. Together with Barbara Attie, she co-produced the award-winning PBS broadcasts *Maggie Growls, Landowska*, and *Motherless: A Legacy of Loss from Illegal Abortion*.